stand up
for something

stand up
for something
the spencer haywood story

by bill libby and
spencer haywood

GROSSET & DUNLAP
A National General Company
Publishers   *New York*

Dedication

For the adult friends of my adult life—Jim and Jill Fulton, Dick and Esther Fraser, Linda and Howard Leight, Eddie and Carolyn Angel, Bob and Alice Longood, Bob and Sue Storwick, Marv Schneider, Wells Twombly and others who have made the going easier.

Lib.

■

Acknowledgments

We wish to thank the family and friends of Spencer Haywood; Sam Schulman, Al Ross, Walter Kennedy, Jack Dolph, J. W. and Donald Ringsby, Bill Gullion; Pete Pfaelzer and John Quinn and the legal firm to which they belong; Will Robinson, Lenny Wilkens, Rod Thorn, Larry Deneholz, Bob Houbregs, the members of the Seattle Supersonics, Gil Lyons of the *Seattle Times*, Chet Nelson, Lynn Howell and the photographers of the *Rocky Mountain News*, Phil Wallace of the Jackson, Mississippi, *Daily News*, Sharon Savage, the staffs and photographers of *Sports Illustrated* and Time-Life, Inc., Dudley, Hardin & Yang, Inc., Photographers of Seattle, and Photography, Inc., of Inglewood, Calif., and all others who contributed in so many varied ways to this book.

■

Note

Since this book was begun, Lew Alcindor has adopted the name Kareem Abdul-Jabbar. References to him by Spencer Haywood or others within this book as Lew Alcindor are not meant disrespectfully.

Contents

Illustrations follow pages 50, 110 and 164

1. Shifting Scenes

He lay in bed all day, watching cartoons and soap operas on television and thinking about the game he had to play that night. He took time out only long enough to drink some orange juice and eat some cold cereal with milk. That was enough to keep him. His mind was on the game, not food. By the time he got dressed to go to the arena in what he calls his Chicago gangster suit he was worked up high.

Indiana, regarded as the best team in the American Basketball Association, with Mel Daniels, regarded as the best center in the ABA, was coming to Denver to take on the Rockets and their controversial superstar Spencer Haywood. An Olympic hero out of junior college, he had jumped the University of Detroit after one season to sign a professional contract with Denver.

He took the suit from a closet packed with fancy clothes. It was raspberry shaded, striped and double-breasted. He hummed a jazz tune as he pulled it on over silk underwear. He is a black man, 6-9 and 215 pounds, and he seemed imposing in the gaudy gangster garb. He knotted the laces of shiny black shoes, pulled a large feathered hat down over one eye, admired himself briefly in the mirror, and cut out of his large, lavish apartment.

1

He went downstairs and got his Cadillac out of the garage and drove it through the chill, darkening streets toward the arena. The car had been built especially for him. It cost him $13,000. But he was to be paid $275,000 for three seasons and he felt he could afford it. And he liked it. Born in a tiny town in Mississippi, reared in the ghettos of Chicago and Detroit, he felt he had some luxuries coming to him. He was earning them with his play.

He was only 19 years old, a rookie in pro basketball, under great pressure, but he was confident to the point of cockiness. After a slow start, in which the team's coach, John McLendon, was fired and replaced with Joe Belmont, Haywood had begun to find his way and had taken the team with him to a long winning streak. As Indiana came in, he was hot, his club was hot, and the town's fans were stirred to a fever pitch.

The team's owner, J.W. (Bill) Ringsby, a trucking tycoon, and his sons Bill and Gary, were busy congratulating themselves for their coup in skirting the rules to sign this youngster before his college class graduated. He won approval to play as a "hardship case," whose mother had been on her knees washing the floors of white people back in Mississippi. "I'll be able to buy her a mansion," Haywood said.

He pulled into the parking lot and faced the lighted arena. "The Ringsbys will get their money's worth," he said. "We're gonna win tonight. We're gonna win a whole lot of games. I'm going to be the best basketball player in the world." Carrying the bag with his basketball gear in one hand, he strode into the arena, past the guard, down a corridor, and into the dressing room. His step was light and jaunty. He was a professional now, on his way to do a job he knew he could do.

The Denver Auditorium is one of those buildings which seem all balcony, closely ringing and hanging over the court. When the people inside make noise, it fills the place and bathes the players with a din of sound that goes beyond that in bigger and newer arenas, which absorb the racket of larger crowds. Now the fans moved in out of the night to fill the building beyond its seating capacity of 7,112 spectators with 300 more settling for standing room

2

spots, and when the Denver team and Haywood came out, the crowd began to make noise and did not stop until the game had ended.

You could see quickly that Haywood was something special. He had good size and strength, but most others in the pro game have that. He had long arms and good reach, but others have that. He had far larger hands than most. He had an extra joint on every finger. Where most of us have three, he has four. His hands were like claws. He was capable of and had with a few steps jumped to touch the top of the backboard. Few can do this.

With his height, long arms, unusual hands, and unique leaping ability, he had become an extraordinary rebounder. He also had physical toughness. And a surprisingly delicate shooting touch. He had quickness, agility, balance, and springiness beyond the norm. He could jump like bigger men and handle himself like smaller men. He was a boy playing among men, but you could see he was exceptional.

Not that he was perfect. Who ever is? He was young, and a certain number of rough edges protruded from his play. He wasn't sure of himself when he was facing a foe and going one-on-one at the basket against him. Usually, he turned around, dribbling, and backed in, using his strength. He forced himself on his foes, infuriating them and arousing referees.

On one play, Haywood hacked Daniels so hard he tore some tape off Mel's wrist. But when he was called for the foul, Haywood protested excitedly. On another play, Haywood was bumped by Daniels and sent sprawling into the spectators at courtside. When no foul was called, Spencer made a fist and shook it angrily at the referee, screaming at him with the sort of anger that had carried him to the league lead in technical fouls. In college he was suspended for three games for punching a player and throwing a punch at a referee, and in pro ball he already had knocked out a Miami player with a one-two combination. Clearly, the youngster did not have his emotions under control.

But his raw ability kept bursting through. In college he had rammed home a dunk-shot with such force he tore away the rim, shattering the plexiglass backboard. Earlier in this pro season he had bent a rim on a similar play. Now

3

in this game he enveloped the ball in his right hand, drove
for the basket, leaped and sailed ten feet through the air to
stuff a shot through the hoop with devastating effect,
bringing a roar of approval from the crowd. A graceful
performer, he moved among the giants to hit short shots
and long shots. He took missed shots off the backboard.
Under pressure, he dribbled the ball downcourt as few big
men can do. He made good plays with good passes. He
worked hard on defense.

He played team ball with his teammates Byron Beck,
Julie Hammond, Junius Keye, Larry Jones, and Jeff Congdon, and they seemed inspired by his play. He shifted in
and out of the forward and center slots on offense and
defense. Guarded by forward Bob Netolicky on offense, he
guarded center Daniels on defense and outplayed them
both. Indiana had an outstanding team, but Haywood and
Denver were too much for them this night. As the home
crowd cheered, Haywood's Rockets pounded up and down
the hardwood court, overpowering the Pacers, pulling
farther and farther ahead.

The din was overwhelming. Belmont, a peppery young
coach, cavorted on the sidelines, urging his charges on,
clapping his hands and shaking a triumphant fist as they
did all the right things. Along the other bench, tough old
pro Bob Leonard, the Indiana coach, pleaded with his
players and screamed at the referees and cursed the
fortunes of the night. Gradually, hope faded, and he sat
back on the bench and hung his head and scuffed his shoes
on the court.

When the Denver lead mounted to an astonishing 40
points, Belmont began to pull his regulars. When Haywood
came out, there still were eight minutes to play and he had
35 points and 21 rebounds, more than Daniels and Netolicky combined. As the fans gave him a standing ovation,
a grin spread over his sweat-streaked, bearded face and he
held a hand aloft with one finger extended as if to say
"we're No. 1" and, possibly, too, "I'm No. 1." And he was
there, then, too, on his way to being voted Most Valuable
Player in the league, leading his team to a division
pennant.

He sat in the joyous dressing room, tired, letting the

sweat dry on him, cussing out the officials, trying to unwind. He said, "Not many games are easy. This one shouldn't have been. But it was. The most trouble I had was from the refs. They keep watching me. I guess I'm a marked man," he concluded. "Well, all right," he said, a grin erupting on his face, which made him look like Bill Cosby. "Well, all right, man, let 'em do the worst. Ain't no one going to stop this cat." And he heaved erect and headed for the shower room.

After he had showered and dried off and returned to his locker, he carefully put on the Chicago gangster suit, which he had designed himself, he pointed out proudly, and the hat with the feather, and he headed out into the night. Working his way through the kids who waited outside, patiently signing autographs for them, he drove the short ride back to his apartment on the twelfth floor of the Brooks Towers.

The apartment was empty. He put some jazz records on the hi-fi, cooked himself a steak, and ate it. Devoured should be the word. He was hungry now. The game was behind him. Life lay in front of him. As he ate, he spoke. "Man, I must be the luckiest cat in the world. I am a poor black boy from Mississippi with a bad life behind me and little education. I have been spat at and slapped and kicked, but no one is ever going to push me around again."

He paused, hard lights glinting in the corners of his eyes. "I can play this game," he said. "I can play it better than anyone. I will make a lot of money playing this game and I will make a helluva good life for myself. I have money in my pocket now for the first time in my life. I have a closet full of clothes. I have a nice big car. I can buy all the jazz records I want. I can get me almost anything I want," he concluded.

"Right now, I want to be the best basketball player. Later, I want to be an actor. I don't think there's anything beyond my reach. About now, I'm going to reach out for some sisters," he grinned. The day was old, but the night was young.

It was after midnight when he left, humming that jazz tune. He "hit the street," as he put it, making the rounds of some friendly clubs, hailed as a hero wherever he went, chatting with chicks until he found one he liked. Later, a party formed at his place. The brothers and sisters rapped against a background of heavy music.

Spencer Haywood leaned on a balcony, the pretty city at his feet. He grinned his Bill Cosby grin and asked, "Hey, man, how long has this been going on? Who the hell could ask for more?"

Winter, 1971-72

He sat in the hotel room stripped to the waist, too disturbed to finish getting dressed, too restless to call down for food. He wasn't hungry, anyway. He sat for a long time, his head down, staring at the carpet. He lay back on the bed. It was mussed and uncomfortable, but he didn't bother to straighten it out. He wasn't looking for comfort. After a while he stood up and went to the big picture window and stared out at Seattle and the fog-shrouded bay beyond. It was a gloomy day and he was gloomy.

He had been speaking and then he had grown silent for a long time and now he had begun to talk again, slowly, but with effort. "All I want is what's coming to me," he said. "I want to tell you there are so many law suits and court cases flying around me I can't even begin to keep them straight. I am suing and being sued, my teams are suing and being sued, even my manager is being sued."

He sighed, dispirited. His face was somber and seemed gaunt. He had lost weight and seemed thin. He said, "I am tired, man. I am tired and I am scared. All I want to do is earn a living playing basketball. I don't know how much I'm worth. All I know is what they tell me I'm worth, and then they won't give it to me. So I have fought for it, and I am being made to look like the worst man since Hitler for it."

Denver originally gave him a contract calling for $275,000 for three years' play. Then some National Basketball Association clubs approached him, offering more money, and Denver gave Spencer a new contract calling for $1.9 million over six seasons of play. He signed it. He wanted to play in the NBA, "the big league," but the war between the two circuits was on, forcing player bonuses and salaries higher and higher. Haywood had grabbed for some of the big money while it was available to him.

Then he became disenchanted with the owners in Denver and suspicious of the value of his contract. He was being paid $65,000 a season, which seemed not to be much for the Most Valuable Player, and most of the money was due him in deferred payments, which he might never get. Older players had counselled him to seek expert aid. So he had turned to a Los Angeles lawyer, Al Ross, who confirmed Haywood's worst suspicions about the pact and agreed to help him get it justified.

The Denver team, torn by dissension, had lost the playoffs, disappointing the Ringsbys deeply. They insisted Haywood had a valid contract and refused to renegotiate it. Courted by other NBA teams, Haywood had jumped the Rockets, hiding out at Ross's house while the aggressive Ross hired a battery of lawyers to combat a battery of lawyers hired by the Ringsbys.

Sam Schulman, owner of the Seattle franchise, not only made Haywood a solid $1.5 million offer for six seasons, but volunteered to stand by him and lend support in any and all court cases. Spencer signed, jumping to the NBA, and now he was caught in a spiderweb of legal technicalities as his right to play in the NBA for the Supersonics was determined. Even the other NBA clubs were protesting his right.

. Spencer Haywood had begun to play for the Seattle team, but continuing court action left his future in doubt. He was making appearances in court in Los Angeles, then flying out to Seattle games all over the map, often arriving just before tipoff, making some, missing others, losing sleep as he flew back to L. A.

"I am not playing well. Man, I am playing poor. But I'm tired and pressing and I can't keep my mind on the game. The Ringsbys treat me like a nigger, they call me a 'black nigger,' and the ABA, the commissioner, Jack Dolph, he just laughs. And the NBA commissioner, Walter Kennedy, wants to throw me out on my ear," he said, shaking his head.

He sighed. "My own teammates resent me. Who'm I, Superman, come to save their souls? The other players, well, hell, Oscar Robertson turned his back on me. Who've I got? Al Ross, yes. My lawyers, yes. I hope to hell I can trust them. My family, I can trust them. But Will Robinson, he's like family, he's like my own father, he coached me and guided me, and he's turned on me. He's with the Ringsbys. They must be paying him off. With promises. Poor black man getting paid off with promises ain't never gonna come true."

Haywood pounded a fist into an open palm. He stared off into space, as though his eyes were on some distant place. He said, "How the hell do I know how good I am? I only know how good they tell me I am. They tell me what I'm worth. But there ain't no way they're gonna give it to me. I've almost reached the point I don't care. I haven't had a date in weeks. I don't want no chicks mothering me, giving me advice. I don't party any more. I just ride airplanes back and forth to court. What I'd like to do is catch a plane clear out of this country. I'm not sure there's anything here for me any more," he said.

Fall, 1971

Spencer Haywood moved gracefully through a scrimmage game with Seattle teammates, other pros in the area, and some collegians. It was informal. The Seattle coach, Len Wilkens, was not there this afternoon, though he often participated. These were voluntary workouts at the Seattle University gym, and while there was not a fan on hand, nor anything at stake, the players were working hard, none harder than Haywood, who was showing some of the brilliance of two seasons back.

"He should be a rookie in pro ball this year," someone said. "No one thinks about that. He's 21 years old and he's got a year and a half of pro ball against the best under his belt. He's come through hell and he's as hungry as a man can be. And he is good. He is going to be something else."

During a break, Haywood leaned back on the gym wall, sweat running down him in streams. He had regained weight. He was bigger than he had ever been, 225 pounds, but trim, solid, and strong. "I feel great," he said, struggling for breath. "I am ready to go. *We* are going to go. We have a team that is going to surprise everyone. They accept me on this team now. I am part of the team. I am a leader. I have to be a leader. I am going to preach love. Man, what we need is togetherness. After the season, the hell with it. But during the season we will love one another and beat the hell out of the other teams."

Driving home, he was happy and humming. He said, "All that court garbage is behind me. I have the new contract, a good contract, and the new team, a good team. We are going to win our division. And I am going to be Most Valuable Player of the NBA just as I was MVP in the ABA." That Bill Cosby grin broke over his face and he laughed. "Why not?" he asked. "Everyone's got goals. This is mine. And I'll do it, man. You'll see."

He had a new apartment, plush and high above Seattle, with a view of the Space Needle from his balcony. There were a couple of girls there, "sisters," as Spencer calls them, ready to cook his supper. He has a special girl, but he still is single and still likes a lot of ladies. "I honor them," he says. "I treat them as nice as I can. I don't use them. I enjoy being with them. They are more friends than girl friends."

The jazz music began to beat. Pals were dropping in. Haywood stood in a corner, smiling, taking the scene in. "It is back to the good life," he grinned. "I dig it. But I am not going to waste it."

He walked out to the balcony, where the air was clear and cool. He said, "I am not going to buy any more $13,000 cars. That money would feed too many hungry kids. If I pass up the next suit of clothes, I can help a man pay his rent. I am going to help the brothers and sisters. Not just my family, *our* family."

He was talking about the family of blacks, and also Indians and Mexicans and all other minority groups; but mainly the blacks. He talked about a fund he is starting to stifle sickle-cell anemia, which strikes mostly blacks. He talked about setting up elaborate basketball clinics for ghetto youngsters. He seemed sincere.

He said, "I come from a family of ten kids. My mom did other people's washing. I never had a father. I picked cotton. I know what it is to go to bed hungry. I learned about life among the pimps and prostitutes and dope-pushers and junkies in the big-town tenements. I don't know how to talk properly yet. I was in high school before I could really read or write. I don't know how to help yet. But if a guy like me with my name making my kind of money can't help, well, then, what's the point of being alive."

He was asked: "Do you hate whites?"

He said, "Yes."

"All whites?"

"No. I'm trying to meet whites, get close to whites, rap with whites, find out about them. There's good and bad of everyone."

"Blacks as well as whites?"

"Yes. But I sympathize with the blacks. I can't call 'em bad. I can't put 'em down. I feel for what life has done to them. I know they want what I want, what all blacks want."

"Freedom?"

"Freedom. And equality."

"How do you feel now that your basketball court cases are behind you?"

"Set free. Like a great weight been taken off my shoulders."

"The court cases affected more than just you. For one thing, they set the right of a college player to turn pro before he graduates, like you did. Is that good?"

"Sure is. A man's entitled to his freedom. If a guy can quit college to work in a gas station, why can't he quit to play basketball?"

"The feeling is, some will be induced to give up on a college education."

"Some don't want a college education. A college education couldn't help me sink baskets. And lots of guys with college educations aren't making $100,000 a year."

"Your case seems to have encouraged others to try to break their contracts."

"I could only break my contract if it wasn't any good. If a contract's good, no one will be able to break one."

"Some people think you're a guy who's always going to be breaking contracts, jumping teams."

"Some people think I'm a bad guy. I don't think I'm a bad guy, but I can't help what people think. I have to do what I think is right for me, not what people think I should do."

"In any event, your case has had far-reaching consequences in sports. You've blazed a trail of sorts. Do you feel like a pioneer?"

"I just feel like a man who had to do something because he thought it was right. I wasn't trying to change anything for anyone else, just for me. If it happened, fine."

"Did you think you'd win?"

"No."

"But still you did it."

"I felt I had to."

"And if you'd lost?"

"I don't know. I'd have been stuck."

"Did you win? The case was settled out of court."

"It was settled. And I got what I wanted."

"How do you feel about doing the book, this book?"

"Like it should be done. The thing that gripes me is all the misinformation that has been spread around. I have been attacked for being a bad guy, for being greedy and disloyal, and I don't think I'm that. I didn't know what was in my contracts. I was 19, 20 years old. I'd had little education. How the hell could I know what was in the contracts? I only knew what they told me was in them. The only advisor I had was a guardian they appointed for me. Who the hell can read those contracts anyway? Can you? Small print, legal jargon. Forget it. I needed help. I got it from an advisor I appointed for myself, Al Ross."

"And you trust him."

"I don't trust anyone. No, I trust him. The thing is, you got to trust someone."

"You feel you were betrayed before."

"Absolutely. All down the line."

"All down the line?"

"Back to Detroit, back to college."

"What happened there?"

"I was screwed. People been trying to screw me ever since I began in basketball."

"Why?"

"If you have something, everyone wants a piece of it. Everyone has their own selfish reasons."

"Including you?"

He laughed. "Including me," he said.

"Will you say that in the book?"

"Yes. I think when the true facts come out, people will look at me differently."

"But if the book is done right, others will be heard, too, everyone who counts, pro and con—you, Ross, Robinson, the Ringsbys, Sam Schulman, Jack Dolph, Walter Kennedy, the Detroit people, and a lot of others. Some probably won't see it the way you do."

"I'm sure they won't." He laughed.

"Some will be against you."

He shrugged, this big man silhouetted against the Seattle skyline, and said, "That's all right. Let it all out."

2. Silver City and the Big Cities

"When you are old enough to get out, you get out," Spencer Haywood says.

He was born in Silver City, Mississippi, on April 22, 1949. This is on the Yazoo River in what is called the Delta country, about 85 miles from the nearest big town, Jackson. When Spencer was growing up, Silver City was a tiny town of fewer than 400 persons.

Times have been changing in recent years, but there was in Spencer's boyhood in his home town sharp divisions between the blacks and whites. The blacks rode in the back of the bus, used the rest-rooms marked "colored," ate in their own places, went to their own schools, lived in their place, and were waited on last in white places. There was considerable segregation and an atmosphere of racial hatred, though the blacks there had not matured to militancy and there was not the open disagreement and violence that was beginning to be put forth in the north by bolder blacks.

Since then, steps toward equality have been taken by the blacks in such places as Silver City, where they have found new freedoms, but the atmosphere cannot be expected to have been altered totally. Such a change cannot be expected within a single generation. But the environment which shaped Spencer when he was growing up was a harsher one for blacks than it is now, and while he is not a boldly militant person, who spits out hard pieces of hatred when he speaks, and is, in fact, agreeable with whites as well as blacks, his harsh origins have helped to form his feelings and he does not disguise his resentments for inequalities or his desires for equality.

Silver City is a cotton-field community in which blacks eke out a meager existence. Spencer's father, John, was a carpenter, and his mother, Eunice, cleaned houses, cared for children, scrubbed floors, and took in washing and sewing. Spencer's father died one month before Spencer was born. Spencer was the ninth child in his family and later there were two more. Of the eleven, seven were boys and four were girls. Some were half-brothers or half-sisters. Spencer's father brought Ollie Mae and Andy and his mother brought Virgil and Lena into their marriage. Together they had Joe, Roy, Andy, Lavarign and Spencer. Then came Floyd and Ivory. Spencer says, "The rules were different for people like us in a place like that. We just lived. You had babies and you worked and you tried to survive. When you got old enough to get out, you got out. Except the mamas and the papas who have to stay to take care of the kids. Except they didn't always stay. You don't admire a man or a woman for running out on his family, but you can understand it when gettin' out is as important as it is there. My daddy got out: he died. I don't know what he died of. In places like that, people like us don't know. You get sick and you live or you die. You seldom see a doctor. I was born at home, delivered by a midwife, a neighbor lady. Sometimes there the mamas deliver their babies by themselves. And then they care for them until they are old enough to get out."

Spencer says, "My daddy was only in his early sixties when he died, but he was probably best off out of it. It would have been better for us if he'd lived because he could of made a living for us as a carpenter and after he died it was hard for my mama to take care of us. As I was growing up, the older kids began to leave to go north, but there still was a mess of us Haywoods to take care of. We didn't have much. We had our house, but we had to pay taxes on it. Daddy built it, and he probably did the best he could with what he had, but it wasn't much, and we wore it out living in it. It was six rooms, I think, just a big old raggedy house, wood frame, paint peeling, holes in the floor.

"We slept three to a bed. Growing up that way was bad because it seemed like the younger one always got the middle and he was always peein' in the bed and the others were always getting peed on and wet and disgusted and yellin' for ma, though there wasn't much she could do about it. It was hot in the summer and cold in the winter. I mean sweatin' hot and freezin' cold. We had no gas. We had a wood stove. And a wood heater which would go out in the middle of the night. We'd take turns getting up at five or six in the morning to go outside into the cold winters to chop wood so there'd be a fire goin' in the heater and a little heat in the house when the others woke up and so there was some wood in the stove so mama could cook some mush or something for breakfast for us.

"We didn't always have enough to eat. We were hungry a lot. The worst thing was going to bed hungry. It hurt in your gut. You curled up in pain and it was awful. You prayed just to fall asleep. The only thing worse was waking up hungry and knowing there wasn't any food to take that hunger from you. And we didn't have the clothes to keep us warm. I had some old raggedy levis and some old raggedy shirts. I was seven years old before I got my first pair of shoes. I had been going to school for a year. To this day my toes curl under. Salvation Army shoes did that. They were too small. I never had a suit of clothes until I was up north and almost out of high school. When I was growing up, I wore hand-me-downs and clothes my mama could get from the Salvation Army. And I used to write my brothers up north for clothes."

He is well-dressed now, with a full stomach, as he speaks of what was then, but he curls over a little from the thought of it, as though remembering has brought the feeling of hunger back to his gut, of shivering back to his skin, and he shakes his head as though to rid himself of it. It is something you do not forget, not ever, no matter what comes later, he says, as if it were a broken bone that was not set properly and did not mend properly and left an arm or a leg forever crooked. His stomach is forever crooked. Trying to straighten it out, he eats ravenously. Restoring his pride, he dresses extravagantly. But his memories remain vivid within him.

He says, "Mama made around $10 a week scrubbing floors and such and she got around $10 a week relief money. That was most of what we had to live on. Mama would go out and wash floors and come home with a little bag of groceries. As soon as we could, we all went out and worked to help out. We started at six or seven, in the fields, mowing lawns, caddying. I started at six, before I had shoes. But there wasn't much for us. We couldn't make much. Those that had gone north sent money home sometimes, but not often. They didn't have to send. And mama would never ask. I picked cotton, did anything for a few pennies. And when I got it, I gave it to mama. A candy bar was a luxury I never knew."

He says he is not seeking sympathy, simply telling it as it was, not only for him but for many others like him and as it no doubt still is for many. He says, "We were poor. We were super-poor. When you don't have anything, you are as poor as you can be. You don't get any poorer than we were. And I knew it, even then. Hell, man, you could see others who had more. All you needed was eyes in your head. We saw how the white folks lived—nice houses, nice cars, nice clothes, food on the table, television sets, money to go to the movies. Even the poor whites had more than we did. It's hard not to hate whites in a situation like that. Hell, when you've got nothing, you hate anyone who has more."

He draws inside of himself for a moment, reflecting on his past. Then he resumes and his voice is edged with sadness: "Mama musta seen how it really was, but she never complained. I remember her crying, though. She was tremendously strong. She was tough. She had no hatred in her. She just knew what had to be done, and she did it. She had no education. She never thought about how hard it was. She just did it. But every once in a while it must have gotten to be too much for her, her kids not having shoes or enough clothes to wear or enough food to eat. And she'd get tired, I guess. She had bad legs and they'd hurt her. And I remember once in a while her sittin' down and just crying. She didn't like for us to see her cry. She wanted to be strong for us, to make us strong. But sometimes it just got to be too much for her.

"She used to say she wished we could have some toys like kids like to have. I never had a Christmas present until I was 16 years old and living with some other people up north. It was all mama could do to scuffle around and get together a Christmas turkey dinner for us. Somehow she always managed. But then we'd go hungry for a month to make up for it. And there was never anything left over for presents. I never had a toy in my life. What the hell," he says, "we managed. We found some fun. We swam in old mud holes. We played golf with broken sticks on a course we made up out back of our crib. We played basketball, but we never had a basketball. We nailed up an old rusty hoop. And we threw tin cans at it. Or we stuffed socks to make a ball. We pretended to dribble by saying 'Bop, bop.' You was allowed two 'bops,' then you had to shoot or pass off."

He leans back, smiling wistfully. "Bop, bop."

He shrugs, as if to say what the hell again. But he can't just put it aside. He thinks of it as hell. He says, "It was hell, a hell-hole of a place. We were niggers in the deep south. We lived on the wrong side of the tracks. You didn't cross the tracks unless you had good reason, such as going to work. Once I was slapped by a white man when I lost his golfball caddying. Once I was kicked by a white man because I ran across his lawn without thinking. You have to have these things done to you to know how they feel. You have to be called 'nigger' and 'eight-ball' and 'boy,' even when you're a man, to know how it feels."

He bears scars from those moments in his past. Bitterly he says, "I didn't know my place. I didn't want to settle for nothing. I wanted more. I wanted to get the hell out of there. That's what we all wanted. As soon as we got old enough to go, we went. We kissed mama goodbye, and we went. Poor mama, the kids running out on her, it had to hurt her, but you had to do it, and she knew it, she could see how it was."

None of his older brothers or sisters finished high school. They didn't stay long enough. Spencer finished, but not there. He started at McNair High School and lasted two years. "It was an all-black school and you couldn't get a decent education there. When I was 14, 15 years old I had maybe a third-grade education. I could hardly read or write. I wasn't thinking of finishing school. You don't in a place like that. There is no point to it. I wasn't even thinking of going to college through basketball. It just didn't occur to me. In a place like that, you're hardly even scouted. Sam Lacey, who played for Cincinnati, is the only pro I know of who ever came from my area, and he made it later."

Spencer Haywood was always tall for his age, but it took a while for his natural talent to come through. He recalls, "The first year I played, I made the varsity, but I wasn't any good. I was damn good at shooting socks and tin cans, but not basketballs. There were older guys ahead of me, and I was just an extra man. And there weren't enough uniforms to go around. The school colors were green and yellow, and the others would go out in green and I'd go out in yellow." He laughs wistfully. "That was one of the worst years of my life," he says. "You have to know what it is to be in yellow when the others are in green. They'd put me in in the last minute or two of one-sided games and I couldn't even make a layup. The second year I began to come on. I got a regular uniform and I made the regular team. I averaged 15, 16 points a game. The coach was Charles Wilson and he was all right. But there wasn't much competition and I doubt if I'd have developed much if I'd have stayed there. I wasn't going to stay, anyway, I was going to get out if it killed me."

He curls his huge hand into a fist and shakes it at the life he led. He thinks of home and he says, "I hate that damn place. An old dirt place where I was treated like dirt. I go back sometimes now to visit my mama, but I hate to go back. I go back now and it's like, oh wow! you're welcome to come here and go there, Spencer Haywood, basketball star. Not the other niggers, of course. 'Oh, they're with you? Oh, well, Mr. Haywood, if they're with you . . . *Mister* Haywood! But do *they* have to come in, too?' I came back from the Olympics and the city decided to throw a Spencer Haywood Day, parade and all. Only I didn't go. It'd never been done for a black before. Everyone said it was an honor. A real honor. Everyone said it was a breakthrough. Well, now, that was cool. All right. I told them they could have their day, but I wouldn't go. I don't know if they had it." He smiles. "I didn't go.

"Why does my mother stay? She doesn't know any better. It's her home. It's the only home she's ever known. Her friends are there. Her life is there. Not her kids. And she misses her kids. But I bought a home for her in Detroit, and she didn't want it. I tried to get her a place in Denver, and she didn't want it. I'd get her a place in Seattle, but she wouldn't take it. I'm building her a new home in Mississippi, but she keeps putting it off. She has no idea of the money I'm making. I tell her, but she doesn't understand. She doesn't know about that kind of money.

"I send her money. She'll never want for anything again. She doesn't have to work any more. But she still works. Not like before. Minding folks' kids and doing a little sewing and things like that. She stopped working and she gained 50 pounds. Her legs are getting worse and worse. She can hardly get around. But she doesn't know what to do with herself if she isn't working, so she works. And she tells me not to send her so much money. She's heard about athletes and entertainers making big money and winding up broke. She keeps telling me, 'Spencer, you save your money, don't send me so much, you look out for your future, I'll manage.' So she stays and all her kids got out."

He got out. It began when he was 14 years old and his brother Joe and sister Lena came back to visit at Christmas time. Spencer recalls, "I took one look at their car and I said, Wow! Joe's made it. I begged them to take me back north with them, to Chicago where they lived. I didn't know what was there. They didn't tell me nothing about life in a ghetto. I figured it had to be better than *this*. I just wanted to see it. But mama said I was too young. I wouldn't give up on it. I hung around their car for days scared to death they'd sneak out on me. When they said they were going, I locked myself in the car and I wouldn't get out. I screamed and cried. Mama hauled me out of that

19

car and beat hell out of me. But I wouldn't let up. 'Just for a visit,' I said. 'Just for a little while.' I begged and I cried. Finally they agreed. On condition I was sent back the next week. I stayed a month. And the minute I got home I started plotting to go back. I worked in the fields and on the golf course and sold empty pop bottles and I saved my money and the day school let out the next summer I was on the bus on my way back to Chicago."

This time he moved in with his half-sister, Lena, and her husband, Clarence. He says, "They let me stay there. They were good to me. But they didn't have much for me. And they had their things to do. It was 'I got a key, you got a key.' So I did my own things. I was on my own. I was only 15, but I was big for my age. Tall, of course. I lied about my age and got a job washing dishes at the Fred Harvey restaurant. I made sixty bucks a week. I got by." He is proud of this. He nods in self-approval, slapping his big hands together. He was 15 years old, and he was a man.

He says, "The moment I got to Chicago I saw what it was. A ghetto. Filthy streets. Rat-infested tenements. People living in rat-traps. People living on welfare. People without hope. But it was better than any life I'd known. A black man could get work there, in the big city. He could buy a car on time and keep it as long as he could hide from the re-po man. He could buy a bottle and get a girl and get together with some people and have a party. A black man could act like a man there. He could swell up his chest and curse at whitey and get drunk or get a fix and say screw you to the world. It was better than being beat down in the south, you see. And I wasn't ever goin' back to live in Mississippi. No way. Not ever.

"I got an education on the streets of Chicago and later in Detroit. By the time I was 16, 17 years old I knew things some people who don't live in the ghettoes will never know. Both places I found out about pimps and prostitutes and pushers and junkies and thieves. The streets was full of 'em. Whatever they were, they were your people, brothers and sisters. Hell, pimps and pushers are people a poor boy looks up to in a place like that. They got the big cars and the fancy clothes and the pretty ladies and the role of bills. Hell, they made it. It doesn't matter how they got it. You know no one's giving them anything. So if they got it, that's groovy, that's cool.

"A poor boy who's never had anything, he wants it any way he can get it. What the hell does he care about rules? What does he care about right or wrong? The poor black boy in the ghetto doesn't think the rules are for him, anyway. Just against him. If a black robs a white, that's like the poor robbing the rich, like Robin Hood makin' out, man, and that's good, not bad. That's cool. You don't think about fighting your way out, earning your way. You don't figure you got a chance the straight way. So you look up to the pimps and pushers who found a way. And the entertainers and the ballplayers who found their way. What else is there? How many senators we got? How many presidents? How many blacks own big businesses. You don't see 'em in the ghettoes man. You see the pimps and the pushers."

Spencer concedes he skirted the ragged edge of disaster in these places. He says, "We had gang fights. We fought each other. But mostly we beat up on whites. I learned to use my fists. I learned to be tough. You got to, to survive. If you're scared, you don't let on. I stole. I carried a .22 in my pocket, snatched purses, and mugged Whitey. We'd steal from stores for food. We'd case a place, see where the people went, and slip in and stuff some stuff in our shirts and slip out. Maybe someone would raise a little hell some other part of the store while we did our thing. I was just lucky I was never caught. I never was sent away. I never served time. I never graduated to big stuff. Friends who were with me there then in those places did. Some of them are in stir. Some of them are shot to death. You don't think of them as bad. I don't. Sure, what they did was bad, but you don't think of it that way. The way you think of it is they was unlucky, they got caught. If you can't sing a song, man, or stuff a basketball, or something like that, you got to find some way.

"I started drinking wine when I was 14 years old. I drank other stuff, but wine was cheapest, so wine it was. I smoked pot, whenever I could get my hands on some. I took some pills. And sniffed heroin. I just never got hooked. Maybe because I never used a needle. Never any hard stuff. I never got to that. If I'd stayed there a little longer, I sure as hell would've. If you're gonna stay there, what the hell's the difference? Like man, it's bad stuff, the worst, it'll kill you; I know that now. But I didn't then. And if I did, I probably wouldn't have given a damn. Wine takes your mind off your troubles, man. A fix takes you right out of this world. And it's a world you want to get out of. I got friends now who are still on the streets of Chicago and Detroit hustling for a buck for a fix. Or down on the farm in Lexington trying to get cured. It's a terrible, terrible thing."

He laughs. "I got hooked on ladies, instead," he says. "You learn fast about sex in the ghettoes, just like you learn fast about everything else. No one's hiding anything from you. The streets are full of whores. They're not bad ladies, just people trying to get by the only way they know how. Sometimes, if I had a few bucks, I'd buy a little bit. Wherever I was living, there would be parties at our place. They'd get a little wild sometimes. You know, the music blasting and the drinking and the smoking and the sexing. A lot of older ladies there, in their 30's, maybe. Sometimes one of them would offer to give little brother a treat and I'd get to go in a bedroom with her. Other times I'd just wait 'till the party wore out and everyone had passed out and I'd pick me out one and climb up on her. Sometimes I'd even hear a party going on in a neighbor's place and I'd lay around and wait until everyone was passed out quiet and then I'd sneak in or pry my way in and find my thing. A lot of the time they never knew what happened to them. Or they didn't care. A lot of moaning and groaning, of course. But liquor and dope put you out pretty good. Hell, man, I didn't know if I was putting it in the right place or not," he laughs. "I'll tell you, at 14 or 15, I had sex with a lot of ladies to this day don't know it happened.

"Later, when I went to high school in Detroit, I pretended I didn't know anything. I was an outsider at first. I stayed away from people. I had shaved my head bald and I didn't have any clothes but maybe an old shirt and some jeans and some gym shoes. The girls didn't come after me, and I didn't go after them. By that time, I wanted basketball more. But after I made it in basketball, then,

22

wow! everyone knew me, all the nice little girls knew me, and with some it was easy. But I was growing up by then and learning to respect a lady, even a teen-age girl, who is really just a little lady, and I wasn't mean or nasty about it or anything like that. I never let on I knew what it was all about, but I did my thing. When you're 14, 15, 16 years old, you want to be a man, you're hung up about sex, and you do things you wouldn't do later. I don't guess there's ever been a time in my life since I was 14 or 15 that I didn't like the ladies, but by the time I was 15 or 16, basketball came first.

"Basketball saved me from becoming an alky or an addict or a hood. When I got into it, I could see it was the way out for me. Someone would say to me, 'Hey, man, you should try this.' And I'd say, 'No, man, I been down that road. My thing is basketball. I can't afford to mess with that crap.' And they'd act hurt, like I'd put 'em down or offended 'em. And it'd make me feel bad. Like, you want to be with 'em. But you got to be hard. My best friend was hooked and I could see myself through him and what I'd be, and I didn't want that for me. And I had a goal. You get a goal, you got to go for it.

"I ran cross-country. Another cross-country runner, Tom Jones, we called 'The Outlaw.' I'd run and be thinking I couldn't run any further when along would come 'The Outlaw.' He'd say, 'Come on. You can still go.' And I'd go. You never knew your limits.

"Used to be you tap-danced your way out. You tapped on street corners for pennies and wound up on stage. Vaudeville's dead. Maybe you learn to blow a horn. I dig jazz the most. I love it. But I never got into it. And it's a tough life, being a jazz musician. Not many get much bread. I thought at first I'd like to be a blues singer. Then I wanted to be a boxer. I even used to go to the YMCA to train. But I'd box these older dudes and get the stuff kicked out of me. I decided I didn't want all that banging on my head. I grew big and I turned to basketball. I found I had a hand for it and I began to look to it for a future.

"I'd never fix a game, but I can see how guys did. I mean I don't have to. I made it. But the thing is, you don't know you're going to make it when you get started. You don't know how you're going to get through high school, much less get to college. And if you get to college, there's no guarantee the pros are going to take you. The cities are full of big cats could play basketball who never made it one way or another. You're 6-9 or 6-10 and everyone assumes you're a basketball player, which is all right if you are, but if you're not, you're a freak. You never had it, so you got to get it when it's being given out. A man offers you money and you ask him what you got to do for it, and if it's not too bad, if maybe you won't get caught, you do it. It's like being a crook. If you're from a ghetto, it doesn't matter what you do, or how you get it, only if you got it. What loyalties you got? To your family. To your brothers and sisters. But to basketball? To some college? Forget it. So you throw your chance away before you get it because you got no way of knowing you're ever going to get it. And you get whatever you can.

"It's a snake pit, but I squirmed out because I grew big and could dunk a basketball," he says.

He played on the playgrounds with players like Dave Bing and Cazzie Russell and Bill Bunting and Reggie Harding, and he read about the Bill Russells and the Oscar Robertsons and the Elgin Baylors. He was playing basketball afternoons on the Crane High School court in Chicago in the summer of 1964 when his brother Roy came to visit. Roy was surprised at the skill Spencer showed him. Spencer says, "All of us in the family had size and could play the game. Andy once scored forty-some points in a game for the Silver City Blues. He was a promising player, but he had to go to work to make out and he gave up the game and nobody's ever going to know how good he might have been. Roy was playing for Bowling Green, college ball, and he later had some trials in pro ball, but he already had bum knees by then. He never really got to use his stuff. He said, 'People tell me you're good.' I said, 'I'm not bad.' Hell, I didn't know if I was good or bad. I took him on, one-on-one. I held my own. He said, 'Hell, you can play.'

"He said I should go back to Bowling Green with him and he'd try to fix it up for me so I could play high school ball around there. He figured I had a chance to make it, and he wanted to help me get it. I said, 'Sure.' So I packed up my one suitcase and took off with him for Ohio. I moved into his dorm while he looked for a place for me to stay with someone. And I played ball with Roy and some of the other players who were hanging around school in the gym. And the guys said, 'Hey, kid, you can play this game.' And I began to believe I could. And I began to play like it. And some of the coaches watched and they said, 'Hey, this guy's gonna be good,' and they wanted me to go to high school near there so they could get me into their college when the time came.

"I was around 6-6 then and I could jump and I had good hands and I'd been learning the game fast from good players. No coaching, but learning from players. Just doing it. And getting better. And seeing how impressed people were. And beginning to be impressed with myself. And it was then for the first time that I really started thinking of maybe getting to go to college so I could become a pro. I wasn't interested in going to college, you see, only because it seemed the only way to get into pro ball. What the hell does a kid like me care about books? What sort of studies had I had? What sort of education had I had? I'd probably never even have gone back to high school if it hadn't been for basketball. But everyone was saying, 'Hey, man, this dude's gonna do it, so I began to think maybe. It wasn't anything real. Nothing you could count on. But it was there.

"But it didn't work out at Bowling Green. Roy couldn't find any place for me to stay, and he couldn't handle me himself. Anyway, he had this idea in the back of his head all along that he'd take me to Will Robinson, who was the coach at Pershing High in Detroit. Roy hadn't played for Will, but he'd played against Will's teams and he knew Will had super-teams and turned out super-players he sent to college and some to pro ball. And Roy knew from his reputation that Will sometimes helped kids like me. Well, Roy took me to Will, and I guess Will saw me for a player, because he fixed me up right away.

"He sort of took to me right off, too, I think, because he became my guardian. Then Will found me a home with James and Ida Bell, who became my joint guardians with Will. Mr. Bell was a foreman at the Chrysler plant in

Detroit and made a nice living and they had a nice home. They had two sons about my age, Greg and James, but the Bells accepted me as another son and their sons accepted me as a brother and I just started living there like it was my home."

There is a family feeling among blacks which seems to exceed that of whites. Black families will take in not only relatives but strangers, and, no matter how poor, share what they have with the newcomer and treat him as one of their own. And no matter what a member of the family does, he almost never is excluded from the home and from its protections and loyalties. Spencer says, "It's like we got to stick together to survive and we see it so we do it without thinking about it. We know what it is for one another. We're all brothers and sisters.

"The Bells were beautiful. They just accepted me. There never were any hangups. Even though I was a problem for awhile. I was used to the streets and life on the streets and drinking and sexing and fixing and I sneaked around some for awhile. But the Bells and Will Robinson straightened me out. They treated me like a son. One Christmas, they gave me my first present—a sweater. They gave me love, so I had to respect them. They kept after me until I straightened myself out. They showed me how I was getting a chance and would be a fool to blow it. They saw to it that I didn't want for anything. They stressed studies. Pershing was a beautiful school. Black and white, but no black-white troubles. No hassle. You could get a good education there. It wasn't a disgrace. And you could play ball there. And Will Robinson made me see for sure I had a future in basketball. For the first time, I had a future."

He smiles a little and shrugs and concludes, "The big-city streets wasn't all bad. They did me some good. They were tough, but life is tough and it helps you to be prepared. I learned some good lessons there, mostly about survival. I learned the value of good things there. You find out what good things mean when you don't have any. I learned a lot from some winos who used to play basketball for bets of juice. They had nothing, but they didn't back down from anything. They did their thing. They said, 'If you don't stand up for something, you'll fall for anything.'

I believe that. And it's been sort of my motto ever since."
How do others see those early days in his life?

Spencer's Mother

"Spencer was always going to go someplace. He was a
nice kid. He always wanted some things he couldn't get.
But that's not bad. He didn't have much. I couldn't give
him much. Lord knows I wanted to, but I couldn't. He
always said he was going to go someplace and get some
things and give me everything. And I thought he would.
Oh, I guess you always feel something special about your
own, but there was something about Spencer, he had this
hunger, I thought he'd get some things, I always thought
it'd be hard to stop him.

"He was in my stomach when his daddy died. He hadn't
even been born yet when his daddy died. His father was a
big man. He was very tall. He had been heavy. Sickness
thinned him out. He was 63 when he died. Oh, Lord, he
left me with all those kids. And others came along later.
And I had to care for them somehow. That's just what I had
to do. How did I do it? Prayer. Just prayer. And work. I had
to get jobs where I could watch the kids. Like at the school.
Or minding other kids. I scrubbed floors, yes. I spent a lot
of my life on my knees. And I sewed. I did what had to be
did.

"It was hard. Lots of time the kids didn't have warm
enough clothes. It hurts a mother when her kids is cold.
People would give me old clothes and I'd do 'em over, fix
'em up, so the kids could wear 'em. Lots of times we didn't
have enough to eat. We had a cow and a hog or two
different times. I could milk the cow, which helped, but
lots of times the cow hadn't been fed good and didn't have
much milk. And if you slaughtered the hog, well, now, you
didn't have him no more, did you? But at least you didn't
have to feed him then. Whatever food I could get, I'd feed
the kids, then I'd eat if there was any left over.

"If my husband had lived, he'd have provided for us,
but, well, he didn't, so that was that. So I did the best I
could. You miss a man, you know. If you don't have one.
You miss your kids having things other kids have. But lots

27

of people was poor where we was. We wasn't alone. That was the lot in life the Lord laid out for us, and we had to have the strength to do the best we could. Sometimes I just wanted to stop. The tears would come. I'd be so tired. My legs would hurt so. Maybe I'd be sick. Maybe it'd be Christmas and there wasn't no way I could give those who was mine anything. But there was no stopping. I had to go on. What would they do without me? I'd have my little cry. They never saw. I hid it from them. They needed their mama to be strong.

"I saw to it that my kids went to school. And knew right from wrong. And knew their Lord. Spencer was never no trouble to me. He got into his little troubles, but a mama expects that. Nothing serious. He was a healthy boy and a big boy and a smart boy. I been blessed with my kids. Not all got to do as well as Spencer, but they all did the best they could. They didn't have much, and they never complained.

"When they got old enough, they left. It would hurt me a lot. But I wanted them to go. There wasn't much for them here in the south. I could see that. It's different for me. This is my place. I don't know about any prejudice or segregation or anything like that. I'm a black woman and I lived a black woman's life. I never gave the whites no trouble and they never gave me none.

"But the young ones, for them it's different; they feel held back, put down. So they got to go. I guess it's better for them in the north. I guess they got a chance there. So they go. And I miss them. Oh, my, how much I miss them, so far away, making their own lives, me not even seeing my grandchildren much. I do have one daughter still here and her child, my grandchild, which is nice.

"Spencer wanted me to leave, to go north with him, but how could I leave? He could leave, but I couldn't. Here is my place, not there. This is what I know. I'm too old to make a new life in the north. I'm too old and my legs hurt too much. He wants me to live fast and live high. Well, I've lived slow and low and hard a long time and ain't no way I can learn how to live different now.

"I'm glad he could get out though. A mama wants to see her babies do good, and I guess he's doing good. A lot of my boys played basketball, but I guess Spencer was the best. It's funny how playing that game pays so good. It's not like bein' a doctor or a lawyer or a carpenter, but it's good to my boy, that's all I care about. He had it hard as a little tyke growing up. His mama knows. He deserves good now. Everyone deserves their chance."

Roy Haywood

"I didn't really grow up with Spencer because I was gone by the time he was born. My mother's sister came down to be with us when my father died, and I went back north with her. I did return home for a year, but then went back north again to stay. Whenever I did see him, I remember him as an energetic little kid, always having fun, always laughing. As he got older, I guess he began to hunger for things. And I guess he felt he got to go to get his chance.

"You depend on a father to bring in the bread, not the mother. Without a father, with only a mother, it's hard on a big family. Most of us were too young to work at anything that would bring in any real dough. There was little welfare. There was nothing that inspired you to stay. I mean if there was something there for us, a future, a chance at a decent life, well, we'd stay. But you grow up knowing you got to go. Poor blacks don't have a chance in the deep south, even today.

"In the north, you're still poor black and you land in a ghetto, but you can see beyond the ghetto there's a world where there might be some small place for you. You go to a school where there's a strong athletic program and you're a good athlete and you say to yourself, well, OK, I might get a break. You live on hope. I grew up playing ball with good players like Bill Bunting and Reg Harding, all of us hoping. And all of us got our shots. And all of us missed. Reg got into law trouble. Well, it doesn't always work out.

"I played ball at Northeast High under Bob Canaberry. I did all right and sent some clippings to Spencer, and later saw how he'd put them in a scrapbook. I guess he was proud of his big brother. Or maybe it was more that it helped him to get his own dream going. When I made it to Bowling Green and he made it to Chicago, he wrote me for some of my old clothes because he didn't have any to wear, and I wrote him, man, you can't wear my clothes, they'd be too big for you, and he wrote back, big brother, I'm 6-6, and I couldn't believe it, because I remembered a little boy.

"I went to Chicago to see him. I rang the doorbell and this big guy comes to the door. I didn't know him and I asked, 'Is Lena home? She's my sister,' I said. And the big guy said, "I know, Roy, 'cause she's my sister, too, and I'm your brother.' And I just looked at him and couldn't believe it. Lookin' at him, I could see then he was still just a boy, but he was so big, as big as I was, and where the hell does it go, your life, when your little brother grows up big without your being there to see it?

"He wanted me to see him play ball so I went with him to the playground and I saw him and I saw he could play, I mean really play. He challenged me and I went one-on-one with him, and he went right with me even though I was older and heavier and stronger and more experienced. I mean I was a fair college player, and here was a kid who hadn't really even started to play high school ball yet; but they learn fast on the playgrounds of black ghettoes in big cities like Chicago and Detroit and Philadelphia and New York, I want to tell you.

"Well, if you got it in basketball, you got a chance; so I figured I had to get him some place where he could get his chance right away, I figured I owed him that much. So I hustled him back to Bowling Green with me and put him up at my dorm and we worked out at the gym while I scouted around for a spot for him. But there wasn't anything there for him. They were impressed as hell, the coaches there, but they didn't have anything for him. Canaberry suggested I call Will Robinson in Detroit. I'd been thinking of that, too. So that's what I did.

"I called Will and told him I had my brother with me and he was only 15, but he was a helluva ballplayer and already 6-6 and needed a place to live and a school to play ball. I guess when I got to the part about Spencer being 6-6 Will started getting excited. I mean he knew I was good, and if I said my 15-year-old kid brother was better and had that kind of size, already, well, hell, it was like offering bread to a hungry man. Ol' Will got overanxious right off. He said, 'Well, bring the boy right on up, ol' Will will see what he can do for him.' 'Can he play for you?' I asked. And Will said, 'We'll see.' We'll see! Ha! Wasn't no way Will was going to let him get away from him.

"Robinson looked through the neighborhood and he found the Bells, whose boys played ball at Pershing and who had a nice home and were nice people and could afford another boy, and asked them if they'd take in a kid who needed a break and they agreed. So Spencer moved in with them and enrolled at Pershing High under Will. The courts fixed it so Robinson and the Bells could be his co-guardians, looking after him, and I went back to Bowling Green.

"Spencer needed help. He'd been running with bad crowds on the streets, running hard. He wasn't a bad boy, but he'd been doing bad things, because that's what you do on the streets. It didn't take me long to see that in Chicago, which was one of the reasons, besides basketball, I wanted to get him out of there. I didn't want that kind of life for him. And I guess he ran for a while in Detroit. But he wasn't basically bad. He just needed the chance to go good.

"I guess the first week he was out for basketball under Robinson at Pershing he wanted to quit because Will ran a tough program and Spencer wasn't used to discipline. Spencer called me up and he wanted to go home or go back to Chicago or come up to be with me. He said that man was just too hard. But I said, 'Spencer, he's a good coach, he turned out good people. What he does, it's for your own benefit.' And Spence insisted, 'I just got to quit.' And I said, 'Look, this ain't the playgrounds. It's real basketball. High school ball under Will Robinson is like college ball. Sure it's tough. It's supposed to be tough. Any good place you play, it's tough. I went though it. All good players went through it. If you want to make it, this is part of it. Just hang on.'

"He agreed, and three or four weeks later he called back and said, 'I'm OK now, I'm makin' it, I'm goin' to make it.' And I said, 'Fine.' I said, 'You're not on the streets now. You got a good home. Those are good people you're with. And coach is a good man. They'll help you. You listen to them.' And he said he would. And he did, I'm sure, because he began to change a lot. He's smart, but he had no real schooling before. He didn't talk well or read or write well, he was self-conscious about it, and he played tough to hide it. Living with the Bells, going to school regular, playing under Robinson, he not only developed as a ballplayer, but as a person."

Will Robinson

"Spencer needed developing when I got him. He was a poor black boy from the deep south who had been mistreated by life, reared in an environment of utter poverty, deprived of cultural opportunities. And he had come to the northern ghettoes and been exposed to the foulest sort of temptations and had given in to some of them. He was a rough, uneducated boy, shy, unsure of himself, putting on a tough act, scared of his ability to survive in a world that does not welcome black people. He had this fine basketball size and this great basketball ability, but let no one tell you that was all he needed, because boys with size and ability come along every year — they're a dime a dozen — and most of 'em don't make it. They don't get what they need to use what they have. I gave that to Spencer. A few years after I began to work with him, he was the youngest player ever to play on our Olympic basketball team, playing a man's role, too, the key man, which is what I done for him.

"Basketball was his out. Most boys in his place never get an out. His brothers and sisters didn't. Oh, they got from the south to the north, but they didn't get 'out,' not really, if you know what I mean; their lives are not what they might be. I use basketball. It is my tool. I take a boy who can play basketball and I make a better basketball player and a better man out of him and I get him a college opportunity and I get him a chance to get out of a life he might otherwise have to live all his days. Over the years I've helped more boys than I can count and I got precious little out of it, but satisfaction, which is something.

"Spencer was rough and adrift and I got him a nice home with the Bells, and between us we stayed after him to

32

straighten him out and develop him. We thought he was worth it. Any boy is. And this boy had some special qualities. As a player and as a person. As a man, he has disappointed me some, but as a boy, he was like a son to me, and I was like a father to him. The Bells became his parents. We counselled him and were strict with his studies and stressed right and wrong, and I worked him hard on the basketball court to bring out the best in him. We gave him love and security. We gave him hope. Between us, we got the job done. Between us, we made a man out of that boy. But it was not a smooth road. There were many misadventures, you might say, along the way."

3. Pershing High and the Heights

Spencer Haywood developed fast as a basketball player under Will Robinson at Pershing High School in Detroit. In his last two seasons as a schoolboy star Spencer averaged around 30 points and 25 rebounds a game and in his last season he led his team, which included Ralph Simpson, who followed him as a college dropout into pro ranks, to the Michigan State Tournament title.

Spencer says, "Robinson was a good coach. He knew the game inside out and he was tough. He didn't take any nonsense from his kids. If you wanted to play for him, you played his way. And everyone wanted to play for him because he turned out good players. Mel Daniels, for example, came just before me. Ira Harge, another ABA star, came just before me, too.

"When practice started, we climbed ropes, did push-ups, sit-ups, ran all day for two or three weeks. We never played a lick. When everyone was dead, then was when he threw the ball out there. Then was when we first started scrimmaging. And we had hard scrimmages. All-out. With the emphasis on fundamentals. I thought I was a pretty good player, but he was climbing all over my butt all the time. He wasn't going to play me for any favorite.

"At first, I got fed up fast. I wasn't used to it. My tail was dragging and my spirit was shot. I figured, who needs it? It was my future, sure, but there are times a kid doesn't look around the corner. I called up my brother and complained. I was ready to quit. I wanted out. I was happier on the streets. He talked me into sticking with it. I knew I should. I just needed someone to say I should.

"It got better. I got better. I got in better shape, I got to know what I was doing and what was expected of me, and I got used to Robinson. I liked the school and the school began to like me when they saw what I could do in basketball. I began to hit the books some and I began to do better in my studies. I had a D average my first year, a C average my second year, and a B average my third year. That's not bad when you realize I was illiterate going in. I could hardly read and I couldn't write legibly and I couldn't talk decent because I didn't know all the words. I began to gain confidence in myself as a person. The Bells were beautiful to me, and so was Will. I began to feel like I had a place in life.

"The basketball couldn't have been better. Robinson taught damn good fundamentals. And he had a style of play with running and movement and shooting that a guy could carry over into college and pro ball. We were in shape and we were prepared. And we had good players. In my junior year, we didn't lose much, but we did lose out on the titles. In my senior year, when Simpson was a sophomore and I didn't have to do all the shooting and could pass off more, we lost only one game, by one point in the city to Northwestern, but we beat 'em by 10 later. We wound up beating Pontiac Central in the state finals in East Lansing at Michigan State University fieldhouse."

By then he had reached the height of 6-8 and he weighed 215 pounds. He was a great jumper, had fine hands and a soft shooting touch. He was all-state two years and national All-America his last year. Although his background was not the best and his grades were just getting better, there was not a college basketball coach in the country who was not interested in him. By Will Robinson's count, 335 colleges contacted him. Some sent letters, some sent telegrams, some sent recruiters, some head coaches

35

telephoned him or came to visit him in person. This is their job and it is what they must do to get players and survive, but it puts cruel pressure on a youngster who has little idea what school would be best for him. Robinson served as Haywood's buffer, forcing the college people to see him, not Haywood, and screening all offers.

"He took a load off my shoulders, but a lot of people got to me anyway," Spencer says. "I know I had offers from every Big Ten school, including Michigan, of course. I had offers from Detroit, of course, and from Bowling Green, my brother's school. I had offers from a lot of Far West schools, including UCLA and USC and the Air Force Academy. I had offers from a lot of Southeastern and Southwestern schools, some of which I'm sure didn't know I was black and some of whom were so interested in getting a good player they wouldn't have cared if he was purple. Most of the offers were legit, though some were shady. Some hinted I could get money under the table for pretending to work at jobs, cars, all the clothes I needed, even ladies. Few of them said much about my studies. I suppose they supposed I wasn't interested.

"It turned my head, some. You know, man, here I was just learning to learn and some of the biggest-name colleges in the country wanted me because I could play basketball. It gave me a sense of power I'd never had before. It gave me a feeling of independence. Robinson was trying to give me advice, but I was wanting to go my own way. I wanted certain things from certain schools. It wasn't money I wanted, not then. It was other things. Odd things. At first I wanted to go to the Air Force because it seemed funny to think of myself as a fly-boy. But when I checked into it, I found out I was too tall for their entrance limits. Then I wanted to go to UCLA because I liked the idea of playing with Big Lew. But then I got to thinking about being in Alcindor's shadow and I forgot about that.

"I finally decided to go to Tennessee. That sounds crazy, I know, and Robinson was dead against it. He figured they just wanted to use me, and he was probably right.But I had met a chick in Knoxville when they brought me to the campus for a visit and I really dug this sister; and even though there sure weren't many blacks in school, there were a lot of them in town, and a lot of sisters I thought I could deal with in the black part of town, and I thought I'd have fun there. It's just a chancy thing, you know, why a guy makes up his mind that he likes this place or that place or wants to go here or there, and a sympathetic sister is as good a reason as any. Ray Mears, the coach, seemed like a nice man. And there was a lot of talk of me breaking the black barrier, blazing a trail in basketball for blacks to follow me in that school and all southern schools. I liked the idea of being a pioneer. So I enrolled. But when I took the entrance exam, I flunked it. I did my best, but I wasn't ready for it and I didn't make it. And the NCAA ruled I couldn't play ball there because of that. So I dropped out.

"Robinson had wanted me to go to New Mexico, where he'd sent Mel Daniels and Ira Harge and had a good arrangement, or Detroit, where he hoped he'd be the next coach. Because of flunking the Tennessee test, I guess, I couldn't get right into a college, but had to go to a junior college first. Bob King, the New Mexico coach, gave me a pretty good rush and arranged for me to prep at Trinidad Junior College in Colorado, and I gave in to him. He sneaked me out by plane in a helluva hurry, as though guys were on my tail, and I guess the recruiters were coming round, and I found myself at good old Trinidad JC.

It was a city of around 8,000 people without any black people. There wasn't anything for me to do there except study and play ball. The studies went OK. I got a 3.2 average out of a possible 4.0, which is a B or a B-plus. And the ball went fine. I made us a good team and we did fine. Vern Moser was the coach and he was fine. I averaged 27 points and 23 rebounds a game and was voted national junior college All-American. But to put it bluntly, I was beyond those boys; it wasn't much of a challenge for me there. And I like to went crazy. There just wasn't anything for me to do. And on the $15 a month expense money I got, there wasn't much I could buy.

"There were about 1,200 people in the school, but only about 75 black dudes. I could rap with some. Mostly, I'd play ball, study, read and sleep. There was nothing to do downtown. There wasn't even a downtown. I'd go to the Student Union and watch the end of the line. There were girls in school I could date, but I never was much of one for dating white girls. I'm not putting them down or it down, but it just isn't my thing. There were only about seven sisters. For 75 brothers. I got one of the sisters. After I went to the Olympics, I got two of the sisters. Two out of the seven."

It was a freak that he got to go to the Olympics. This was in 1968 when black athletes were threatening to boycott the Olympics in Mexico City later that year. The black track stars, who are the stars of our Olympic team, felt they were "used" by lily-white National AAU officials and suggested that a refusal to participate in the international competition would focus world-wide attention on their civil rights cause. San Jose State professor Harry Edwards was an unofficial leader of these protestors, whose number included John Carlos, Tommie Smith and Lee Evans. In the end, Carlos and Smith gave their black-gloved salute to our national anthem on a victory stand. But, in the end, they had reached that stand, they had participated in the Games. Black basketball players did not know this when they had to make up their minds about taking part in the Olympic trials; they had to make up their minds first. And Lew Alcindor, Elvin Hayes and other black star amateurs and collegians of that year bowed out.

Vern Moser said Spencer Haywood was the best basketball prospect he'd ever seen, but who listened to Vern Moser? However, driven by desperation, National AAU officials invited junior collegians to join with senior college players and other amateurs in trying out for the U.S.A. basketball squad in hopes of rounding out an acceptable team. And they turned up a new star in Spencer Haywood from Trinidad Junior College, who stole the show at the Albuquerque, New Mexico, trials, made the team, and became, at the tender age of 18, not only the youngest player ever on a U. S. Olympic basketball team, but the star of the team.

Big, strong and springy, quick, agile and tough, the inexperienced youngster made a deep impression on observers and pulled in a great deal of favorable publicity as he toured with the team in warmup tests in Madison Square Garden and other major arenas against pro players and pickup teams, then awed all who saw him and garnered headlines for his performances in pacing his club to a clean sweep in the Olympic tournament in the beautiful, large, circular indoor stadium erected outside Mexico City expressly for these classic contests.

This was not this country's best Olympic basketball team by any means, hardly comparable to the one led by Bill Russell or the later one led by Jerry West and Oscar Robertson, but because of Haywood it was able to maintain a U.S. record of never having lost a single game, much less the gold medal, in basketball play, a record which is not as easily maintained as it may seem, a record which may not endure much longer as several other countries stress the sport, while our country's players stress pro play.

Bearded, but just a boy, really, a bearded boy, he somehow seemed a man as he played his games before crowds of more than 20,000 persons. There is an image of him there which remains in the mind's eye, sweating, struggling, but gracefully guiding his older teammates to the top, assuming a leadership beyond his years, grabbing a rebound when it was needed, netting a basket when it was needed, working hard, working, working, working. Coach Henry Iba said, "He is so sincere and dedicated and works so hard, I can't believe it."

Spain fell, 81-46. Senegal, 93-36. The Phillipines, 96-75. Panama, 95-60. Italy was supposed to be tough, but was beaten handily, 100-61. Yugoslavia was supposed to be tough, but was beaten decisively, 73-58. Puerto Rico turned out to be tougher than expected, almost upset the favorites, but fell at the finish, 61-56. In the semi-finals, the U.S. beat a big Brazil team, 75-63, while Yugoslavia upset Russia to gain another shot at the top club. In the finals, the U.S. prevailed, 65-50.

"It was a great experience, from start to finish," says Haywood. "I know some of the brothers backed out. I suppose I sympathized with some of their sentiments. But I wasn't any part of that. They didn't let me in on it. No one spoke to me about it. When I was invited to take part in the Olympic trials, it was an opportunity I never dreamed of getting. Man, there was no way I wanted to pass that up.

"In New Mexico, I met Bill Russell and he spoke to me

and I answered him. I thought, 'Wow, I'm talking to Bill Russell.' I couldn't believe it. I looked at the way he was dressed. You had to figure he had money in his wallet. He seemed smooth and straight. I was just a kid, you know. I was really impressed. I thought more than ever I wanted to be just like him. I knew then for sure I wanted to play pro just like him. And he'd been an Olympic star and won a gold medal, so I wanted that, too.

"Even though some of the big-name ballplayers had pulled out, we had some good talent at the trials and we got some good guys going, like Jo Jo White and Charlie Scott, who are top pros now. I found out I could play with them, and by then I was beginning to feel I could play with anyone. At first, just making the team was a thrill, but then I saw it was my place to lead it so I just took on that responsibility and did it. Hank Iba was the coach, slow-down style, but I just did my thing his way.

"I only averaged 19 a game, but I rebounded regularly and stressed defense. We stressed team play and defense and a disciplined offense, which was good because we didn't get to play together long and had to go a little cautious. I gained a lot of confidence on the pre-Olympic tour we took around the country, but when we got to Mexico City I felt unsure of myself at first. I'd never been to a foreign country before and I wasn't used to a lot of different kinds of people being around speaking a lot of different languages and I'd never played before the kind of crowds we played in front of.

"I'd get so nervous before games I'd start shaking in the locker room. A couple of times I stumbled running out on the court. All that was expected of us was to win every game and not ever lose even one because no U.S. team ever had. Yet people kept saying we were the worst U.S. team ever and were bound to lose, which fired us up. We were determined to prove we were better than people thought we were. And no one wants to be the first to lose, you know. Once we began playing, it was all right. We began winning and it was all right.

"It wasn't all easy. I mean some of the big centers I faced had a lot of size on me and not much skill so they tried to make up for it by pushing me around, but I just pushed back and I held my own. The writers kept saying I was the star, so, OK, I played like that. I figured if I'm supposed to be a man, I'll be a man. And we kept on winning. Puerto Rico scared the bejabbers out of us, but we got by them and pretty much breezed in after that. We never did get to play Russia, which was a disappointment, but we'd have beaten them, I'm sure. We twice beat the team that beat them.

"When we won the final and took the victory stand and they draped those gold medals around our necks and played the national anthem, it sent shivvers down my spine. I mean I'm no super-patriot. I know a lot that's wrong with this country. But, it was the situation. Here I was, 19 years old, the youngest guy ever to play on an American basketball team in the Olympics, the star of the game, how many years out of Mississippi? And all those people from all those other countries who always started out rooting against us because we were the big guys they wanted to see knocked off wound up cheering us. It was some kind of feeling. I don't know where my gold medal is. I don't have a trophy case. I don't even keep many trophies. I spread them around. I give them here and there. It wasn't the medal. It wasn't the anthem. It was winning. It was doing that thing.

"The city is a beautiful city and the people are beautiful people. It was a tremendous experience meeting people from all different countries and all different ways of life, everyone all gathered together in sportsmanship, you know, to compete, to win, but to have a good time, to have an experience. Well, it was an experience, a beautiful experience," he concludes, his eyes shining. He is smiling. The memory of it obviously is a pleasure to him.

Now, less pleasant memories intrude. Although normally athletes who prep at junior colleges spend two years at the junior college, then two years, their junior and senior seasons, in senior college, those with a B average or better in their studies are eligible to move up after one year, and Haywood had that, and the desire to move up, but he had lost his desire to attend New Mexico. And he was being earnestly recruited by Detroit, which wanted the Olympic hero to play his college ball in his "home town."

41

Spencer recalls, "I had been reading an article in *Sports Illustrated* Magazine about how black athletes are mistreated in many colleges, how they are pushed around, used up and shoved out. They recruit you with honey, but after they get you they handle you with vinegar. They don't care about your studies, and after your eligibility is used up, they don't care if you graduate. A lot of athletes never do graduate from college, which is why it's a bunch of bull about it being so bad when guys quit to turn pro. This stuff scared me, and a lot of the guys I got to talk to said it was so. I asked Greg Howard and some of the other athletes at New Mexico how it was for them there, and they said it was bad. What the hell did I know about New Mexico? It didn't sound like a place for black guys.

"Robinson was pressuring me to enroll in Detroit. Bob Calihan, the coach there, was pressuring him to get me. Calihan was due to retire as coach there and Robinson had been promised he'd replace him. If he got me to go there, I guess. Will had the record as a high school coach in Detroit. He'd turned out the best players and the championship teams. But he was a black guy, and black guys don't usually get the college coaching jobs. So I guess he had to show them he could deliver by delivering me. But that was all right. I wanted to help Robinson. He'd helped me. And I figured we could have a helluva team at Detroit. And I'd be back among people I knew. And maybe I'd even get to play for Will again before I graduated. So I enrolled in Detroit."

Bob King says, "What can I say? We recruited him and we thought we had him and we lost him. We wanted him. Who wouldn't have wanted him? He had to go to a junior college first. We didn't send him to Trinidad. No one sends anyone anywhere. We helped arrange it so he could go there if he wanted to, which he did. And he agreed to come to New Mexico. But when it came time, he backed out. I don't know who he spoke to. He didn't speak to me. I don't know what anyone could have told him, because we take as good care of our athletes here, black or white, as they do at any school in the country. We do everything that is within the rules. Some of these kids don't feel bound by rules. Whatever he read, he didn't read anything bad about New

Mexico because we weren't in that article. Whatever, he just went back to Detroit and we lost him. We had no hold on him. We couldn't stop him from going. We couldn't stop people from influencing him. I guess this is a kid who is pretty easily influenced. In any event, he didn't stay at Detroit long."

Haywood lasted one year at Detroit. He played his sophomore season under Calihan and finished fourth in the nation in scoring with an average of 31 points a game and led the nation in rebounding with an average of 21 per game. Sometimes he was sensational. In one game, on a driving layup, he flew through the air with such force and stuffed the ball down through the basket so hard that he tore the rim right off the glass backboard, shattering it. Other times he displayed an uneven temperament. Scrambling with a foe for a loose ball in Toledo, he was called for a foul. When he protested too strongly, the referee ejected him from the game. So Spencer punched him. Haywood was suspended for two weeks.

Spencer says, "The man had been making bad calls. This was a bad call. When I complained, he said, 'Don't talk back.' Like I was a boy. And he was smiling. So I said, 'Hell, I'll wipe the smile off your face.' And I did. But I didn't get him a good shot. And they pulled me off him. And later the sportswriters said I should be barred for life. But they don't bar the big ballplayers, you know that? It was interesting to find that out. Hell, I know I was wrong. The man was only trying to do his job. It's just that he did a bad job. And probably should have been out looking for other work. But I haven't punched any referees since. A few players, but no refs."

Still, Spencer came back in full stride. Although his absence cost the team a possible bid to the National Invitational Tournament in New York, Detroit still finished fine at 16-10 and clearly was one of the coming teams of the country. However, by the time the next season rolled around, Haywood was gone, and so were Detroit's chances. Calihan had retired from coaching to the athletic director's chair, and his replacement was Jim Harding, not Will Robinson. And with the coming of Harding came the going of Haywood.

The change in coaches probably was the prime reason for Haywood's defection. Spencer says, "That was the big thing, yes. I liked Calihan. He was a good guy and a good coach. But when I went there, I went with the understanding that he was on his way out as coach and Will was on his way in. I'd heard hard things about Harding. All the guys had. He was supposed to be a bad man. He was such a bad man, when he was at LaSalle, half his team quit him. And while I never played under him at Detroit and don't know the man, I guess he is bad, because after he got to Detroit half his team quit him. I guess he lived up to his reputation. I didn't wait around to find out for myself. I had no desire to play under him. He hadn't recruited me. I hadn't been told he'd be my coach when I agreed to go there. A guy has a right to know things like that.

"More than that was the shaft they gave Robinson. They bought him off with a promise like *they* been doing all their lives, then backed down from it. And Will deserved that job. He really did. Anyone around Detroit, anyone who knew anything about basketball, knew that. I was disgusted. I could see their word meant nothing. But I could see that even before that. I'd had bad tonsils all my life. I never had the money to get them taken out. Sometimes I'd get attacks of tonsillitis and be terrible sick. Then it'd pass until the next time. That's the way it is with tonsils. But I guess they keep getting worse and worse. I had a bad attack the one season I played with Detroit, but they didn't want to have them taken out then because they didn't want me out of action. They promised they'd pay to have them taken out after the season, but they never did. I had 'em taken out, but I wound up paying, out of my Denver money, which is why a guy like me wants to turn pro, so he can make his own money, so he can pay for his own operations, so he don't have to rely on anyone's promises."

He shakes his head, his expression angry. The veins in his neck stand out. His muscles bunch up and he slaps his fist into his palm in frustration. He says, "They didn't do me any favors at Detroit. They gave me a full scholarship and $25 a week and they arranged for me to have a flashy car to drive. I drove an Austin-Healy, a sports car. I like that sort of luxury. That was all right. But I also worked at

Jack's Place, a clothing store, for $1.75 an hour to have a few extra bucks in my pocket and a place where I could get some rags cheap.

"The school put me in a physical education program. They must have thought that's all I could handle. We had a big argument, because by then I had it in my mind that I'd be going into pro sports and maybe later into acting or announcing and I wanted to take a radio and television course instead. I won the argument. I worked like hell catching up on all I'd missed earlier, and I got a 2.9, which is all right, but no thanks to them. Then when I got sick, they said, keep playing, son, we need you, we'll take care of you later. Well, later never came. Just like when Will got me to go there: 'Don't worry, Will, we'll take care of you later.' Well, later never came for him, either.

"I thought of going to Michigan State. John Bennington, the coach there, wanted me. I'd have had to sit out a year to be eligible, but that might have been all right. I really did want the college. At Detroit, one of my teachers, Father Brown, really turned me onto books and I got 2.9, 3.0 grade averages and felt I was getting somewhere. But then Cincinnati of the NBA started sniffing around, then Denver of the ABA, and with Denver we found out I could turn pro right away and start making my own living, good money, right away, so that sounded good.

"I mean I was making $15 a month in school, and when suddenly someone says you can make $100,000 a year, you start listening. There were strings to it. They weren't prepared to pay me $100,000 a year straight salary. But they said they'd give me money for my old age, and it would amount to around $300,000 for three years. They put out the line and they had me hooked. I hadn't thought I was eligible for pro ball until my college class graduated, but they said they could get me in on a hardship gimmick, since my family was needy, which it certainly was, as long as I sent home some money, which I would have done anyway.

"Robinson thought it was smart, so I went along with it. I mean I wanted school, but I didn't want to be a scientist; I wanted to be a basketball player, I wanted big bread, so why not get on with it? So I made the big jump from

45

Detroit to Denver, from college ball to pro ball, and, as it turned out, from one snake pit to another. But college ball hadn't impressed me that much. And don't tell me how I screwed Detroit. They treated me like a black stud. Don't tell me how the colleges do this and that for the boys. You ask the players. Black players. Or white players. Not while they're in college, afraid to talk. Ask the pros. Or any of the guys after they've left college. Find out how many graduated. Find out how many feel they were treated right. OK, I wasn't happy, so I left. That's my business, right? That's my right. Right?"

Bob Calihan

"We first tried to recruit Spencer Haywood when he was a high school boy in Detroit. We are a Detroit college, we're interested in good athletes for our teams, and we were especially interested in an outstanding athlete in our own town. We approached him through Will Robinson, his coach, a fine coach who turns out fine players, and a person who'd always helped us to recruit players we wanted because he was interested in placing players in good colleges. He might have had ties elsewhere, such as at New Mexico. I know some of his players went there. But that was none of our business. We couldn't, wouldn't, and didn't ever make him any promises in exchange for any players, not even a Haywood.

"I think it's proof of this that we lost Haywood to Tennessee. He failed to get in there, but that was something else; he intended to go there. Then he turned up in the southwest, prepping at Trinidad Junior College. It was said that he was supposed to go to New Mexico, but until a boy actually enrolls at a senior college, or signs a letter of intent to enroll at a senior college, there is no rule against other colleges continuing to seek him. We did keep in touch with Will, saying we still very much wanted Spencer, and we were very pleased when he enrolled here. Aside from the natural talent he brought to our team, he brought a big name from the Olympics, he already was a hometown hero from his high school exploits, and we felt the popularity of our team would reach a new peak.

"I made it clear I might not coach throughout his college career. I'd been coaching 21 years, I'd been athletic director a few years; I felt it was time to retire from the coaching, and I felt it was time to concentrate on the athletic directorship. It's very difficult to combine both jobs. Both take a lot of time and attention. But we didn't know who the new coach would be. We certainly didn't promise Spencer or Robinson or anyone else that it would be Robinson. We might have said we would consider Robinson. And we did consider him. And it is no reflection on him that we did not choose him.

"We chose a coach with college coaching experience. He had the reputation of being a tough coach. He is. But that's not necessarily bad. He played his own college ball under Henry Iba, one of the great coaches and a strong disciplinarian, and he brings many of the same qualities to his own coaching. Some players did quit after Harding took over. But some I think simply were following Spencer. And some didn't want to go through the schedule we faced without Spencer that we had arranged with Spencer. And some simply didn't like a stern coach. Possibly I wasn't stern enough. But Harding is still here and he's won twice as many games as he's lost over his first seven seasons here with boys who are willing to make sacrifices to succeed.

"Will Robinson seemed to have a strong effect on Spencer, and I'm sure most of it was for the good. Will had taken an underprivileged boy from a poor background, straightened him out and helped make a new life. And he'd given him fine coaching in basketball. Possibly, Will was so disappointed when he didn't get our coaching job he influenced Spencer to leave school. But I don't know that. I just know that Spencer left.

"If he was disappointed that Robinson didn't get the job, he didn't say so to me. If he was disappointed that Harding did get the job, he didn't say so to me. He certainly couldn't have had any valid objections to Harding's coaching because he never stayed around long enough to be coached by the man. You ask if we failed to fulfill a promise to pay for a tonsillectomy for Spencer, but I honestly don't recall him complaining of any tonsillitis during the season. And if he wanted money for an operation after he left school, he'd be responsible for that then, not us, wouldn't that be so? I don't think we failed on any promises to him. Everything was legal and above board.

"Had he stayed with us, he might have become one of the best college players ever. He certainly was one of the outstanding sophomores I ever saw and the best we had while I've been at this school. He had size, strength and all sorts of natural skills. He did have trouble controlling a hot temper. The incident in which he punched a referee was very unfortunate, embarrassing to the team and to the school. Possibly, his punishment should have been more severe. But it was a first offense and we try to help troubled youngsters, not dismiss them. Possibly the official made a bad call, but I don't think that's the point. If he made a mistake, Spencer made a bigger one.

Still, Spencer tried hard for us, and for the most part I certainly had no complaints about his performances. With him, we began to dream some pretty good dreams. We scheduled games in Madison Square Garden and Chicago Stadium. We thought we could be a threat for the NCAA title. He left and we were destroyed. We won six and lost 19 the next season. We've come back since then, but not to the top. We haven't had any players of his ability. They don't come along very often. And when they do, you don't get many of them. And the one we got, we didn't keep long. If you get them often, you're a UCLA and you've got a dynasty going. Well, that's the way it is.

"I think after the glamour and excitement of the Olympics, college ball seemed a little tame to Spencer. Perhaps the publicity went to his head. Certainly, he was hungry for big money. And I can't blame him for leaving if the money is as big as it is supposed to have been. I think the super player who can play many years and make big money for many years probably should get into professional ranks as soon as he can. And I think the player who is uninterested in a college education might as well turn pro if it is possible for him to do so. But I think the dangers in signing players for pro ball before they complete their college education is that many who could make use of a

48

college education will not get it and many who expect to play pro ball will not make it. A college education can be of tremendous value to a person all his life, while most never will be high-paid professional athletes and many who do make the pros will last only a few years. That is the record, but few view it realistically.

"Spencer was a good student here. He wasn't going to graduate *magna cum laude*, but he took the courses he wanted to take and went to his classes and he did well enough. One of the reasons he said originally he wanted to come here was we are known to have a fine radio-TV course and he wanted to prepare himself for a future along those lines. We encouraged his interest in studies and were disappointed when he lost interest in school. I'd certainly be less than honest if I didn't admit as athletic director I was deeply disappointed when we lost him from our basketball team. He destroyed our dreams. But he is entitled to make any life for himself he wants to make. And in his case I'm not sure he made a mistake. But I do think many who might follow his example will be making mistakes. And I think the NBA and ABA and all professional sports leagues will be encouraging many youngsters to make serious mistakes and will pose a threat to college athletics if they raid campuses without regard for anyone's welfare beyond their own bank balances. For all I know, Will Robinson advised Spencer to stay. I know some of these young men need good advice."

Will Robinson

"I gave Spencer good advice, but he didn't always take it. He listened to me about running around, about wasting himself, about learning how to really play this game, using what God give him, and he became a tremendous high school player. There wasn't a college in the country didn't want him. I took the pressure off him. I protected him. But still some got through to him. I didn't want him to go to Tennessee. I didn't want to see a black boy go back down south. They've had since the Civil War to start doing right by blacks, are they going to start now, with a boy like

Spencer? They just wanted to use him, put him in a showcase. But he got it in his mind he wanted to go, be a pioneer. Only it didn't work.

"I've always had good relations with New Mexico. Sent Mel Daniels and Ira Harge there. And I believe black boys, my boys, were treated well there. Spencer had to prep first and they arranged for him to go to Trinidad Junior College in Colorado and Spencer took my advice on that, and it helped him being there. And he got to go to the Olympics from there, where he showed the results of my coaching. He needed me, so I went, all the way to Mexico City, with my wife, to help him, with the result he was voted the outstanding player in Olympic basketball, a boy who'd been prepared properly to fill a man's role.

"We decided it would be best for him to go to Detroit, however. I was led to believe I would be the next coach there. It wasn't only Bob Calihan, but others there. And I should have been the next coach there. I had the best coaching record in Detroit. I had turned out the best players. I was a living legend there. And I got along with whites as well as blacks. The timing was right. This was right after the riots, and it would have been a beautiful marriage for integration, a wonderful example to set for the citizens. I could just feel it in my well-being. It was right. As it turned out, it was a tragedy. I am still depressed by it. Such an opportunity never will arise again.

"I made the athletic officials there the best offer any coach ever made a school. I said I would bring Spencer and other top boys and the first year I would take the team into the NCAA tournament and the second year we would win it all and by the third year our basketball program would be an artistic and financial success such as that school never dreamed of having. They'd be in the big time, they'd probably be building a beautiful new fieldhouse, they'd be on top of the world, or I wouldn't take a dime, I'd bow out without salary and without fuss.

"Why didn't I get the job? Race, of course. It's just this: Had I been white and not black I don't think there would have been any question but that the job would have been mine. That is a disgrace, of course. But then that school has a long history of mishandling athletics and athletic oppor-

50

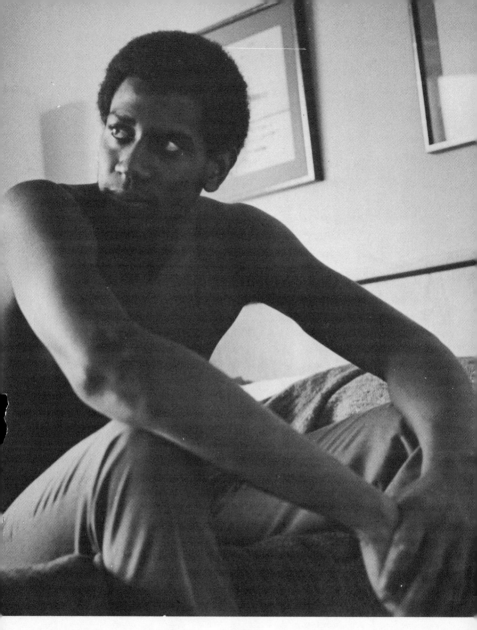

Brooding, Spencer Haywood sits out an uncertain time in his young life as he waits for a resolution of his controversial flight from the Denver Rockets of the ABA to the Seattle Sonics of the NBA and the resultant court case. There were many moments of waiting and wondering and worrying between appearances in a federal court and in Seattle uniform on NBA basketball courts around the country.

(PHOTO BY DUDLEY, HARDIN & YANG)

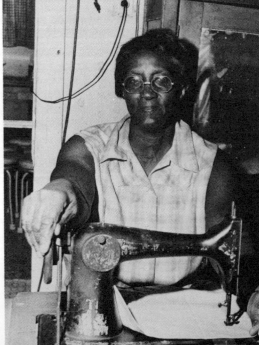

A youthful Spencer Haywood is shown at the age of thirteen. Right, his mother sits at her old sewing machine. Above, she sits with her grand-daughter, Pinky, left, and daughter Ivory outside her old River Road house in Silver Springs, Mississippi, as it is to-day, where Spencer was reared yesterday. Ivory, incidentally, is the leading scorer on her Humphrey's County basket-ball team with an average of 25 points per game.

(MOTHER PHOTOS BY PHIL WALLACE, JACKSON, MISSISSIPPI, DAILY NEWS)

Haywood's coach, friend
and guardian while he at-
tended Pershing High School
in Detroit, was Will Robinson.
At left, Haywood tosses in an
easy two-hand dunk-shot in
practice at the University of
Detroit.

In action in the Olympics in 1968 Spencer Haywood led the Americans U.S.A. to another gold medal in basketball, a medal they were not expected to win. Here, in the final game against Yugoslavia, he blocks a shot by Peter Skanski—a move that was to become familiar to players in both the ABA and NBA.

(PHOTO BY WIDE WORLD PHOTOS)

At another happier time, a smiling Spencer Haywood is shown at the press conference at which was announced his new, third contract, said to be worth $1,900,000 for six years' play, with the Denver Rockets and J. W. "Bill" Ringsby, right, and his son, Don Ringsby, photo at left.

(JOHN WHITWORTH FOR THE ROCKY MOUNTAIN NEWS)

In ABA action with the Denver
Rockets, a menacing and dominating Spencer Haywood displays some
of the moves that made him not only
Rookie of the Year, but Most Valuable Player in the circuit and the
key man on the divisional pennant-
winner. Above, he grabs the ball and
protects it from the Stars' Craig
Raymond, center, and Tom Washington, right, while preparing to
pass off. At left, referee Earl Strom,
one of several NBA officials who
jumped to the ABA, watches with
awe as Spencer stuffs the ball
through the basket two-handed. In
these games in January, 1970, the
Rockets were rolling along on an
eighteen-game winning streak.

Client Spencer Haywood makes a point to manager Al Ross of All-Pro Management outside a Los Angeles courthouse during the pursuit of his controversial legal case, largely heard by Judge Warren Ferguson, below, whose rulings have shaken the establishment.
(PHOTO BY BILL RAY © TIME, INC.)

Judge Warren Ferguson
PHOTO BY ASSOCIATED PRESS)

Spencer Haywood's enormous and unusual hands are displayed against an average hand. His fingers have an extra creased and knuckled joint on each beyond the average. The upper portion is lighter in coloration, as though added later by some mad scientist. Haywood's hands cup a basketball as easily as another's might enfold a grapefruit. (PHOTO BY DUDLEY, HARDIN & YANG)

tunity. Where are they in the sporting world? What have they accomplished? It's a good school, I suppose, and that is the first consideration, of course. But they wanted excellence in athletics, too. After they got Spencer, they went out and scheduled themselves against the best teams in the biggest arenas in the biggest cities in the country. They can't pretend they haven't gone after this thing; they just haven't gotten it. With me, they'd have gotten it.

"When we decided it would be best for Spencer to get out of there, it wasn't only the way they'd treated me badly, but the way they'd treated Spencer badly. He'd had the tonsillitis, but they insisted he keep playing until the season ended. Then when it ended, they backed down on their promises to pay for an operation. They weren't going to give him the best coaching. They weren't concerned with his getting the best education. So what was the point of his staying there? His mother was still on her knees washing floors back in Mississippi. His brothers and sisters were hungry. He needed money. And pro teams were offering him money. It didn't make sense for him to wait two more years.

"The offers for him came to me. European teams called or wrote asking his services. In some countries over there, such as Italy and Spain, they play a lot of basketball on a professional level, and I suppose they were impressed by the Spencer Haywood they'd seen in the Olympics. Some players such as Wayne Hightower played in Europe a while before returning to the U. S. to play pro ball. Bill Bradley played in Europe, too. But I told Spencer I didn't feel it would serve his purposes best. He wouldn't be improved by good coaching and competition, and he wouldn't be in the spotlight over here. The Harlem Globetrotters contacted me about Spencer. Wilt Chamberlain passed up his last year of college to tour with the Globetrotters before going into the NBA. But I didn't feel the fooling-around approach would be good for Spencer's image. He wasn't established in the public eye as Wilt had been.

"We really got interested when a representative of the Cincinnati Royals of the NBA contacted us. I don't remember who it was, because we weren't interested in his particular pitch and we didn't go into it much, but it did

59

set us to thinking along the lines we later followed. He said Cincinnati wasn't in a position to play Spencer right away, but they could pay him right away, sign him to a contract, get the rights to him and use him as soon as he was eligible. In the meantime, they'd have put him in a position to help his family. This wasn't as far out as it sounds at first. The owner of the Royals had signed Jerry Lucas to a personal services contract while he sat out a season, then used him the next season. And after Spencer later left Denver and signed with Seattle, the court ruled that since his contract with Seattle was valid, other NBA teams had no right to get him through the draft.

"When a representative of the ABA contacted us with an idea we could go to Denver to play right away, we were interested. These teams never sent their own people. They always saw to it their own skirts was clean. They always worked through third parties. This time they worked through a guy by the name of Steve Arnold, who had a business with a guy named Marty Blackman in New York, and who did business with the ABA. He said he'd heard we were unhappy in Detroit; he said Denver was interested in turning Spencer pro right away, and if we were interested in joining the Denver team he thought something nice could be worked out. So I got Spencer and flew him to Denver where we met with Arnold and Blackman and the owner of the Denver team, Bill Ringsby, and his son, Don, and we negotiated all night and we worked out something nice for Spencer.

"I represented Spencer and I advised him and I gave him good advice. He wanted to play in the NBA against the best players, but I told him the NBA wasn't going to let him play with them for two years and he could worry about that later. I said this was war, between the NBA and ABA, and he could take advantage of it by signing with the ABA for the sort of money he couldn't command if there was peace by the time he graduated. Spencer was worried about the money up front, but I was more concerned about the money in back, the money that guaranteed his security, his future. I saw to it that he had an annuity written in. I saw to it that it was written in that they paid for a college education for Spencer so he could finish his schooling whenever he wanted and that was put in. I didn't get a dime out of it. It was all for Spencer.

"Later on, they fixed up an even better contract for Spencer, and I advised him to take that. But then Spencer wanted an even better contract yet, and he stopped wanting to take advice. The more money he got, the more he wanted. He wanted to see it in piles around his feet. He got greedy. What good is $75,000 a year or $100,000 a year or $150,000 a year to a player if taxes are going to take most of it and he's going to spend the rest and he'll have none of it left later? The only good contract for a player is a contract that gives him the money to live good now and help the people he should help and gives him more money every year of his life later in life, when he can't play basketball any more. I helped him get that, and the gratitude I got was I lost him.

"From the moment he got to Denver, he started getting away from me. These other people started talking to him, giving him bad advice, these other players and people from other teams and these lawyers and agents, like Al Ross, who stole my son from me, because Spencer was like a son to me. I never gave Spencer a bad word of advice in my life. And I never got nothing from him, not even a thank you, much less a thin dime. I got him to Denver and the good pro contract. Right up to there, he was all right. From then on, he got to going wrong, he got mixed up, he got led down a crooked road."

4. Denver and Dollars

Although many details of the Spencer Haywood case are in dispute, some are not.

In August of 1969 at the age of 19, Spencer Haywood signed his first contract with the Denver Rockets of the American Basketball Association. Spencer signed and so did Will Robinson, representing him as his guardian. J. W. (Bill) Ringsby, the Rockets' owner, and his son, Don, represented the Denver team. The contract was worth approximately $450,000 in round figures for three years of Spencer's service to the team. He was to be paid $50,000 a year for three years, then was to receive an annuity from age 40 of $15,000 a year for 20 years. Spencer also asked for seasonal expenses, so his yearly salary was increased to $51,800 to cover an additional $1,800 for winter apartment rent. And he received a $10,000 advance.

That fall, the Ringsbys invited Haywood and Robinson to hear a presentation by a New Yorker, Ralph Dolgoff, of a plan he had developed for the investment of contracted monies. The plan promised greater returns for lesser expenditures than previous programs and greater tax shelters for all concerned. Many ABA teams were impressed by the Dolgoff plan and were using it to shape the contracts they were offering players. It was the basis of the large contract Carolina offered Billy Cunningham to jump from Philadelphia of the NBA, for example, although he then decided not to make the leap. (He was forced to, finally, in 1972.)

In October of 1969, Haywood and Robinson signed a new contract with the Denver Rockets. Under this contract Haywood was to receive the $50,000 seasonal salary originally set for three years, but he was also to have $3,000 a year invested for him for 10 years in the Dolgoff plan. This investment was to generate $300,000 for him by the time he was 60 years of age. Again, he could begin receiving money from the age of 40, but the less he took, the more he would receive later, since the more that remained in investment, the greater the eventual returns. Spencer also purchased Bill Ringsby's car from him for $9,000, the payments to be deducted from Haywood's annual salary, reducing it to $47,000 per year. This contract also was considered to be a three-year, $450,000 pact.

In April of 1970, after NBA scouts had begun to court Haywood, when Denver wanted greater assurances he would remain with their ABA team, when Haywood wanted more money, Spencer signed still another new contract, a third pact, with the Rockets. This contract was announced as a six-year, $1.9 million pact. Since Spencer, turning 20, still was under the legal age of 21, his signature was matched by that of Ben Gibson, a Denver banker, who became his guardian and was to advise him on the contractual details. Gibson represented a bank which handled accounts for the Ringsbys and the Rockets, who recommended him to Haywood. In the new contract, Haywood was to receive $50,000 per year for two more years, as covered by the remainder of the earlier pact, but reduced to $47,000 per year to cover the car payments, and $75,000 a year for four additional years, plus the proceeds from $10,000 a year invested by the Rockets for ten years into the Dolgoff plan. Thus it was considered he was to receive $400,000 in straight salary over six seasons and it was estimated the investments for him in the Dolgoff plan would generate an additional $1.5 million for him between the ages of 40 and 60.

There was a $100,000 insurance policy contained in the

pact, plus a promise to pay him $50,000 if traded. And $5,000 was sent the Bells as a "bonus."

Spencer ratified this in court in June.

During this time, Haywood had established himself as a professional player of tremendous value to the Rockets or any team which could obtain him. For a 19-year-old boy who should have been in his junior year of college ball, he had had a remarkable rookie season in pro ball: he wound up as the leading scorer and leading rebounder in the ABA, the Rookie of the Year and the Most Valuable Player in the circuit, surpassing the performances recorded by such established stars in the ABA as Rick Barry and Mel Daniels. If the level of competition was unequal to that in the NBA, it was sufficient to make the domination of such an inexperienced youngster truly meaningful.

The previous season, Denver had finished third in its division, 16 games off the pace of the pennant-winner. Haywood joined a team which had one shooting star in little guard Larry Jones, but no other consistent scorer, no effective rebounder, no star center in a game which is dominated by the big men. At 6-9, Spencer was best suited, by pro standards, to play out of the corners in a forward position, but because he was the best they had, the Rockets often had to match him against seven-foot centers, yet he not only outscored them, but also outrebounded them consistently.

Byron Beck, Julie Hammond and Junius Keye were the other tall men on the team, while Jeff Congdon and Lonnie Wright were the other backcourt "little men." These men were, at best journeymen performers, although one or two had good potential. John McLendon, the coach of the team, tried to build a new team around his new star, Haywood, and his old star, Jones. He was not successful at first. A black man who had coached such black schools as Cleveland State, Tennessee State and Kentucky State to national titles in small-college competition, he had gotten one earlier "color-barrier-breaking" opportunity in the old ABL and now a new one in the ABA, but when his team won only 9 and lost 19 of its first 28 games, and was stuck in the cellar ten games off the top, he was dismissed and replaced by Joe Belmont.

64

Belmont, a former Duke University and National AAU performer and a referee with limited coaching experience, had been signed by Denver as a super-scout, but he stepped into the top spot on short notice and rapidly rebuilt the Rockets to respectability. A warm, eager young man, enthusiastic on the bench, he seemed to instill a lot of spirit into the team, and such strategy as he used, such as making Beck his regular center and settling Spencer in at a forward slot, paid rich dividends. The Rockets soon went soaring on a 15-game winning streak, which projected them back into the pennant race. They wound up winning 42 games and losing only 14 out of 56 run by Belmont and finished in front in the division by six. Fans in this mile-high city got sky-high over the team, and in the end the club was encouraged by the enthusiasm of 21 sellout audiences.

Haywood was the hero, the largest man in sports in this beautiful big-little town, which has only one other major league franchise—the long-suffering pro football Broncos. The fans drove over snow-drifted roads from surrounding communities, hustled through freezing nights and packed the warm old auditorium to watch this wunderkind work his miracles, raising a racket that threatened to raise the roof above the balcony of this beat-up building as the Rockets, moved by momentum, beat up on all visitors. And when Haywood and his helpers took to the road, where they continued to win, he and they developed into a great attraction, one the three-year-old circuit sadly needed for survival.

At the time, it had become apparent that Haywood and Daniels and Roger Brown and a few others in the ABA could have been stars in the NBA, as Rick Barry was before joining the new league, and as Connie Hawkins had become after leaving it. Hawkins was MVP of the old ABL at 19, and Haywood, who plays much like Hawkins, early in the season was proving the most advanced prodigy to turn pro since then.

Haywood was happy. At first it was fun. The money he was making was more than he ever dreamed of making in his life. And he was having a good time with it. He had bought the $9,000 car and spent another $4,000 to have it customized especially for him. He had spent twice that much on a new wardrobe and had himself designed many of his clothes, "Chicago gangster suits." He had moved from a modest apartment to a plush pad and was throwing fancy parties for friends and the "sisters" he adored. He also was trying to do some good with his money. He had given his mother some and was buying her a new home, and he was setting up his brothers in business and sending a sister to school. He was even helping the guys and gals who ganged around him, a soft touch for a hard-luck story. He didn't seem to mind. He was taking acting lessons and envisioning himself as the first black cowboy in movies and on TV, so that there would be more money later.

"I have a good time coming to me, don't you think?" he asked, grinning broadly. "What have I had in my life? Nothing until this. I just want to enjoy it a while. I'll worry about later later. Some day I'll marry and have kids. Some day I'll have responsibilities. Some day I'll settle down. Some day I'll be an old man. But that ain't today. Today is now. And you're only young once. I'm young and single and I'm making money and if I'm blowing some of it there's more where that came from. I'm no fool. When the time comes to worry, I'll worry. But you only live once and I got a lot of living to do right now." He was like a child at Christmas time. There were toys all around him, within reach, and no one to slap his hand. And who would have wanted to? He was happy, living a life many would want to and never will, even for a passing moment.

He stood in his plush place, almost awesome in his joy, and said, "Denver is my town now. The Ringsbys gambled on me and hit the jackpot. It's not as tough as I thought it would be, you know that? I was scared coming in, a 19-year-old college kid trying to play the pros, but I've found out I can play with them, I can play better than them. Maybe it's because it's the ABA and not the NBA. There's better players in the NBA, I know. And better teams. But there's good players in the ABA, too, and I've found out I'm as good as they are, and I'm making our team the best team, and I'm not afraid of the NBA any more, either, because I'm sure now I can play with the best. It's a helluva thing to find that out, you know."

"Spencer Haywood," said his coach, Joe Belmont, "can be the best basketball player in history. He is more agile and has more all-around ability than any man his size who has yet come along. He is one of those like Oscar Robertson and Lew Alcindor who was good enough to have made it big in pro ball right out of high school, and is making it big when he should still be in college ball, before any of the others had to do it. And he is going to get a lot better. For one thing, he is going to get bigger. He is going to add weight. He is strong, but he is going to get stronger. With his reputation, he has a lot of pressure on him, but he has more poise than any boy his age I've ever known and unusual desire. He wants to be the best. He doesn't want to settle for anything less. And he may not have to."

That Belmont was a booster was, of course, understandable. And others were impressed, too, if a little more reserved. Bob Leonard, a great college player at Indiana University and an experienced pro player and coach in the NBA, who was coaching Indiana in the ABA, said, "If I had a man as big and agile as Spencer, such as Gus Johnson, I think Haywood could be stopped. When he drives, he doesn't always look for the open man. And he doesn't always go all the way, but stops, turns and backs in. And, he, himself, is not good defensively. But he has the ability to learn. He has the tools to be great. He really seems to love to play. And, most important, maybe, he has a mean streak in him. He'd cut your throat for a field-goal. That's a great asset in a player."

Al Bianchi, also a former NBA player and coach, who was coaching Washington, said, "Haywood always goes to his right. He has to learn to go to his left, too. And he doesn't block shots anywhere like he should. With his agility and jumping ability, he's got to get better. But he could get it all in time."

This was before a Washington game in Denver. In the Caps' dressing room, Rick Barry said, "Spencer's been a center and he's learning to play forward. He's not used to facing the basket and he can't put the ball on the floor and make the moves to beat a man one-on-one, like, say, an Elgin Baylor can, but, hell, that's fast company. At the All-Star game, I gave him some tips on how to play Mel

Daniels and Spencer put 'em right to use and made them work for him, which is rare in a kid. And he was the MVP of that game. If he gets good coaching, he can get to be one of the greats. He has great things going for him."

Some 7,000 fans filled the small building to see the Sunday afternoon game. Barry, the old rebel, showed them something, and Haywood, the new one, showed them something else. Barry the successor to Elgin Baylor as the finest forward in the game, battling back from knee injuries, hit every kind of shot imaginable and kept the Caps in the contest until he was benched after nine minutes of the third quarter with four fouls. The game got away from his team then, during that time. He returned angrily to finish with 55 points, within two of the league's one-game scoring record, set the previous season by the storied Hawkins, but it was insufficient to save his side.

Meanwhile, Haywood, who would like to succeed Barry as the best at their spot, picked up pointers from Rick as he went along, played all 48 minutes, wound up with 31 points and 16 rebounds and passed off for 12 more baskets. On one play, he faced the basket, went one-on-one against Ira Harge, faked him out going to his left, wrapped the ball behind his back and stuffed a score. On one drive, he went all the way through to score, sending Harge stumbling off stride. On another drive, drawing Barry on defense, Spencer sought an open man, found him and fed off while in the air for an easy bucket. He darted out with a long arm and blocked a shot 20 feet from the basket on another play. Paced by Spencer, the Rockets won by nine as the crowd cheered delightedly.

In the dressing room, Spencer seemed dissatisfied, and was goddamning the referees for fouls called on him and some not called against him, which is his usual way, when they wheeled in some Vietnam veterans to meet some players. One was legless. He reached eagerly for Haywood's hand. Spencer shook it, sucked in his breath and turned away. Softly aside he asked, "What the hell have I got to complain about?" After that, he dressed in silence. Outside, he found some kids carrying on profanely. They were black kids, waiting for him, working off excess energy while waiting by throwing bottles, wrestling with one another and cursing contentedly. Haywood bawled them out, loaded them in his big car, drove them back to their tenement, unloaded them at a playground and shot baskets with them until it was too dark to continue.

Back at his apartment, Spencer stretched out on a sofa and said, "I want to make a lot of money and do a lot of good with it, for myself, and for others. I want to put on free basketball clinics for poor kids. I want to donate dough to poor blacks in Africa. I'm no militant. I'm not turned on by violence. I don't hate everyone. I want to help Indians and Mexicans and every other poor put-down minority as much as I want to help blacks. I take each man as he comes. But I'll never forget being poor and hungry and being slapped and kicked and it has got to change my life some. I got to go after the big dough because I got big plans. Some for myself. I want to help my friends and my family, but I also want to help myself. I have put some money in a pile and said this is for them, and I hope it works for them, and I am putting the rest in another pile and saying this is for me and I will make it work for me."

The season was wearing on and he seemed altered from earlier, less content with his life. He confided, "I want to live the good life because what other life do I have? It's been bad, but it's been getting better, and I want to make it the best. If I have to become the best basketball player in the world to make the most bread, that's what I'll be, because I want to be that and because I want the bread. I'm spending too much, you know that? It's all gone before I get it. All right, I had my fling, maybe it's time now to cut down on the fun and games. I want to have something left.

"Denver isn't paying me enough, you know that? When I signed with them, I didn't know what was a lot. And I wasn't sure what I could do on the court. Now I know. And now teams like Milwaukee are offering me a lot more money than I'm making with Denver to jump from the ABA to the NBA. Can you imagine me playing with big Lew Alcindor? Who'd ever beat us? But I don't know if I can jump. Milwaukee says I can, but I don't know if I can. I always wanted to play in the NBA, not the ABA, but now I don't know if I can. I always wanted to play with the best. Maybe there'll be a merger. Maybe I won't have to jump.

Maybe Denver will do better by me. But I'm not sure any more."

He sighed and said, "I don't know about the Ringsbys any more. Bill Ringsby calls me 'boy.' I tell him, 'I'm not a boy, I'm a man. Call me by my name, Spencer.' Maybe he didn't mean anything by it. But sometimes they treat people bad. They had no business firing John McLendon. He was a good coach. He got off to a bad start this season, but he was a good coach. Joe Belmont's a good coach, too. He's a good man. I got nothing against Joe Belmont. But I still wish they hadn't fired John McLendon. We're winning with Belmont. But there's trouble on the team. Larry Jones is unhappy. He's jealous of me. He has a right to be. He's making $23,000. He's been the top scorer in this league. He came in without a big name, so they bagged him cheap, but now when he asks for more dough they say no. Well, I'm going to get mine because that's my right, and if anyone tries to cheat me out of it or con me out of it or take it from me, I'll fight them. I've paid my dues. I'm paying the price. I'm playing this game as good as anyone. And I'm going to get as much out of it as anyone."

He shook his head as though to shake off bad thoughts. He seemed to pull himself together. It was time to take off to pick up some lady visitors at the airport. As he dressed in some fancy duds, he started to whistle a song. "Oh well," he laughed, "There's always the sisters for comfort. They're even parachuting in these days."

Two nights later he was on the move again, dropping into Dallas where the Rockets were ripped by 13 despite his 37 points. Spencer said, "What I get means nothing. It's what we get that counts. I had a good night, but we had a bad night. I could have had a better night and so could we. If I get seven more points and my man gets seven less, we win. Or maybe if I get a basket or a rebound or a steal at just the right time, it turns things around. I could see it going wrong, and it made me mad and I stopped playing for awhile, which was stupid." Belmont said, "Spence was all right, but he got mad a little and then he slowed down a little. I tell him we can win without him, but it's a helluva lot easier with him. I tell him he's got to go hard all the way or I'll have to give him rests, but when I pull him, he begs back in. I'm gonna start giving him more rest," he smiled, "between games."

Spencer was playing more minutes than any player in the league and he admitted he was tired. In Los Angeles, he turned down a request to appear at a sportcasters' luncheon so he could rest. He lay on his back in his motel bed all day except for four times when he got up to eat, stuffing himself with everything he could find in the restaurant. "I have to build up," he said. "I've lost 15 pounds this season and I'm down to 210. I'm not used to this grind of traveling and playing 80 games a season. You go and you go and you go. It seems like you spend half your time in airport waiting rooms or airplanes or living out of a suitcase in some hotel room, and every time you turn around you're out on a court to play another game and you have to look around to figure out where the hell you are and who the hell you're playing. I need 14 hours sack-time a day. I can't nap in planes the way some old cats can. They've been around and they're used to it. They take what they can get. I guess you get used to it. But it must take time. It's a hell of a grind. You go and you go and you go. When the hell do you sleep?"

He could not sleep. He lay in the dark room talking instead of sleeping. He talked about his dreams of being the best in basketball and making the most money and having the nicest apartment and the most girls. "Everything about me is outsized," he said, smiling. He snapped on a lamp for a moment and reached out his long arms and displayed his large hands and showed his long fingers and how each finger had an extra joint and bent in three places instead of the usual two. The top digit on each finger is whitish, looking as though it might have been added by a mad scientist. "It's my secret weapon," he grinned.

Smiling, he looked very much like Bill Cosby. "I've heard that," he grinned. "I'm even used it. I had one chick believing I was his brother for an entire evening. In the end, I confessed I really wasn't a Cosby. Who I was was Bill Russell, who always was my idol. For a while, I wanted to be just like Russell. Now all I want to be is myself," he said. And he turned off the light and lay back down on his bed in the darkness.

At the Sports Arena that night, a teammate, vagabond pro Ben Warley, said, "Spencer is some kind of someone. He is a young old man, real good people. He has great talent, but he is modest and willing to work hard at making the most of himself. And he may become the most man this game has ever known." Over in a corner, Larry Jones simply said, "He's a fine young player." And dismissed it. There was no enthusiasm in Jones's voice or manner. Clearly he was not a member of the Haywood cult.

Someone whispered, "Jealousy rears its ugly head." And noted confidentially, "You are the star of the team for a couple of years, the scoring star of the league, and then a new star comes in who outscores you and makes more money than you do and, zowie, there is a division. So sometimes Larry doesn't throw the ball to Spencer and sometimes Spencer doesn't throw the ball to Larry, and when someone throws the ball to Spencer, Larry is mad, and when someone throws the ball to Larry, Spencer is mad, but we've been winning, so it's OK. But how long can we go on winning?"

"Doesn't the coach see it?"

"There isn't much he can do about it."

"And the owners?"

"They pat us on the back when we win and kick us in the teeth when we lose. They don't want to know why something is happening, only what's happening. They just care about the score. They're front-runners. We're like tenant-farmers harvesting a crop for their table."

"How come you're still winning?"

"Haywood, mainly. And momentum. But the NBA scouts are sniffing around Spencer, and he's getting it in his mind he's worth more money than he's getting. We may be at the top of the hill. On the other side it's all downhill."

Before the game that night, Bill Sharman, the former star NBA player and coach, a brilliant coach who has won wherever he has gone with whatever he had, said, "We try to beat this team by stopping Haywood. We try to stop

Haywood by forcing him outside. He can hit from outside, but he can't dominate you there the way he can inside." The L. A. Stars, Sharman's club, worked on Spencer all night, double-teaming him a lot, roughing him up a lot, screening him off from the inside, closing off the basket area to him. So he scored 43 points, mostly on long outside shots, surpassing his previous pro high of 41, and sneaked inside for 19 rebounds. But his team lost to the Stars. Later, Sharman appeared relieved. "The boy almost beats you by himself," he said. "He almost certainly will become the greatest player at both ends of the court ever." Veteran sportscaster Sam Balter said, "Haywood is the first truly complete basketball player to come along."

Told these things in his dressing room, Spencer sighed and said, "It is all very nice to hear these things, but it doesn't make my job any easier. If I don't become the best in history, I'm letting everyone down. That is some kind of burden to tote around with me. But I guess I'll just have to get used to it. It's what I want, too." He was sprawled all over his bench, sweaty and weary. Belmont, deeply disappointed in the outcome of the game, came over and was gentle with his prodigy, putting his arm around him and talking quietly to him. "You just keep growing and doing your thing," he urged, wetting his white shirtsleeves on his star's black shoulders.

Back home, against Pittsburgh, Denver won as Spencer scored 36. Two nights later, in Washington, he scored 43. The next night, back home against New Orleans, he scored 46. Two nights later, back in Dallas, he scored 47. "If the NBA is any faster and rougher than this league," he said, "it'll surprise me."

It was getting rougher and rougher for him as foes tried to frustrate him, double-teaming him, holding him, shoving him, working on him as the way to whip Denver. But he kept bombing the baskets and hitting the boards, and once in a while he punched an opposing player, and all the time he screamed bloody murder at the officials. Stories that the NBA teams were interested in stealing him away broke in the newspapers and soon the Ringsbys had called Haywood in and he had signed that third contract.

He kept getting better, game by game, until the Rockets

clinched their divisional pennant with several games to go. Then, in the last game, he set a new one-game league scoring record with 59 points against Sharman's Stars in Denver. When he was taken from the game with two minutes remaining, Spencer received a standing ovation that lasted two minutes. For the season, Haywood had new league record averages of just under 30 points and 20 rebounds a game, his team took its title by six games, and he was MVP.

The playoffs were something else. Spencer was sensational individually, but the Rockets started to struggle collectively. Barry was brilliant in the opening series as his Washington Caps pressed the Rockets to the limit. At his best when it counts the most, as usual, Rick averaged 40 points a game in the seven-game set. He and Haywood had a fight in one game which wound up with players on both sides wrestling on the court. After winning the first two games in Denver, the Rockets lost the next two in Washington. The Rockets then won again in Denver, lost again in Washington, but wrapped it up with a romp at home in Denver.

Sharman's Stars were a different story in the semi-finals. The Rockets won the opener, but then lost four straight and the series. Spencer wound up right behind Barry in playoff scoring with an average of just under 37 points a game and the best in rebounding with an average of just under 20 a game, but suddenly it was all over for the Rockets. They had shot skyward, then thudded back to earth, and there was deep disappointment in the organization. The Stars could go no further, losing to Bobby Leonard's Indiana Pacers in six games for the ABA championship.

Haywood traveled over the summer, touring with an all-star team as far away as Panama and just packing and picking up and going, visiting friends in Detroit and Chicago and New York and Philadelphia whenever he felt like it. He had the money and a restless urge. He felt dissatisfied. He talked to other players. He asked them about their contracts and other players' contracts and they asked him about his. He studied it and tried to make sense of it, and he began to feel it wasn't what it should have been.

For one thing, he saw that he'd have to play for Denver for ten years, not six, to get all of the future returns from the investments made for him, and there was no indication how much he'd be paid over the additional four years. Anyway, he hadn't wanted to tie himself to the team for that long. And he wasn't satisfied with the $50,000 a year he was making. He now was the MVP of the ABA, but he was making less than lesser players. Others had seniority on him and had worked their way up the salary scale with years of successful service, so perhaps they rated more, but he wasn't looking at it that way. Also, he couldn't see where he had any guarantees he'd ever make the kind of money he was supposed to make later on, even by the time he was 60. Who knew about investments?

He began to go in to the Ringsbys to see if he couldn't get a better contract, but they indicated to him they'd given him about as many better contracts as they were going to. Their feelings should have been understandable to him in this, but he had been growing more and more mistrustful of them and their motives and he resented their attitude. He began to feel strongly that he should have had expert legal and business counselling and advice in the signing of his contracts, and he resented it that neither the Ringsbys nor Will Robinson had recommended he have such on his side. Robinson tried to cool him off, but Spencer no longer trusted Robinson; he wondered if Will wasn't being influenced by the Rockets. Soon he no longer was even speaking to his old mentor. This left him feeling alone.

Spencer had been spending his money as fast as he made it and he had made contact with Al Ross, a Los Angeles lawyer, who managed many athletes, such as Deacon Jones, Rick Barry, Carl Eller and others, under the banner of All-Pro Management, to handle his money and put him on a budget and maybe make investments for him and earn some side money for him in the form of commercials or endorsements or TV appearances. He asked Ross then to study his contract, too. It was time for Spencer to start preseason training with the Rockets and he reported to camp, but in a bad frame of mind, without enthusiasm. He almost seemed relieved when he broke his hand and was sidelined early in the exhibition schedule. Then Ross told him the contract was terrible, and it didn't guarantee him anything that had been promised him, and had many unfair clauses in it, and, since he had signed it while a minor and without real legal and business advice, he probably could force Denver to give him a better contract.

Haywood, who originally had signed with All-Pro Management to handle his account for 25 percent of any new business it brought him, now signed a new personal contract with Ross to handle all his affairs for 10 percent of all his income, this pact to supersede the old one, and he moved into the attorney's Beverly Hills home while Ross began to negotiate with the Ringsbys for a new deal for his new client. There were some stormy meetings, in Denver, in Los Angeles, at the L. A. International Airport and the International Hotel. ABA commissioner Jack Dolph got into the act to seek to save the young superstar for his young circuit. There was talk of ABA owners wanting Denver to trade or sell Haywood to another ABA team that would satisfy him, or even of wanting the Ringsbys to sell out to new owners in Denver who would satisfy him.

At a time when some of sports' most powerful moguls were seeking him, Spencer supposedly was hiding out, but he did not do it discreetly. One afternoon, several youngsters showed up at Al Ross's office asking for autographs by Haywood. Wondering how in hell they knew Spencer was around, Ross searched his suite for his client and found him in a small room, napping on a couch, and with him found his answer. Haywood had been keeping in shape by running in a public park wearing a gaudy warmup sweatsuit bearing the names HAYWOOD and DENVER ROCKETS boldly emblazoned on the back. The attorney confiscated the outfit and he, himself, often wears it these days when he works out with whichever of his nomadic clients happens to be in town, telling them how much better at basketball he is than they are.

Meanwhile, Ross could not get what he wanted from the Ringsbys and he was beginning to hear not only from other

ABA teams, such as Carolina, but from NBA teams, such as Seattle and Los Angeles. He began to talk business with them. NBA Commissioner Walter Kennedy got into the act for fear one of his league's teams would sign a player whose original college class had not graduated. Such a signing would violate the "four-year rule," which protected the universities from pro "raids," a rule which Denver and the ABA had ignored by invoking the "hardship" escape clause which permitted "needy" players to sign up. Sam Schulman of Los Angeles, the owner of the Seattle franchise, asked the NBA for permission to sign Spencer, but was denied this at a meeting in San Diego. The maverick Schulman went ahead and signed Haywood anyway, for $1.5 million for six playing seasons to be spread over 15 years — $100,000 cash per year.

From the time Haywood left Denver and arrived in Los Angeles, the tale of his new leap made headlines on sports pages across the country. As the rumors and charges flew back and forth, the controversy grew into a major and messy sports scandal. Before long, legal action ensued, followed by court hearings and proceedings. The Rockets charged Ross with luring Haywood from them and secured a temporary injunction against his serving Spencer. The Rockets sought to force Haywood to fulfill his contractual obligations to their team. Ross and Schulman charged that the Denver contract was invalid, charged the NBA four-year rule was illegal, and asked approval of the Seattle pact. High-powered and high-priced legal firms representing the Rockets, Ringsbys, Ross, Schulman, the Sonics, the ABA and the NBA were hired and bent to the battle.

The season had begun. The Rockets, minus Spencer, struggled as losers, and Belmont swiftly was fired as coach. He was replaced by Stan Albeck, who would be replaced at season's end by Alex Hannum. The Sonics, with star center Bob Rule injured, also were struggling, but before long coach Lenny Wilkens was waiting for Haywood, who had to help. When Judge Warren Ferguson ruled in L. A. that the four-year rule was, indeed, illegal, and gave Haywood legal permission to play for Seattle pending the outcome of the case, Haywood did begin to play, but he did not play well and he did not help the team much. He seemed to be resented by some of his new teammates. They did not quite know what to make of this controversial, apparently temperamental, certainly high-priced young superstar, who, though billed as their saviour, had yet to prove himself in what they considered to be the real big league.

Spencer also was flying back and forth between court appearances and games with the Sonics in Seattle and all the other NBA cities across the country, making some, missing others, missing sleep, tired, unsure of his future, almost aimless. When he did play, his presence was protested by other NBA teams, even those which had expressed interest in signing him. Even when he did not play, his presence was protested. One NBA team blamed Seattle and Spencer for an injury a star player suffered in a game because he was distracted and disturbed by Haywood's presence on the bench. It almost got to be ludicrous after a while, but the beleaguered black youngster was not laughing.

He was in a Seattle hotel room at twilight. He'd had the "Do Not Disturb" sign hung outside the door all day. He had not let the maids in to make the beds. He did not want to be bothered. He had not bothered to eat all day. He lay on the rumpled bed, not sleeping, tired but unable to sleep, staring at the ceiling. He got up and pulled on his pants, but he did not bother to put on shoes or a shirt, and he stood and stared out the window at the grey day for a long time. He sat on the edge of the bed and stared at the carpet or off into space. He spoke sometimes, but there were long silences from time to time. He seemed sad.

"I'm tired," he said. "I'm bone-tired physically. I feel all used up mentally. I can't think straight any more. I have been pulled this way and that way until I feel like I'm just going to come apart. I am so sick and tired of all the hasslin' you wouldn't believe it. You probably figure I brought it all on myself. I guess everyone does. I'm supposed to be a bad man. Greedy Gus. Out for himself. Hell, who isn't? I don't know how much I'm worth. Only what they tell me I'm worth. Then they won't give it to me. Hell, that contract Denver gave me ain't worth the paper it's printed on. Three of them they give me and none no better than trash. How the hell did I know this? What am I, a lawyer? Did I have a lawyer? Hell, no. Did they? You bet your boots they did. I do now.

"You go into things with good expectations. High feelings, you know. Then it turns sour. I went to Detroit on trust. Then they did me dirt, and they did Will Robinson dirt. So I left Detroit to turn pro with Denver, and Detroit and the NCAA and the public still haven't forgiven me for turning pro before I graduated from college. Why? Isn't it my business? If the man wants to pay me to play, why shouldn't I be free to make a buck? What is it, robbin' a bank? Ain't I free? Are all athletes slaves to the system? Who the hell was going to worry about whether I graduated anyway? Who the hell was going to give me a buck, a nice place to live, some decent clothes, a nice car to drive? Who the hell was going to give my mom a few bucks so she could start living decent? How does the system protect me? So the NBA was mad as hell at the ABA for letting Denver sign me, but they weren't going to let New York or L. A. sign me.

"Then Denver treated me like dirt. They misled me at every turn. And Will Robinson turned on me and sided with them. And so I finally got someone with some sense on my side. And all the ABA teams wanted me and all the NBA teams wanted me. And when I left Denver to sign with Seattle, all the ABA teams were mad at Denver for letting me get out of their league, and all the NBA teams were mad at Seattle for getting me into their league. The same teams that wanted me suddenly wanted me out when they didn't get me. It seems like the only people ever on my side are the ones that got me at the given time. And right now I'm not sure my own teammates want me. Some are nice, but some seem to think I'm diseased. The public thinks I got the plague."

He shook his head, torn by his troubles. Softly, he asked, "Am I right? Am I wrong? Have I done wrong? Did I ask too much? Should I have just accepted things as they were? Shouldn't I fight? Didn't Rick Barry fight? Isn't Curt Flood fighting? Like the man said, 'If you don't stand for something, you'll fall for anything.' So I'm standing up for myself. And maybe they'll knock me down. I don't know if I can win. I don't know what I'll win. I don't even know if I want to win anymore. I just want to play basketball. But when they let me, I don't play good anymore. My mind's on a million other things. And in the long run they may not let me. Maybe it's ending for me.

"Maybe I should just pack up and get out. Sometimes I think I'd just like to drop out of sight. Sometimes I think I'd like to go to Russia or Cuba or somewhere, anywhere, anywhere else but here. I don't want to hassle any more. I don't know if it's worth it. I'm tired. Tired of hasslin'. Tired of hating. Tired of being hated. Tired of being a bad man. Tired of not living. I haven't had a date for weeks. I don't want no sisters giving me advice. I don't speak to friends. I don't even call home to my momma. I've had advice 'til it's coming out of my ears. It doesn't mean anything to me anymore. I can't figure out what's right and what's wrong anymore. I'm just tired."

And he sat on the bed in silence for a long while in the darkening room, without bothering to turn on the lights, without wanting to be bothered.

5. Court to Court

The controversial court case centered on a single rebellious individual, Spencer Haywood, but it touched on many sensitive matters of sports business. And while the case eventually was settled out of court, there were rulings along the way which have had great impact on sports. In fact, even the out-of-court settlement of the case seems to have had an unsettling effect on the old order.

Also, the attitudes and intricate manueverings of athletes and the sportsmen who control their destinies are interesting, as revealed on the following pages.

Essentially, there were some basic legal issues in dispute. The Denver Rockets contended that Los Angeles attorney Al Ross took their star Spencer Haywood from them and induced him to breach their contract with him. Haywood, through Ross, contended the Rockets, through the presiding Ringsbys, Bill and Donald, had induced the minor Haywood to sign contracts which would not deliver what was promised him and without proper representation.

The National Basketball Association, through Commissioner Walter Kennedy, contended that one of its members, the Seattle Supersonics, owned by Sam Schulman, had no right to sign to a playing contract a player whose original college class had not graduated; such a signing would be a violation of the NBA's four-year rule. The American Basketball Association, through Commissioner Jack Dolph, contended Haywood had no right to live up to his new contract to play for Seattle in the NBA, since he already had an old contract to play for Denver in the ABA.

Additionally, the NBA, as does the ABA, allots rights to players through a rotating draft system. The Buffalo Braves of the NBA contended they should have the right, which they later exercised, to draft Haywood if their turn came up first. Seattle countered with the contention that since it already had Haywood under an NBA contract, he was not eligible to be drafted and then signed by any other NBA team.

Beyond this, there were many variations of basic issues in dispute, many of them brought up through other cases past, present or pending.

Major league professional sports organizations have adopted certain rules to protect their operations. Essentially, court rulings that theirs are not typical interstate commerce operations have protected them from antitrust charges. But they seem to live in constant fear that test cases in the courts, with consequent judicial rulings, or Congressional hearings, with the enactment of new legislation, will alter the status quo.

The franchise-holders in a given league operate as a private club. They vote to approve or disapprove the sale of franchises to new owners and to add or not add new franchises and owners. They vote to approve or disapprove the transfer of franchises from one city to another, usually on the grounds that a franchise is not being satisfactorily supported in a city, whether or not mismanagement may have been the fault that support was not forthcoming.

Thus, in baseball, it is legal for the Washington, D. C., franchise to be moved to Minnesota, for a new one to be established in Washington, and then for a new owner of the new franchise in Washington to move it to Dallas-Fort Worth. And for a franchise to be moved from Milwaukee to Atlanta, and an expansion franchise to be located in Seattle and then after one year to be transferred to Milwaukee.

In basketball, when the ABA was formed, a franchise was located in Oakland, across the Bay from an existing NBA franchise in San Francisco. The NBA star in San Francisco, Rick Barry, jumped to the ABA team in Oakland, but he was prevented by a court ruling from playing for his new contract-holder until an option year on his old contract had expired. When the Oakland franchise was shifted to Washington, Barry signed a new contract with San Francisco and contended he did not have to go since he had signed a contract to play with an Oakland team, but the courts again ruled against him. The franchise was later transferred to Virginia, and the San Francisco franchise now operates in Oakland. Meanwhile, Barry was traded to New York. So he signed with the Nets in hopes he could stay with them, but when his original contract expired in 1972, a court ruled he had to then return to San Francisco and the NBA. Rick is one player who has never won a case.

In some sports, players in the past were free to sign with the team of their choosing in the beginning, but then were bound by contract to the league for the remainder of their careers in that sport. The owners were free to transfer these contracts by trade or sale from one team to another. In all professional team sports now, the rights of teams to new players are allotted through common drafts held within each league. And these players are bound by the contracts of each league. In major league professional baseball, basketball and hockey, these contracts contain reserve clauses which, in essence, bind the players to the teams which hold their contracts throughout their careers. In football, there is an option clause which permits a player to play a year beyond his contractual obligation to a team, then seek to sign with another team, with his original contract-holder to be recompensed, by decision of arbitration if necessary.

Baseball abandoned its open marketplace for new players and adopted a free-agent draft when bidding for the best prospects produced payments beyond reason for unproven talent. However, when a new league is formed to compete with an old league in a given sport, such as the AFL rising to compete with the NFL in football or the ABA rising to compete with the NBA in basketball, you have not one team drafting a new prospect, but two, one in each league. The competitive bidding for services again produces big bonus payments and astronomical salaries. And as their contractual obligations expire or can be broken, players are tempted economically to jump from one team in one league to another team in the other league. If the new league can survive long enough and apply enough pressure to the old league, the old league usually will weary of the war and sue for peace in the form of a merger to insure survival.

The NFL was bending under a bonus barrage by the AFL but did not break until the AFL began to raid the NFL of its most precious stars—quarterbacks. After Oakland of the AFL signed Roman Gabriel of Los Angeles of the NFL to a contract, and Houston of the AFL signed John Brodie of San Francisco of the NFL to a contract, the NFL agreed to merge and these jumps were knocked down in mid-air. Gabriel already had agreed to return to L. A. and honor his contract there, and he did not press a court case to gain the additional monies promised him. However, Brodie did press for full payment of the $750,000 promised him (for three years' service) and now has a contract granting him payment in full (part already received, part to be received in the future, without any additional service). He will be paid $52,500 a year for ten years beginning the year he retires. The leagues cooperated in honoring this debt.

Although sports tend to run in cycles of domination by one team or another—baseball's Yankees in the 1950's, basketball's Celtics in the 1960's, football's Packers in the 1960's, hockey's Canadiens in the 1960's—the purpose of the draft is to provide an equal distribution of talent and, hopefully, over a period of time, balanced competition. Generally, the teams with the worst records one season get the earliest choice of the new players available for the next season. And the purpose of the reserve clauses is similar, but it also protects the investment in money and development each franchise makes in its own talent. Theoretically, if there were no restrictions, a few franchises in the best economic situation could afford to acquire the best players and dominate their leagues to degrees that would produce uninterest and declining attendance and fewer TV and radio bids. Also, it is argued, the fan who purchases season tickets has a right to know he will see his team's star players. However, it also is argued that the fan has no protection against his favorite stars being traded or even his favorite teams being transferred. And number one draft choices frequently are traded away, too.

It is said that the four-year rule in football and basketball protects youngsters from the temptation to give up on their college studies prior to graduation. Realistically, these rules have served to protect the interests of the colleges, who by playing football and basketball provide training for players during their maturing years and even produce star attractions for the professional leagues in those sports which have no investment in minor league operations as development grounds. And for all but a few exceptionally talented youngsters, college ball is the only road to pro ball in these sports, whether or not they are interested in studies. There has been no four-year rule in the professional baseball and hockey leagues, which have minor league systems and so seem more interested in developing their own stars than urging youngsters toward degrees. A degree never has been a requirement for admission to any professional sports league, anyway.

The Spencer Haywood case as much as anything else hastened merger plans between the NBA and ABA, pending Congressional approval. The rights of professional sports to regulate itself have been debated on the floors of the Senate and the House many times in the past and are being so again. Former Senator from California Thomas Kuchel, an attorney representing the two leagues before Congress, has said, "The business of professional basketball is in deep economic trouble. Many of the teams in the two leagues are consistent money losers. It is unrealistic to expect that owners will continue to subsidize them regardless of economic considerations.

"Unless merger is promptly consummated, it is my belief that a substantial number of franchises may fall. After the inevitable shaking out and shrinking down, professional basketball would be confined to a relative handful of the largest cities. This would be to the detriment of the basketball fans of the country, and of the players, many of whom no longer would have opportunity.

"The conditions presently confronting professional basketball result from the annual rites of self-destruction between the two leagues. Teams are quite literally forced by the need to maintain league status to bid against each other annually for those college players entering professional ranks with reputations as potential superstars. The yearly bidding war with its fantastic contracts for a limited number of untested rookies will inexorably end in ruin."

Robert Nathan, a consulting economist retained by the two leagues, has testified he considers a merger essential on economic grounds. He contended that without it the bidding war for the services of the best players will cause clubs to overextend themselves to points of collapse. In his survey, he used statistics of 11 ABA teams for four seasons (39 of a possible 44 team years), and 17 NBA teams for six seasons (67 of a possible 81 team years):

"On two occasions, teams in the ABA incurred operating losses in excess of $1 million per year. In one third of the years, operating losses were between $500,000 and $1 million. In nearly half of these observations, losses fell between $250,000 and $500,000.

"The NBA financial picture is somewhat better, but hardly affluent. Of the 67 operating years examined, 25 were profitable and 42 were not. Nearly half of the annual losses were over $250,000. Nearly a fourth were over $500,000. Two cases had annual losses over $1,000,000."

He reported additionally that only two of the 17 franchises were found to show a profit for the entire period studied.

Nathan noted that average starting salaries of draft choices ranged from around $8,000 per year for the 1960-61 season to $12,000 per year for the 1966-67 season. With the arrival of the ABA, however, these rose to $46,000 per year for the 1970-71 season.

In general discussion of the salaries of "superstars" signed by the ABA, he noted that the top pact reported paid a player $317,000 per year for three years (including bonus, salary and other compensations) and the lowest $46,000, with the average around $117,000.

Following the signing of Haywood to play six seasons for $250,000 a year with the total $1,500,000 to be paid out over 15 years at $100,000 a year, the NBA and ABA signed such rookies as Jim McDaniels by Carolina for $2,900,000, Artis Gilmore by Kentucky for $2,200,000, Johnny Neumann by Memphis for $2,000,000, Elmore Smith by Buffalo for $1,800,000, Sidney Wicks by Portland for $1,500,000, Ken Durrett by Cincinnati for $1,500,000, Austin Carr by Cleveland for $1,400,000 and Howard Porter by Chicago for $1,200,000 to pacts ranging from three to twenty years. But these are reported figures, and while many are reliable, much of the money is in deferred payments from investments in such as the Dolgoff plan, which may or may not operate to perfection and the ability of the athletes to eventually collect anything like the amounts mentioned is, as the reader shall see, in deep dispute.

In testimony during the Haywood trial, attorney William Barnard, representing the ABA and the Denver Rockets, contended the highest annual salary in the ABA was $75,000 per year, but attorney Charles Phillips testified that two players who jumped from the NBA to the ABA were receiving $200,000 or more per year—Zelmo Beaty, who transferred from Atlanta to Utah, was being paid $200,000 by the Stars, and Joe Caldwell, who was being paid $220,000 by Carolina. He added, however, that some of this was in deferred income. Caldwell, for example, was drawing $150,000 a year for five years of play and $70,000 a year for the following five years above and beyond any new playing contract for that period.

Rick Barry, the first famous league-jumper, was worth only $15,000 a year, although he was a college superstar, when he signed with San Francisco before the basketball war. He signed his second season for $30,000 with a bonus deal based on attendance that boosted his take to $45,000. He was offered $40,000 for his third season with another bonus deal that might raise his take to $75,000, but signed instead for $75,000 a year for three years with Oakland. The three-year $225,000 contract was considered enormous at the time, but now seems small. Barry also had a percentage in the franchise, but when it was sold some legal language was employed stating that only the assets were sold and he did not receive a cent of the sale price.

When the Oakland franchise was shifted to Washington and then Virginia, Barry still was being paid at the rate of $75,000 a season. Seeking to reacquire his services, San Francisco signed him to a six-year pact providing him, on an escalating scale, $544,000 for three years, an average of around $180,000 a year, and $600,000 for the next three years, an average of $200,000 a year. However, the courts did not permit him then to drop his ABA pact and pick up this NBA contract. When he was traded to New York, the Nets sought to pacify him with terms better than he had with Virginia, though not as good as he would have gotten with the Warriors, and based on an escalating scale to encourage him to remain with them. He signed with them for $335,000 for three years, an average of $110,000 a year, and $540,000 for three more years, an average of $180,000.

Since Barry went from the NBA to the ABA, others have followed for far fatter contracts. Barry blazed the trail. Caldwell and Beaty are two who took advantage of the situation, for example. Neither was a $100,000-a-year player in the NBA, but the ABA's need for stars escalated their value. Others have used the threat of a move to promote improved pacts. Billy Cunningham is the best example. He agreed to jump from Philadelphia of the NBA to Carolina of the ABA, when his NBA contract expired, for $500,000 for five years plus $200,000 projected in later payments on Dolgoff plan investments. Also, Carolina agreed to pay him to keep him happy until his NBA contract ran out. However, when Carolina was late with an $80,000 payment, Cunningham canceled the pact, succumbing to offers to stay in Philadelphia for five years at approximately $150,000 per year. The courts later ruled he must honor the Carolina contract beginning in 1972.

Connie Hawkins cashed in on a jump from the ABA to the NBA, but there were special circumstances in his case. He had a lavish law suit pending against the NBA on the charge that it had blackballed him for a presumed implication in a "fix" scandal which never was proved. NBA lawyers advised the owners they would lose the suit. NBA owners also by then were anxious to get this superstar out of the ABA. Years ago, Hawkins had been MVP of the old ABL while making $6,500. Now he dropped his lawsuit and signed with Phoenix of the NBA for $400,000 for four years, plus $30,000 a year from age 42 to the age of 69, an annuity of consequence. Other NBA owners share with the Suns the cost of this settlement.

At this point, although limited indoor seating does not provide the owners of professional basketball teams with the income potential of, say, the owner of a major league baseball team, pro cagers have become by far the highest paid performers in salaried team sports. A study of secret reports and inside information indicates that in the 1970-71 season there were 44 players whose average yearly earnings, including promised future payoffs, were in excess of $100,000. Every team in the NBA had at least one $100,000-a-year player, while all but Dallas, Pittsburgh and the Floridians in the ABA had at least one. New York of the NBA had five and Indiana of the ABA had four. These were the 1969-70 playoff champions. The NBA had 29, the ABA 15. A few are fringe members of this category, but most are clear-cut. A few others may belong, but are not clear-cut.

These are the 44 members of this non-exclusive club in the 1971-72 season, some whom already have or will soon have switched leagues.

NBA Members

Willis Reed, New York
Walt Frazier, New York
Bill Bradley, New York
Jerry Lucas, New York
Earl Monroe, New York
Wilt Chamberlain, L. A.
Jerry West, L. A.
Dave Bing, Detroit
Elvin Hayes, Houston
Wes Unseld, Baltimore
Jo Jo White, Boston
John Havlicek, Boston
Elmore Smith, Buffalo
Chet Walker, Chicago

Elgin Baylor, L. A.
Kareem Abdul-Jabbar, Mil.
Oscar Robertson, Milwaukee
Pete Maravich, Atlanta
Lou Hudson, Atlanta
Billy Cunningham, Phila.
Hal Greer, Philadelphia
Howard Porter, Chicago
Ken Durrett, Cincinnati
Austin Carr, Cleveland
Sidney Wicks, Portland
Len Wilkens, Seattle
Spencer Haywood, Seattle
Connie Hawkins, Phoenix

Nate Thurmond, Golden State

ABA Members

Joe Caldwell, Carolina
Jim McDaniels, Carolina
Roger Brown, Indiana
Mel Daniels, Indiana
Rick Mount, Indiana
George McGinnis, Indiana
Artis Gilmore, Kentucky
Dan Issel, Kentucky

Johnny Neumann, Memphis
Rick Barry, New York
Zelmo Beaty, Utah
Julius Erving, Virginia
Charlie Scott, Virginia
Ralph Simpson, Denver
Larry Cannon, Memphis

As a general rule, the established star, already under contract and working his way up the pay scale through years of prime performance, has not netted the contracts lured by super-rookies in open bidding between the warring leagues. They already are under contract, bound to their team in their league. Most are disinclined to jump to another team in another town in another league, uprooting their families and disturbing business interests they have built up.

Wilt Chamberlain may have been tempted by an ABA pitch to star on an ABA team in L. A.'s Sports Arena, but he already had the top veteran's pact in the NBA, reportedly $180,000 annually. Others also have handsome contracts. One veteran star, for example, receives $125,000 a year, tax-free. He pockets the money, the club pays the taxes. So it was no surprise when Jerry West reportedly asked $300,000 a season from the L. A. Lakers in 1972. However, for the most part, unproven rookies have been the ones to benefit most from the player war. Sought also by the ABA, Lew Alcindor, Elvin Hayes and Pete Maravich commanded bonus contracts surpassing the salaries paid most veterans in the NBA. Alcindor's pact averaged $280,000 a year—$1.4 million for five years. And since then the war has intensified and lesser performers have drawn larger contracts. Sought also by the NBA, Artis Gilmore, Jim McDaniels, Dan Issel and Charlie Scott signed for something that averages close to $300,000 a year for each.

A main problem is that these players really are unproven. Most make it, but a few do not. Many high-priced rookies or sophomores in pro ball today are subs and some have been cut, yet they must continue to be paid. Philadelphia signed Dana Lewis to a multi-year contract worth $350,000, guaranteeing him $175,000 even if he was cut, then cut him. San Francisco signed Cyril Baptiste to a fat pact with some guarantees, then dropped him like a hot potato. The L. A. Stars went for a bundle for Simmie Hill, then sliced him, and he's been bouncing from team to team ever since. Phoenix went for a bundle for Greg Howard, then passed him on. Chicago went high for Jimmy Collins but then got low mileage from him. Many clubs have been stuck for much money. Many clubs have kept mediocre players because of what they paid for them and have cut better players who cost less. In some places players are being played because of what they are being paid, not because they are the best on the team. And the reluctance of team owners to be embarrassed by dropping some of these deprives more deserving players without big names of opportunity.

It is possible that the potential income of some pro basketball teams has been underestimated. For instance, the New York Mets led the baseball major leagues in attendance during the 1971 season with 2,266,680 fans drawn at home, while the New York Knicks led the basketball major leagues during the 1970-71 season with 893,487 at home. The Mets' Shea Stadium holds 55,000 persons and their schedule gives them 81 home games. The Knicks' Madison Square Garden seats only 19,500 and their slate, including playoffs, gives them only 48 dates. However, the top price of a Met ticket is $4 and the assumed average $2.50, so the team gross probably was around $5,700,000. The Knicks' top tickets are $8.50 during the regular season and $12 for the playoffs, probably averaging $7.45 and so producing a gross of $6,650,000, or nearly a million dollars more than the Mets.

The Lakers sold 656,582 tickets at an average price of $5 for the Forum in suburban Los Angeles and thus grossed around $3,280,000. Milwaukee with fewer seats, but higher prices, is estimated to have grossed around $2,900,000. To gross $3,000,000, a baseball team with an average ticket price of $2.50 must draw 1,200,000 fans. According to a survey conducted by Leonard Koppett of *The New York*

Times in *The Sporting News,* who assembled many of these figures, only 11 of the 24 teams in major league baseball accomplished this in 1971, and only two of these teams were in the American League (Detroit and Boston). Presumably, the rest operated in the red. However, presumably most NBA and ABA teams also operated in the red, even with the addition of radio and TV revenues. Any profits are projected for the future, especially by ABA clubs, who accept losses as the only way to wage war, force a merger and eventually bring the best into their buildings and earn themselves an equal cut of radio-TV returns.

Members of the NBA Players' Association have protested the planned merger on the grounds that it would eliminate all their bargaining power. The least they wish to settle for is a contract guaranteeing veterans the option to negotiate with other teams.

Ira Millstein, former Justice Department attorney, now a counsel to the NBA Players' group, says, "In order to reduce or stabilize the price to be paid for talent, the two leagues wish to eliminate all competition between them by the familiar avenues of combinations and agreements not to compete. This plan is a per se violation of the Sherman Act. . . . Schemes by competitors to eliminate competition between them in the acquisition of raw materials so as to lower the cost of doing business have always been held to be so. . . ."

North Carolina Senator Sam Ervin, Jr., says, "I believe that if a basketball player is good enough, he should be paid the highest price that bidders for his services are willing to pay. I do not believe contracts for player services will rise indefinitely beyond what a team can pay. If they get too high, the teams will just stop bidding beyond what they are able to pay. . . ."

Charles Maher of the *Los Angeles Times,* in a detailed study of the situation, quoted Ervin as adding, "Simply to say that salaries are too high is to ignore the freedom to bargain which our economy allows to those who are selling personal services, and that includes everyone who is selling such—doctors, lawyers, Indian Chiefs, ditch diggers. . . .

"The monopolistic conditions which exist in other sports (that is, the absence of competitive bidding for talent) keep the salaries of professional athletes below what they should be.

"Everyone can use figures to his own advantage, but the rise in players' salaries makes a very interesting comparison with the increase in the value of professional basketball franchises.

"The value of the Boston Celtics as measured by purchase prices went from $2.8 million in 1965 to $6.2 million in 1969, which is an increase of 121 percent. The value of the Houston Rockets (previously the San Diego Rockets) went from $1.7 million in 1967 to $5.7 million in 1971, which is an increase of 235 per cent.

"Thus, the players' earnings are really just keeping pace with the value of the clubs.

"I don't believe that their losses are as great as the owners say. All the basketball teams are allowed to treat their players as capital assets and the owners can depreciate their value. . . . When a new owner buys a team, he assigns as much as possible of the purchase price to player contracts and depreciates them.

"To grant them special considerations because of so-called economic necessity would be absurd."

Lawrence Fleisher, general counsel of the players' group, added, "Today's owners, the great majority of whom came into the business within the last three years, are generally extremely wealthy men who have been successful in operating large businesses. They are told by their financial advisors that basketball appears to be the sport of the 70's with an unlimited horizon of potential income from pay TV and further expansion.

"The tax laws allow them to offset any actual losses from the operation of the team against their huge personal income and allow them to take deductions for amortization of player contracts.

"Since 1966, seven new franchises have been granted by the NBA. The aggregate entry fees paid have totaled $19.6 million—a bonanza shared equally by the existing franchises. If congress approves this merger, the teams of the ABA will pay $12.5 million to the NBA as their entry fee—for a grand total of $32.1 million.

"It must be kept in mind that these enormous sums have

not been paid by innocent newcomers to the world of business, but by sophisticated and highly successful entrepreneurs dedicated to further profit."

Jack Kent Cooke, owner of the Los Angeles Lakers and Kings, has conceded, "As pure businesses, sports would seem to be bad business. Few franchises return profits comparable to that possible for monied men with other investments. But sports franchises remain sound investments because seldom if ever are they sold for less than the original purchase price. The value of most professional sports franchises has increased so steadily that most owners know they can always sell for a sum far greater than their purchase price and operating losses."

The proprietors of sports franchises hire and fire coaches at a rate that has degraded the profession. Some owners have averaged a different coach or manager every year of their operation. Some have had two or three a season. Some are fired in mid-season. Many after only a few games of a season. And players are traded from team to team and city to city regularly. Some players have been traded six or seven times in their careers. Some have changed uniforms sixteen or seventeen times, often two or three times a season. Each time, they face uprooting or separation from their families. Professional sports can be a most insecure life for the journeyman performer.

Traded to Philadelphia after more than a decade of playing baseball in St. Louis, Curt Flood sought to upset the system in court, but he has been denied. He contends, "It is absolutely unfair to tell a veteran with a family settled in a home, with children settled in school, with business interests established in town, that he must simply pick up and play elsewhere as ordered or else forfeit all monies he is capable of earning in his profession. It is in violation of all the rights granted all other citizens. An insurance salesman can be transferred from St. Louis to Philadelphia, too, but he has a choice of quitting and seeking another position selling insurance with another firm in St. Louis or a city of his choice."

Rick Barry points out, "I was condemned by fans, writers and broadcasters for jumping from San Francisco of the NBA to Oakland of the ABA, then for seeking to avoid having to move with the Oakland franchise to Washington or Virginia. But these same people do the same things they damned me for. I was called disloyal. Where is the loyalty of a writer for a newspaper in Detroit when he jumps to a newspaper in San Francisco because it pays him more money or gives him more exposure or better benefits? Where is the loyalty of a sportscaster to a station in San Francisco when he jumps to a station in Washington because he feels it is better for him? Why should the basketball fan be permitted to change from Joe's Service Station to Sam's because it's a better job, while the basketball player has to stay put? It doesn't matter what athletes are paid. Many who are higher paid in other professions have rights of choice denied us. In my case, I didn't want to leave the Bay Area because I'd rather live here, not because I'd make less money there. It's the free choice I want, but don't have because of a double standard imposed on athletes."

Spencer Haywood says, "We all want the most money we can get, just as any man does, but it's more than that. In my case, I came to feel I wasn't being treated fairly and wasn't going to be treated fairly. I lost respect for my employers and wanted to go to work for someone else. Someone else wanted me. They were willing to pay me. I felt I could be happy there. It's just that simple. Or should be. Don't tell me how overpaid we are. What does that have to do with anything? If the owners couldn't afford it, they wouldn't pay it. That's pretty simple fact, too. I didn't have any gun to hold at anyone's head. I had my talent. I wanted to offer it in the open market. I had a contract, but I felt it wasn't a fair one and I felt I had a right to fight it in court."

Al Ross adds, "Almost all of the rules in professional sports protect the owners and not the coaches and not the athletes. It is not fair for the owners to say a player is forbidden to leave college and enter professional ball and earn an honest living with his talent whenever he wants to do so and is wanted. It is not fair for the owners to say that they will decide for which team each player must play and that he is bound to his contract for his entire career. It is not fair for them to say the player must play for whatever one team wishes to pay him and no more, no matter what another team is willing to pay. These owners want competition on the court, but they are not willing to be competitive. They want to decide the rules for all among themselves in secret meetings, than act in concert with gentlemen's agreements to support the slavery they impose on individuals. They employ the best lawyers and business and tax consultants they can hire to do their business for them and draw up contracts, but when a young boy brings a lawyer or manager to advise him, the owners scream that agents are destroying the integrity of sports. The stand of the owners is indefensible."

Sam Schulman noted: "Once we concluded Spencer Haywood did not have a legally binding contract, we considered him a free-agent, free to be signed by us and by anyone else, no matter what my fellow NBA owners contended were in their rules. We considered that their rules had no legal standing. They change the rules to suit themselves very often, anyway. Many of the same men who were upset with me for signing Spencer Haywood were perfectly prepared to sign him themselves, to break the rules themselves. The commissioner, Walter Kennedy, has one set of rules he applies to some owners, another set for others. I could not respect his leadership."

Kennedy commented: "Without leadership, without respect for leadership, without rules, without respect for rules, there would be chaos. We are in a form of partnership and we have agreed on certain rules to protect the balance of power which is necessary to our survival, and for one of our members to operate with reckless disregard for the rules and for his partners is to jeopardize all we have worked to create."

ABA Commissioner Jack Dolph said, "Even in war there must be some rules to regulate conduct. If a player does not have a valid contract, he should be free to bargain for his services with those teams which have rights to him. But if a player has a valid contract, he should respect it."

And the Denver Rockets' Don Ringsby added, "We considered that Spencer Haywood had a valid contract with us. It was signed when he was a minor, but it was signed with the consent of a responsible advisor, and it was signed again in court after he became an adult. We consider that the contract would have lived up to every letter contained in it, but that is not the point, the point is it was a valid contract and should have been respected as such."

In the NFL, football player Dave Parks fulfilled his contractual obligations to San Francisco, left the 49ers and was signed by New Orleans. San Francisco received repayment after arbitration presided over by commissioner Pete Rozelle. There have been other such cases, although the players argue that a gentleman's agreement on the part of the club owners not to sign players who seek to leave teams is seldom violated and works a hardship on players such as Joe Kapp who seek to make their own deals.

When Spencer Haywood, claiming an invalid contract with the Denver Rockets of the ABA, turned up in Los Angeles alongside attorney Al Ross and declared he either wanted his Denver pact clarified and promised monies guaranteed or a similar pact set up with another team, a storm of controversy and a flurry of activity was stirred up. Much of the activity was behind the scenes and has not previously been revealed.

6. Fight to the Finish

Under pressure from Al Ross and their fellow ABA owners, the Ringsbys reluctantly agreed to discuss a new contract for Spencer Haywood, but several meetings and telephone conversations failed to produce an agreement. At one point they were very close to settling for either $125,000 or $150,000 a year in straight salary for six years, but it fell through.

A Denver newspaper reported that Haywood was seeking a $3.25 million contract, but Ross denied this and Don Ringsby later denied saying any such thing. When Haywood later signed with Seattle, he signed for less than the $1.9 million he said he was seeking to have guaranteed in Denver; he signed for $1.5 million.

Not only Seattle, but Los Angeles, Phoenix, Chicago, Cincinnati, Buffalo, Atlanta, San Francisco, Milwaukee, Boston and New York are reported by Ross to have expressed interest directly and through third parties in signing Haywood. In most cases persons representing these clubs made the initial pitches to assess the situation. In some cases, the owners or general managers of the clubs followed up with more pointed interest.

Meanwhile, ABA commissioner Jack Dolph and other club owners in the infant circuit sought to save the young superstar for themselves. Carolina offered to purchase Haywood's contract from the Ringsbys for $1,000,000, but was rejected. Utah offered to trade Zelmo Beaty for him, but was rejected. Kentucky offered Cincy Powell and other players for him, but was rejected. Denver did offer to trade Haywood to Kentucky for Dan Issel and Lou Dampier, but was itself rejected this time. Some of these clubs approached Ross directly. Kentucky offered $1.1 million for 5 years, Carolina offered $2.1 million for six.

Reportedly, Dolph and the ABA owners minus Ringsby met in secret session and agreed by a two-thirds vote to attempt to purchase the franchise from the Ringsbys for $2,000,000 and install a new owner in Denver who could satisfy Haywood, but the Ringsbys deny a firm bid ever was made.

There was a plan in which Sam Schulman would sell his Seattle interests, purchase the Denver franchise and shift it into Los Angeles to operate in the Sports Arena in opposition to the Lakers in the Forum. Schulman and Laker owner Jack Kent Cooke are not friendly. An expansion franchise would have been located in Denver to be run by former Notre Dame and Denver coach Johnny Dee with graduating Notre Dame superstar Austin Carr awarded to this team. Meanwhile, the rights to UCLA's graduating superstars Sidney Wicks and Curtis Rowe would be awarded Schulman to go with Haywood in his new Los Angeles franchise.

There was another report Schulman simply planned to sign Haywood to a personal services contract, then start his new ABA team in the Sports Arena in Los Angeles with Spencer and the UCLA stars. Schulman denies that he wanted to sell his Seattle interests or would sign Spencer for that city and then take him from the town, but he admits he seriously considered the L. A. Sports Arena project pegged on the attractiveness of the former UCLA players, provided he could sign them.

It is a fact that a team composed of UCLA grads Kareem Abdul-Jabbar, Gail Goodrich, Walt Hazzard, Keith Erickson, Wicks, Rowe and Steve Patterson, surrounded by competent players, operating under the nickname, perhaps, of the Los Angeles Bruins, would be the best in basketball.

Meanwhile, Jack Kent Cooke of the Lakers asked NBA commissioner Walter Kennedy if there was a way legally to sign Spencer. He was told "no way." Sam Schulman of the Sonics asked Kennedy to put it to a vote. This was done at an NBA meeting and he was denied, 15-2. Dick Bloch of Phoenix was the only owner who sided with Schulman. Schulman says he offered to sign Spencer for the NBA and open him to the draft, but the owners said no.

Nevertheless, Schulman eventually went ahead and signed Spencer, but for Seattle. Many of the teams which had been interested in Haywood protested the act. Jerry Colangelo of Phoenix said, "This opens up a Pandora's box." Bob Breitbard of San Diego, who later sold his franchise to Houston, said, "I'm just flabbergasted." Jack Kent Cooke of Los Angeles said, "I think it's a very unfortunate incident." Reportedly, Mr. Cooke asked his fellow owners to impose the harshest possible penalties on Schulman.

Dick Motta of Chicago said, "I'm glad to see Haywood in the league, but why in Seattle and why not in Chicago? We were told we couldn't go after him." Paul Snyder of Buffalo said, "If he belongs anywhere, he belongs in Buffalo or on one of the teams which most needs help and should have first rights to him." Joe Axelson of Cincinnati said, "I'm not sure he belongs in this league."

Red Auerbach of Boston said, "Seattle has no right to do this." Ray Patterson of Milwaukee said, "I think Sam has no chance of keeping Haywood. I'll be damned if we want Schulman in this league if he pursues this course." Bob Cousins of Atlanta said, "This threatens to wreck this league."

Walter Kennedy said, "There is no chance Seattle will be permitted to play Haywood."

Franklin Mieuli of San Francisco, who was preparing to transfer his franchise to Oakland, said, "We wouldn't want to expel Seattle from the league because it wouldn't be fair to hurt the city, but we might consider acting against Sam

Schulman." Others were less charitable. Joe Axelson said, "There's always a lot of feeling against a city where it rains so much."

When Spencer reported to the Sonics and made his first appearance on the Seattle court, he received a standing ovation. By then, his case was in the courts. It was not clear if he would be cleared to play, however, and he did not play that night. When he played his first game for Seattle, on January 14, 1970, in Baltimore, he was booed. The Bullets protested the game. In Chicago, Spencer did not play, but an official complaint asking $600,000 in damages was lodged when Chet Walker was injured in the game because just sitting on the bench Haywood "created a destructive and disruptive atmosphere."

Schulman soon seemed exasperated. Reporting he had received what he considered to be "a very malicious, vindictive letter" from Elmer Rich, president of the Chicago Bulls ("We'll kill you before you kill us. . . .") and noting the comments made by his fellow owners and by other officials of the other teams, the Sonics' owner said, "My colleagues have short memories. When they wanted players, I did everything in my power to help them whether or not it was clear they were entitled to these players.

"I was instrumental in this league being able to sign Lew Alcindor in Milwaukee and taking him away from the ABA. I was instrumental in arranging for the return of Rick Barry to this league, although the courts later ruled he could not play here. I was instrumental in the settlement of the Connie Hawkins suit so that he could be signed in this league. I might point out rights to him were not obtained by pure draft but in an award to Phoenix after it had lost a coin-flip with Milwaukee for the rights to Alcindor. And we took Hawkins out of the ABA.

"Whenever called upon by my colleagues, I have served as a neutral mediator and negotiator without any benefit to myself except as a member of a league that might be strengthened by my acts. But when I seek to obtain a player for myself for the benefit of my team and so the league, the other owners turn on me. Well, it seems they speak out of both sides of their mouth! They were perfectly prepared to sign him themselves. They were not prepared to fight for him, to agree to accept all court costs and consequences, and I was, which was the main reason, not money, I have him and they do not. I am deeply disappointed in them, to say the least.

"As for Mr. Kennedy, well I'm not disappointed in him because I long ago came to expect such conduct from him. He is a puppet president, manipulated by the more powerful owners. His deportment depends on who the owner he's dealing with is. I am continually frustrated by his inability to make decisions on his own. I think a shrewder commissioner would see that I will win this fight in court.

"In any event, I am in this fight to the finish. I am not going to back down to the obligations I have assumed to Spencer Haywood, who has been tempted and deceived every step of the way, and I am not going to back down to the obligations I have to my own principles. Even as I speak to you, NBA teams are negotiating with college and contracted ABA players to secure their services. The hypocrisy of the situation is appalling."

The press generally seemed to be against Haywood and Schulman. Bill Ringsby said, "The players are going to destroy themselves and us with their greed," and the writers supported this stand. Wendell Smith, a Negro writer in Chicago, referred to Spencer as the "superstar renegade." A piece was prepared presenting Spencer's side in *Sport* Magazine and Roger Stanton, a white Detroit writer, wrote, "He is ungrateful, misguided, uneduated and irresponsible. What a shame a man with all this basketball talent went down the drain so fast. . . . Haywood has had many terrible decisions in his young life and hurt a lot of people. In his greed for wealth, he has stopped at nothing."

A wide array of legal talent converged on the courtroom in Los Angeles where most of the case was considered under the jurisdiction of Judge Warren Ferguson. Among others, Eugene Wyman, Frank Rothman, John Quinn, Howard King, Greg Bautzer and Pete and Marianna Pfaelzer represented Haywood, Schulman and Seattle; Frederick Furth, William Barnard and John Boone represented Denver and the ABA; Robert Gibbs represented Buffalo; G. William Shea represented the NBA; and the firm of Ball, Hunt, Hartz, Brown and Baerwitz (the Brown being former California Governor Pat Brown) represented Ross and All-Pro management.

Along the way, there was issued a critical ruling permitting Haywood to play for Seattle pending settlement of the case. There were also other temporary injunctions granted, denied or revoked on one side or the other; and after a while confusion clouded the contest as it proceeded in starts and stops, and then in spurts with the collection of depositions, with sworn testimony on the stand and with lawyers' arguments before the bench. The case dragged on between January and March 1971.

A main portion of the Haywood argument was presented by Frank Rothman in court on February 26, as follows:

"What the draft says is this: It says we have 17 member teams in the NBA. Team Cleveland drafts a young athlete out of college. The other 16 teams say we now agree in concert that we will boycott that athlete, we will not deal with him, we will not talk to him and we will not permit him to play with any other of our 16 members teams. He can only play with the one team who has drafted him. And he can only play if he can arrive at a monetary agreement with that team. So if Spencer Haywood—using him just as an example—has a mother and father and family and children living in L. A. and he wants to play in L. A., but he was drafted by Cleveland, he could do nothing but play for Cleveland. Or, secondarily, if he felt that he was worth a hundred or two hundred or three hundred thousand dollars a year and Cleveland thought he was worth $5,000 a year that is all he gets and he has no bargaining rights except the bargaining rights to say I won't play basketball. Now the problem is very mildly alleviated, very mildly alleviated because there is an ABA. And so you get some competitive spirit between the two. But the facts are that steps are being taken to eliminate that situation and that is the basis of the antitrust suit filed by the Players Association in New York to prevent a merger of the two because of the unfairness to the players. So I think that the college draft is a clear, outright boycott."

Pete Pfaelzer stated the remainder of the Haywood argument: "You take an underage boy and without providing him adequate representation you give him contracts telling him they are worth such and such and ask him to sign them on faith when in fact it is highly questionable that they are worth such and such. The owner of the Denver franchise, J. W. 'Bill' Ringsby, told Spencer Haywood before he signed the third contract with the Rockets, 'Spencer, we are going to make you the highest-paid basketball player in the country, we are going to pay you one-point-nine-million-dollars for six years of play,' and he told the press this and it was so published, and he added a note to the side of the contract which said, 'Spencer, this contract totals up to one-point-nine-million for six years, personally guaranteed,' and signed with his name, but if all pro sports contracts are like this one I hate to think what a small percentage of the amounts that are published and the amounts that the athletes believe they will receive . . . they actually . . . receive.

"Denver actually was paying Spencer around $50,000 a year for three years and $75,000 a year for three years, plus $10,000 a year for ten years put into the Dolgoff Plan investment program. They also paid Haywood's guardians the Bells and Will Robinson $5,000 each and were paying on a $100,000 insurance program for Spencer. However, in essence, they were committed to pay $60,000 a year for three years, $85,000 a year for three years and $10,000 a year for four more years, a total investment of $575,000 over a 10-year period, which is a long way from $1.9 million and actually averages out to less than $60,000 a year.

"And the fine print in the contract is fascinating. The later benefits for Spencer were vested at the right of 10 percent per year. Every year he failed to play for them up to the end of ten years would have cost him ten percent of his future payments. And if he failed to fulfill his six-year obligation to them, he would get none of the promised later return. Presumably, if he was traded within these first six years, he would get nothing. What was to stop Denver from trading him after five years? Who is to say a new owner would live up to an old contract? What if the team folded? Or the league folded? Both very possible in ventures of this sort, by the way.

"From year six through year ten, Haywood had to serve them to guarantee he got his future benefits, but he had no contract covering this. He owed them services for no set sum. If Denver had chosen to offer him $50 a week to sweep out the john, he could take it or leave it. I rather imagine they wouldn't do that, but who knows? What if he got injured and was unable to play beyond six years? Or in less than six years? The Rockets owned the Dolgoff investments, not Spencer. Then, too, he had to wait 20 to 40 years to collect, until he is an old man.

"Finally, there can be no way $1.4 million in future returns possibly can be guaranteed from a program such as this. It is an investment program, pure and simple. The shrewdest manipulators cannot guarantee any returns over the long run. The market rises and falls. The value of mutual funds alters. What it amounts to is they took a little-educated, unsophisticated, underage boy and said you don't need advice, you can take our word, we'll give you a piece of pie in the sky. And the boy signs. And when he comes of age, they tell him to sign again, and he does.

"Now he has advisors who inform him the contract was misrepresented to him, which is why it went to court, to prove the point, to break the contract, and he has signed a new contract with another team in another league, and that league says he can't play in their league because his college class hasn't graduated and because he hasn't gone through a draft, which will tell him which team he can play for, and which team will tell him how much he can play for a year from now."

In a summary judgment, Judge Ferguson ruled that the four-year rule was illegal, that it denied an individual the right to play his sports professionally even if he has no desire to continue in college, even if he is ineligble for college and college athletics, and that one such as Haywood had a right to play for any professional team which wished to sign him.

This shocked the basketball establishment. NBA Commissioner Walter Kennedy said, "This could kill college athletics and seriously injure professional athletics." NFL Commissioner Pete Rozelle said, "It could destroy college football and basketball." San Francisco Athletic Director Pete Peletta said, "It's a prostitution of athletes and athletics. Those moneybags should go on trial."

Northwestern football coach Alex Agase said, "This could eliminate all superstars from college competition." Furman basketball coach Joe Williams said, "This will take a great deal of incentive out of recruiting good players." Surveying opinion, *Sports Illustrated* magazine quoted one college commissioner as saying, "We could always go back to using student athletes."

There were a few who reacted calmly. University of Pennsylvania Athletic Director Fred Shabel said, "I don't think I should deny anyone the right to chart his own life." LSU basketball coach Press Maravich said, "You can always get the education, but you can't always get the money." Speaking of his star, Marquette basketball coach Al McQuire said, "I've looked in his refrigerator and I've looked in mine, and mine has meats, pastries and other goodies. There are two sides to this street."

Walter Byers, executive director of the NCAA, admitted, "I think Judge Ferguson was on sound legal ground. Remember, the four-year rule was not put in by the colleges, but by the pros to enable them to secure talent for themselves with a minimum of inconvenience. Some of our members want us to fight this, to go to Congress. That's just whistling up a wind tunnel."

Indiana University sophomore star George McGinnis promptly put himself up on the open market and was snapped up by the Indiana Pacers of the ABA, and Mississippi sophomore star Johnny Neumann put himself up for grabs and was grabbed by Memphis of the ABA.

The NBA and ABA decided to limit the signing of undergraduates to "hardship" cases, invited all who felt they qualified as "needy" to apply, stand investigation and be placed on a special list for a special annual draft. The draft was conducted and several collegians were chosen. Presumably this group action will be binding only until a member team elects to sign a player outside of this draft, and perhaps puts its rights to the player to a court test if challenged.

USC football coach John McKay said, "We may not be able to recruit needy kids in the future."

Judge Ferguson also ruled that, having a contract with Seattle, Haywood could not be made to submit to a draft and to play for Buffalo or any other team which then drafted him. This did not have immediately drastic consequences, except to beat the Buffalo bid, but it could have such in the future should teams in a league choose to sign players prior to a draft and, again, put its right to do this to a court test if challenged.

NBA commissioner Kennedy seemed crushed and commented, "I can't believe an operation such as ours can be denied the right to govern ourselves."

Lawyer Ross countered with the comment, "Leagues have the right to make any rules they wish, and they will be upheld, as long as they are legal. Legal is legal and illegal is illegal. The rights of team owners and players are the same as for all citizens, or should be, no more and no less. Some rules work a hardship on business operations, but they protect the individuals, which is as it should be."

Ross himself came in for some uneasy moments during the trial. When the original 25 percent pact Haywood had signed with All-Pro Management and the later 10 percent pact he had signed with Ross were revealed, Judge Ferguson wondered if, since Ross heads up All-Pro Management, Haywood had to pay 35 percent of his income to the same person. He quizzed Spencer on this.

Part of the judge's cross-examination of Haywood follows:

Witness: "We don't have that contract [the first one] any more."

Court: "You don't have that contract any more?"

Witness: "No."

Court: "I was just told that you have it."

Witness: "No, no, that contract does not exist. I only have one contract with Mr. Ross."

Court: "You see the problem, Mr. Haywood. You see why I am worried about you."

Witness: "I only have one contract with Mr. Ross."

Court: "You don't have a contract with All-Pro Management?"

Ross, from courtroom: "Can I speak, your honor?"

Court: "No, siree."

When Ross made an exasperated sound, Judge Ferguson held him in contempt of court, ordered him to appear in his chambers the following morning and expressed to Spencer the suspicion that, whether he realized it or not, he really did have two contracts for management totaling 35 percent. He concluded with the comment, "Everybody is after this kid's money."

However, in his chambers the next morning, it was clarified that the 10 percent personal pact with Ross did, indeed, supersede the 25 percent contract with All-Pro Management, that Ross and All-Pro were rendering a total management service for Spencer for 10 percent of his income, and the contempt citation was dismissed.

Grinning, Ross swabbed sweat from his flushed face like a condemned man who has just been cleared and admitted later, "For a minute there, I thought I needed a good lawyer." The towering Haywood hung an arm on his attorney's shoulders and said, "You're my man, man. You don't think I'd let any judge come between us, do you?"

On the witness stand, Spencer confirmed that he had been prepared to return to Denver rather than cause Ross to suffer any harsh consequences, that as late as Christmas day he had been ready to drop the whole case just so he could go back to basketball when a meeting with Sam Schulman at the Beverly Hills home of the Sonics' owner resulted in his decision to hang on.

It came out that Will Robinson had not legally become his guardian until August of 1968, shortly before the Olympics in Mexico City and less than a year before negotiations with professional teams began. Haywood testified he had asked Robinson if they shouldn't have legal advice, but was told that it wouldn't be necessary. And when he had asked the same of Don Ringsby, he was told, "We don't deal with lawyers and peddlers." As for the advisor, Denver Banker Ben Gibson, who was provided for him prior to the signing of the third pact, Haywood said he

108

never discussed the contract with him and never gave him any advice. Haywood said he had no understanding of the technicalities revealed in the small print in his pacts.

Haywood testified he left Detroit and went to Denver on Robinson's advice, but later came to mistrust Robinson and wonder if he was on the Denver payroll. Later testimony by the Ringsbys did reveal that Robinson had been put on the Rockets payroll as a scout by Don Ringsby and was paid $5,000 cash by Bill Ringsby and $2,000 a year for the next five years.

Haywood testified he first heard from a representative of All-Pro offering management services in February of 1970, but that he did not ask Ross for legal services and sign with him for these until October of 1970. He said that he had made the second contact with Schulman with a telephone call to him on Thanksgiving Day. He testified he'd asked $1.9 million from Seattle—$316,666 a year cash for six years' play, payable over 10 or 20 years, and Schulman had countered with an offer of $80,000 a year for six years payable over those six years, and that they compromised on $250,000 a year for six years' play payable over 15 years. They shook hands on the agreement on December 4 and signed the actual contracts December 28. He said that during this time the Ringsbys had gone as high as $125,000 a year in their offers to him and had offered to trade him to another team in the ABA. He was tempted to return, but eventually decided he no longer wanted to play for them under any circumstances.

In J. W. "Bill" Ringsby's deposition, he was examined by Pfaelzer. His testimony follows in part:

On his first meeting with Spencer:

"He stated what he wanted to begin with. We stated what we felt we could afford to pay him. We discussed the possibility of his being able to make our club, to make the team. We discussed the possible value that he might have to our club. We discussed his future. We discussed many things. We talked about his residence in Colorado, in Denver, and how we felt and we feel that the people in Denver, Colorado, are very good to the black people. They have, generally speaking, much better homes than they do in other areas. They are looked upon with more respect, I think, than they are where there are overpopulated areas of black people. We discussed that he would have a good living situation in Colorado and discussed the future of the Rockets with him, among many things."

On the compensation Haywood would receive:

"'Well, he first requested, as I recall, well, he asked for a million dollars. He actually thought he wanted a million dollars. Of course, how he wanted it, I don't think he even knew how he wanted it when he asked for it, but he wanted a million dollars to start with. . . .'"

Mr. Ringsby said he first offered $35,000 a year and Haywood countered with a request for $60,000 a year, and that Spencer asked for a two-year contract while Denver wanted a five-year contract and they settled on $50,000 a year for three years. He added, "This was voluntary on my part, it was not asked for and I don't believe Spencer discussed it up to that point. I said, 'In addition to that, I will give you $15,000 a year for 20 years after you become 40 years of age if you will play for the Denver Rockets for 10 years.' Mr. Haywood said, 'Well, that's very good, but what if I don't play for 10 years?' Then I said, 'Well, if you don't play for 10 years, we will give you one-tenth of it for each year that you do play."

Mr. Ringsby said he suggested Spencer get a tax advisor or counsel. He noted in an aside that while Arnold and Blackman did "bring" Haywood to them, "We did not pay them anything. The league did. They did try to collect from us after it was all over, too. I mean they did want money from us, but we had no agreement with them. We had no promise to them or anything." He testified that Will Robinson had sought a scouting contract from them, had been put on the payroll as a scout, had been paid $5,000, had promised to deliver them a player and had done so, Ralph Simpson, who left Michigan State to sign with the Rockets as a hardship case. Concluded Ringsby: "I believe that Mr. Robinson is still on the payroll and still scouts for the Denver Rockets and probably will be for some time."

He said that when the Dolgoff plan was brought to his attention and a presentation made to him, he brought it to the attention of Haywood and Robinson and recommended

110

PLAYER

AMERICAN BASKETBALL ASSOCIATION
UNIFORM PLAYER CONTRACT

AGREEMENT made this **1st** day of **April** , 19**70**

between _____ **THE DENVER ROCKETS** _____ (hereinafter
called the "CLUB"), a member of the AMERICAN BASKETBALL ASSOCIATION, (hereinafter sometimes

called the "ASSOCIATION"), and **SPENCER HAYWOOD** of the City of **DENVER**
(hereinafter called the "PLAYER").

IT IS AGREED AS FOLLOWS:

1. **Employment and Term Thereof.** The CLUB hereby employs the PLAYER as a skilled Basketball Player
for the term of __6__ years from the first (1st) day of October, 19**70**, subject, however, to termination,
extension or renewal as specified herein. The PLAYER'S employment shall include attendance at training camp,
playing the games scheduled for the team during the schedule season of the American Basketball Association,
playing all exhibition games scheduled by the team during and prior to the schedule season, and playing the
playoff games for which the player is to receive such additional compensation as is provided by the ASSOCIA-
TION. Regular players will not be required to attend training camp earlier than four (4) weeks prior to the
season starting date of the team of which the player is a member. "Rookies" may be required to attend training
camp at an earlier date. Exhibition games shall not be played on the three (3) days prior to the opening of a
team's regular season schedule nor on a day prior to a regularly scheduled game. The All-Star game shall for
the purpose of this paragraph not be considered an exhibition game. Exhibition games during the regularly
scheduled season shall not exceed three (3).

2. **Compensation.**

a. **Salary.** For the PLAYER'S rendering services described herein, and for his agreement not to play basketball or engage in activities related to basketball for any other person, firm, corporation or institution
during the term of this contract, and for the option hereinafter set forth giving the right to renew this contract, and for the other undertakings of the PLAYER herein, the CLUB agrees to pay the PLAYER each
year during the term of this contract the sum of $47,000.00 first 2 yrs/$75,000 last 4 yrs.
in twelve (12) equal semi-monthly payments beginning with the first of said payments on November 1st of
the season above described and continuing with such payments on the first and fifteenth of each month until said sum is paid in full. Provided, however, if the CLUB does not qualify for the playoffs, the payments
due subsequent to the conclusion of the schedule season shall become due and payable immediately after the
conclusion of the schedule season.

b. **Expenses.** The CLUB promises and agrees to pay the reasonable board and lodging expenses of the
PLAYER while playing for the CLUB in other than the CLUB'S home city and will pay all proper and necessary expenses of the PLAYER and his meals enroute.

3. **PLAYER'S Duties and Obligations:**

a. **Duties.** The PLAYER agrees:
(1) To report at the time and place fixed by the CLUB in good physical condition; and
(2) To keep himself throughout the entire season in good physical condition; and
(3) To give his full time and best services, as well as his loyalty, to the CLUB, and to play basketball
only for the CLUB unless he is released or his contract is sold or exchanged by the CLUB; and
(4) To be neatly and fully attired in public and always to conduct himself on and off the court according
to the highest standards of honesty, morality, fair play and sportsmanship; and
(5) Not to do anything which is detrimental to the best interests of the CLUB or of the American Basketball Association or of professional sports.

b. **Compliance With CLUB Rules.** The CLUB may from time to time during the continuance of this contract establish reasonable rules for the government of its players "at home" and "abroad," and such rules
shall be a part of this contract as fully as if herein written and shall be binding upon the player; and for
violation of such rules or for any conduct impairing the faithful and thorough discharge of the duties in-
cumbent upon the player, the CLUB may impose reasonable fines upon the player and deduct the amount
thereof from any money due or to become due to the player. The CLUB may also suspend the player for
violation of any rules so established, and during such suspension the player shall not be entitled to any compensation under this contract. When the player is fined or suspended, he shall be given notice in writing,
stating the amount of the fine or the duration of the suspension and the reason therefor.

c. **Participation in Other Sports.** The PLAYER and the CLUB recognize and agree that the PLAYER'S
participation in other sports may impair or destroy his ability and skill as a basketball player and his participation in basketball out of season may result in injury to him. Accordingly, the PLAYER agrees that
he will not engage in professional boxing or wrestling; and that, except with the written consent of the
CLUB, he will not engage in any game or exhibition of basketball, football, baseball, hockey, lacrosse, or
other athletic sport, under penalty of such fine and suspension as may be imposed by the CLUB and/or the
Commissioner of the ASSOCIATION.

4. **Physical Condition and Injuries.**

a. **Physical Condition.** If the PLAYER, in the judgment of the CLUB'S physician, is not in good physical
condition at the date of his first scheduled game of the regular playing season scheduled by the ASSOCIA-
TION for the CLUB, or if, during such regular playing season, he fails to remain in good physical condition, unless such condition is a direct result of participating in any basketball practice or game for the
CLUB, it is mutually agreed that the CLUB shall have the right to suspend such PLAYER until such time
as, in the judgment of the CLUB'S physician, the PLAYER is in sufficiently good physical condition to play
skilled basketball. In the event of such suspension:

*The third contract signed by Spencer Haywood and his "guardian"
Ben Gibson and by J. W. and D. W. Ringsby on behalf of the Denver
Rockets in part—the first part and the last part is shown here and on
the following page. The annual salary as typed in is shown as $47,000
for two years and $75,000 for four years.*

15. Option to Renew. On or before the date of the expiration of this contract, the CLUB may, upon notice in writing to the PLAYER, renew this contract for the further term of one (1) year following said expiration date on the same terms as are provided by this contract, except that:

a. The CLUB may fix the rate of compensation to be paid by the CLUB to the PLAYER during said period of renewal, which compensation shall not be less than ninety per cent (90%) of the amount paid by the CLUB to the PLAYER during the preceding season, and

b. After such renewal, this contract shall not include any further option to the CLUB to renew the contract. The compensation in subsection a. herein shall mean only the salary as prescribed in paragraph 2 above.

16. Retirement. If by reason of his becoming a member of the Armed Forces of the United States or any other country, or if for any other reason whatsoever (including, without limitation, illness or injury not incurred in the performance of services under this contract), the PLAYER shall retire or withdraw from professional basketball as a player prior to the expiration of the term of this contract, and subsequently shall return to professional basketball as a player, then the time lapsed between such retirement or withdrawal and such return shall be considered as tolled, and the term of this contract shall be considered as extended for a period of time beginning with such return and ending after a period of time equal to the portion of the term of this contract which was unexpired at the time of such retirement or withdrawal; and the option to renew hereof contained in paragraph 15 shall be considered as continuously in effect from the date of this contract until the end of such extended term. During the period of such retirement or withdrawal the PLAYER shall not be entitled to any compensation, expenses or other payments under this contract.

17. Waiver of Claims. The parties to the contract, if involved or affected in any manner whatsoever by a decision of the Commissioner and/or the Board of Trustees and/or the Member Clubs, as provided in the Bylaws and Rules and Regulations of the Association, agree to release the Commissioner individually and in his official capacity and to waive every claim he or they may have against the Commissioner and the ASSOCIATION, and every Member Club and its directors, officers, stockholders or partners, for damages and for all claims and demands arising out of said decision.

18. Whole Agreement. This agreement contains the entire agreement between the parties and there are no oral or written inducements, promises or agreements except as contained herein. No change, termination or attempted waiver of any of the provisions of this contract shall be binding unless in writing and signed by the party against whom the same is sought to be enforced and approved by the ASSOCIATION as provided in paragraph 9.

19. Governing Law. This contract shall be governed by the laws of the State of ___COLORADO___

EXAMINE THIS CONTRACT CAREFULLY BEFORE SIGNING IT.

IN WITNESS WHEREOF the PLAYER has hereunto set his hand and the CLUB has caused this contract to be executed by its duly authorized officer.

WITNESSES:

THE DENVER ROCKETS   CLUB

By _D. W. RINGSBY, PRES. AND GEN. MGR._

SPENCER HAYWOOD   Player

Player's Address___DENVER, COLORADO___

BEN GIBSON, GUARDIAN

I, Spencer Haywood, being of lawful age and no longer a minor acknowledge that I know each of the terms and provisions of the above agreement and do hereby fully approve, ratify and affirm the same in its entirety on this _____ day of June, 1970.

Spencer Haywood

Rider Attached

THIS AGREEMENT made and entered into on this 1st day of October, 1970, between Ringsby Truck Lines, Inc., a corporation (hereinafter call "Ringsby") and Spencer Haywood, an individual, (hereinafter referred to as "Haywood"), in consideration of the mutual promises and agreements herein contained and further consideration passing to Ringsby otherwise than in this agreement, it is agreed between the parties:

1. INVESTMENT FUND: Commencing on the 1st day of October, 1970, and on this same date each year thereafter for each of the next nine (9) years, Ringsby shall invest Ten Thousand Dollars ($10,000.00) annually in a "growth mutual fund" under the "Dolgoff Plan", in such proportionate amounts as it may desire which investments, together with the earnings and accumulations thereof, shall hereinafter be referred to as the "Investment Fund". The Investment Fund so created shall be and remain the sole absolute property of Ringsby and it may invest and reinvest, from time to time, the securities or other assets of the Investment Fund as it, in its sole discretion, shall deem beneficial so long as the funds shall be in "growth mutual funds". Nothing contained in the agreement or otherwise, shall be construed to give Haywood any property right or interest nor security interest of any kind or type in the Investment Fund nor shall the same be construed to be a trust of any type or kind.

RIGHTS OF HAYWOOD: The rights of Haywood shall be only as specifically hereinafter provided and Haywood agrees on behalf of himself and his personal representatives, heirs, legatees, distributees, beneficiary or beneficiaries and any other person or persons claiming any benefits through or under him be virtue of this agreement that this agreement and the rights, interests and benefits hereunder shall not be assigned, transferred, pledged or hypothecated in any manner by Haywood or by any personal representative, heir, legatee, distributee, beneficiary or beneficiaries, or other person claiming any benefits through or under Haywood by virtue of this agreement and shall not be subject to execution, attachment, garnishment or other similar process issued by any Court. Any attempted assignment, transfer, pledge or hypothecation or other disposition of this agreement or of any such rights, interests and benefits contrary to the foregoing provisions, or the levy of any execution, attachment, garnishment or other similar process thereof, shall be null, void and of no effect.

3. INSURANCE: Ringsby shall apply for one or more policies of insurance upon the life of Haywood on which premiums shall be paid and shall have death benefits of no less than One Hundred Thousand Dollars ($100,000.00) to be payable to such person or such persons as shall be designated by Haywood. The policy or policies of life insurance provided for in this paragraph shall be the sole property of Haywood and as incidents of ownership therein, including the right to designate or change the beneficiary thereof, shall be vested in Haywood.

■

The agreement covering investment fund and insurance details and the rights of Haywood and restrictions imposed upon him as covered in his third pact with the Denver Rockets, and the rider to the contract, are shown on this and the following pages.

4. <u>USE OF INVESTMENT FUND</u>: During the term of this agreement, Ringsby shall have the right of use of the Investment Fund in such manner and for the purposes hereinafter set forth:

(a) To use all or any portion of the Investment Fund as collateral for one or more loans to Ringsby which loans shall be in such terms, conditions and at such rate or rates of interest as may then be prevailing and as may be agreed to by Ringsby and any lending institution. Ringsby shall have the right for such purpose to hypothecate, assign, pledge or otherwise transfer as a security interest such securities (or other assets) as may then constitute a part of the Investment Fund.

(b) Ringsby shall have the right to liquidate such part of the Investment Fund at such times, and from time to time, as it may deem necessary so as to provide funds to pay any and all taxes that may be levied by any governmental authority, including Federal and State Income taxes, in respect to or upon such Investment Fund; any and all interest charges that may be incurred for loans made to said corporation which loans are provided for in Paragraph (a) above; and any and all premiums that may be paid by Ringsby upon such policy or policies of insurance as provided in Paragraph 3 above.

5. <u>PAYMENT</u>: Payment from the Investment Fund to Haywood shall be made at such times, in such manner and with such conditions as are hereinafter set forth:

(a) At any time after the date of the final investment by Ringsby, Haywood shall have the right to direct the payment to himself of an amount equal to ten per cent (10 %) of the then value of the Investment Fund as of the date of the direction of such payment.

(b) In each succeeding year for a period of thirty (30) years, or until the Investment Fund is exhausted, which ever shall first occur, after the election to direct payment is made as provided hereinafter, and on the same date in such succeeding year, an amount equal to the amount paid pursuant to Sub-paragraph (a) shall be paid to Haywood.

(c) The exercise of the right to direct payment shall be made by written notice from Haywood to Ringsby at least ten (10) days prior to the date that payment is directed to be made:

(d) For purposes of this paragraph, the then value of the Investment Fund, as of the date that a payment pursuant to Sub-paragraph (a) is to be made, shall be determined by ascertaining the fair market value of the Investment Fund less all accrued and unpaid taxes levied by any governmental authority, including Federal and State Income taxes

- 2 -

in respect to such Investment Fund; and less any and all unpaid loan
or loans (including accrued and unpaid interest charges thereon) due
any lending institution, the proceeds of which loans were used to pay
the premiums upon the policy or policies of insurance provided for in
Paragraph 3 above; and less any and all unpaid insurance premiums upon
the policy or policies of insurance referred to in Paragraph 3 above.

6. CONSIDERATION FOR AGREEMENT: Haywood agrees that if he ceases to perform
service to Ringsby with or without cause at any time during the period set forth in
Paragraph 1 hereof, this agreement shall terminate and Ringsby shall be relieved of
all obligation hereunder. In the event of the death of Haywood during the term set
forth in Paragraph 1 hereof, and if Haywood shall have rendered services to Ringsby
as agreed, the personal representatives or legatees of Haywood shall be entitled
to receive the entire proceeds of One Hundred Thousand Dollars ($100,000.00) life
insurance as provided in Paragraph 3 above. In addition to consideration rendered
by Haywood to Ringsby prior to the time of the election to direct payment as provided above, Haywood shall, and he does hereby agree that during the period payments
are made to him from the Investment Fund, he shall render advisory and consulting
services to Ringsby in regard to the business carried on by it. In the event that
Haywood shall forfeit all rights to any and all payments from the Investment Fund.
Haywood agrees that, although his rights to receive payments as provided for under
Paragraph 5 of this agreement may be vested, that he has no property interest in the
investment fund until payments are actually received and that he shall not and cannot
in any way pledge, assign or mortgage this agreement in any way. Should Haywood
at any time pledge, assign or mortgage this agreement, all rights and obligations of
Ringsby are immediately relieved and Haywood, upon such assignment, pledge or mortgage
will automatically and immediately lose all vested rights under this agreement.

8. BINDING AFFECT: This agreement shall be binding upon and inure to the
benefit of any successor in interest or assignee of Ringsby and shall be binding
upon and inure to the benefit of personal representatives, heirs, legatees, distributees and beneficiaries of Haywood.

IN WITNESS WHEREOF, the parties have caused this agreement to be executed on the
day and year first above written.

I, Spencer Haywood, being of lawful age and   RINGSBY TRUCK LINES, INC.
no longer a minor acknowledge that I know   By: _____
each of the terms and provisions of the above
agreement and do hereby fully approve, ratify   _____
and affirm the same in its entirety on this
8th day of June, 1970.   _____

_____
Spencer Haywood

- 3 -

RIDER TO CONTRACT

It is mutually agreed that if Haywood is injured in performance

of services hereunder or while playing or practicing basketball

or while going to or coming from any basketball game or practice
off season/to the extent that he is unable to further perform within   sessi

the meaning and intent of Paragraph 4. b. of the Contract he shall

be entitled to full salary during the term of such disability but not

longer than the term of this Contract, less any compensation or

insurance provided by the Rockets. If the Denver Rockets should
trade Haywood to any other club without his approval, then in that
event the Denver Rockets agree to pay Haywood $50,000.00 as
consideration for said trade.

DENVER ROCKETS

By _DWRimsley_
        President.

Spencer Haywood
Spencer Haywood

I, Spencer Haywood, being of lawful age and no longer a minor
acknowledge that I know each of the terms and provisions of the
above agreement and do hereby fully approve, ratify and affirm
the same in its entirety on this _8Th_ day of June, 1970.

Spencer Haywood
Spencer Haywood

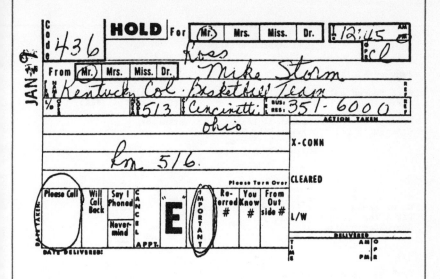

A handwritten note covering an incoming telephone call to Spencer Haywood's manager, Al Ross, is shown here. On the following page is one of the typewritten pages of notes out of Ross's file summarizing one of those busy days during Haywood's "holdout." The phone call, mentioned in the notes, covered an offer from Kentucky of the ABA of $100,000 up front and $200,000 a year for five years for Spencer's services. Other notes are Ross's reminders to himself about what others said, what he thought , about meetings set and to be set.

REGARDING SPENCER

January 9, 1971

Mike Storen called (12:45) in Cinncinatti, Room 516. Quality
Court,(513) 351-6000   (Spencer Room #610)

Wendell Cherry-President of League & Ex. Attorney
& Kentucky Col (502) 425-6140 Home
               (502) 897-6111 Home
               (502) 589-3790 Office

100 M at Exec. of K
5 years - 200 M per year (cash)
Play with Denver or another team in League - ABA
No deferred-Treat this year as full year
200 M for balance of this year
Guarantee by league
Indemnify as to all costs and will fight NBA and Denver

Has K
    &
Has 100   check with them
Fed up with Ringsby and want to do this immediately

Conveyed offer to me today

Points
1.) Court Suit - Denver K
2.) Certain point reached with Ringsby
3.) Sonic K for X $
4.) Uncertainties with Ct, NBA and Playing

We want him in league

Resolve $

Where Ct. for 2-3 years

Can handle league member better than NBA Ct. battle can do better
than two leagues battling

Committee knows what I am doing - with full knowledge, will invoke
his power

Must get together the sooner the better and do it.

Tinkham lost control of his client - Will solve per relationships

No problem - no cut, no trade, no option, no injury, all other things
offered

Stu Kadison and Pete Plealzer met at Century Plaza 1/9/71 with
Galanz'

1 IRELL & MANELLA
   CHARLES H. PHILLIPS
2 KENNETH A. GOLDMAN
   Suite 900 Gateway East Building
3 Century City
   Los Angeles, California 90067
4
   Telephone: 277-1010 and 879-2600
5
   Attorneys for Defendants
6

7

8   UNITED STATES DISTRICT COURT

9   CENTRAL DISTRICT OF CALIFORNIA

10

11 THE DENVER ROCKETS, a general   )
    partnership, and RINGSBY TRUCK   )
12 LINES, INC., a corporation,   )
)   CIVIL NO.
13   Plaintiffs,   )
)   70-2575-F
14   v.   )
)
15 ALL-PRO MANAGEMENT, INC., a   )   AFFIDAVIT OF
    corporation, and AL ROSS and   )   SPENCER HAYWOOD
16 MARSHALL BOYER, individuals,   )   IN OPPOSITION TO
)   PRELIMINARY RESTRAINING
17   Defendants.   )   ORDER
    _____   )
18

19 COUNTY OF LOS ANGELES)
) ss.
20 STATE OF CALIFORNIA   )

21   I, SPENCER HAYWOOD, BEING DULY SWORN, DEPOSE AND SAY

22 AS FOLLOWS:

23   1. When I first signed a contract, in 1969, to play

24 basketball with the Denver Rockets (hereinafter "Denver"), I was

25 an untried rookie with only two years of college basketball

26 experience. I do not have a copy of that first agreement, but I

27 believe that its general provisions are along the lines outlined

28 in the affidavit of D. W. Ringsby (although I note that the affi-

29 davit of J. W. Ringsby is in conflict therewith).

30   2. During the fall of 1969, I attended a meeting in

31 which Mr. Dolgoff tried to explain to me and to my then guardian,

32 William Robinson (hereinafter "Robinson") what he called the

W OFFICES
& MANELLA
WAY EAST BLDG.
TURY CITY
IGELES, CALIF.

■

*Shown on this page and on the following pages are the first four
pages of an affidavit given by Spencer Haywood to the United
States District Court in Los Angeles regarding his side of the case
in one of the many legal actions which took place. Brackets or under-
lining for emphasis were doodled onto the transcript by his attorneys.*

"Dolgoff Plan". Also present at that meeting were D. W. Ringsby
and J. W. Ringsby. Although I listened to Mr. Dolgoff, I knew
at the time that I did not understand how his plan operated.
However it sounded good to me, and I had a great amount of faith
in Messrs. Ringsby, who had brought Mr. Dolgoff out to talk to me.
I therefore agreed that we could substitute his plan for the
deferred compensation plan contained in the first contract.

      3. The meeting between me and J. W. Ringsby, referred
to commencing with paragraph 7 of his affidavit on file herein,
actually resulted from a call which he placed to me, rather than
from me to him. At the meeting, Mr. Ringsby told me that he had
read reports in the press that I had been approached by teams
from the National Basketball Association with offers of more
money than I was getting under my then existing contract with
Denver. I told him that I thought I should get more money, at
least as much as the other highly paid players, and he stated
that he would make me the highest paid player in professional
basketball, which he stated that I deserved to be. Specifically,
he offered to give me a six year contract for a guaranteed total
of $1.9 Million. From Mr. Ringsby's statements, I understood
that part of this sum would be payable in the form of annual
salary during the six year period and the balance would be
deferred, but I also understood that at the end of ten years, I
could withdraw 10% per year for the ten years thereafter, thus
giving me the total $1.9 Million by age forty. In his statements,
Mr. Ringsby made it clear that the total of $1.9 Million was to
be guaranteed.

      4. At the conclusion of that meeting, I was in fact
happy; I did ask Mr. Ringsby to write down what we agreed to; he
did so, but unfortunately I threw the paper away after the subsequently prepared ABA contract form was signed.

      5. The press conference referred to in Mr. J. W. Ringsby's

LAW OFFICES
LL. & MANILLA
ATEWAY EAST BLDG.
CENTURY CITY
, ANGELES, CALIF.

affidavit was his idea, not mine, although I had no objections.
The press conference was in fact held and he stated to those
present that we had just agreed to a six year contract for a
guaranteed sum of $1.9 Million.

6. There are numerous untrue or inaccurate statements
in the aforesaid affidavit of J. W. Ringsby. Among them are as
follows:

(a) In paragraph 3 thereof he refers to a guaranteed annuity for a period of fifteen years. I believe that the
initial contract provided that such payments would continue for
twenty years, as set forth in the affidavit of D. W. Ringsby.

(b) Regarding paragraph 6 thereof, the true facts
are that during the months in question I was approached by a
salesman employed by All-Pro Management, Inc. (hereinafter "APM"),
following which I contacted Al Ross with respect to possible
representation in connection with endorsements, etc.

(c) With respect to paragraph 7 thereof, as noted
above, he called me and asked for the meeting. I did not say that
I wanted to have a press conference. That was his idea. I did not
make any of the other statements therein attributed to me.

(d) The inaccuracies and falsities in paragraph 8
thereof are so numerous that they are difficult to summarize.
What was actually said at that meeting is set forth above in this
affidavit. I made no statement that I was happy with my contract.
In fact I stated that I wanted more money. I made no statements
with respect to agents bothering me, or the like. The paragraph
commencing at page 2 line 29, and continuing through page 3 line
13 is totally false. Mr. Ringsby neither said to me nor wrote on
any piece of paper any calculations by which he had arrived at the
figure of $1.9 Million. With respect to the court-approved
guardian in Colorado, I stated why not use Will Robinson.
Mr. Ringsby said that I was a Colorado resident and could not use

LAW OFFICES
IRELL & MANELLA
00 GATEWAY EAST BLDG.
CENTURY CITY
LOS ANGELES, CALIF.

-3-

1 Robinson. I did not request that Ben Gibson be my guardian for

2 this purpose. Mr. Ringsby suggested Gibson and I agreed although

3 I had only met the gentleman a few times.

4   7. Quite some time later I was presented with the

5 written agreement attached as Exhibit C to the affidavit of

6 D. W. Ringsby. I signed that contract without making any real

7 effort to read or understand it, both because I then had the

8 utmost faith in both J. W. Ringsby and D. W. Ringsby, and also

9 because I did not believe that I would understand all of the fine

10 print anyway. I was not present when Ben Gibson signed as my

11 guardian, nor did he ever attempt to explain to me what the

12 contract provided; nor did he ever discuss the terms of the con-

13 tract with me in any way; nor did I ever appear in court in

14 connection with any proceedings for the approval of the contract.

15   8. On or about June 8, 1970, Donald Ringsby called me

16 and asked me to come in and sign a ratification. I did so simply

17 because he had asked me.

18   9. I reported on schedule for practice in connection

19 with the 1970-1971 season. I played in the first two exhibition

20 games, but then sustained a leg injury which kept me out of action

21 for several games. In a subsequent exhibition game, against

22 Indiana, I broke my hand. That was on or about October 6, 1970.

23 My hand was placed in a cast, and remained in a cast until quite

24 recently. Nevertheless, at the time of the first regular season

25 game, on October 14, 1970, the trainer, Lloyd Williams, insisted

26 that I should play even though my broken hand was in a cast. I

27 called Dr. Brown, who was treating me, and he told me that under

28 no circumstances should I play until at least November 6 at the

29 earliest. Since coming to California in October, I have been

30 under the treatment of Dr. Milton M. Birnbaum, M.D. Attached

31 hereto as Exhibit A is a true and correct copy of a letter from

32 --

LAW OFFICES
NELL & MANELLA
GATEWAY EAST BLDG.
CENTURY CITY
OS ANGELES, CALIF.

-4-

Al Ross, Esq.
1900 Avenue of the Stars
Suite 2250
Los Angeles, California 90067

Gentlemen:

This is to confirm the understanding between Al Ross and myself as follows:

1. I hereby engage you as my exclusive personal representative to perform the following services for me:

(a) Negotiate any and all professional contracts which are offered to me .

(b) Collect all income.

(c) Maintain a commercial and other bank accounts under my name at such bank or banks as you may determine from time to time.

(d) Pay all accounts of mine which shall be due from said account.

(e) Do all necessary year end tax planning and prepare Federal and State Income Tax Returns.

(f) Advise and counsel me on a savings and investment program as required.

2. You agree to exert your best efforts to make available to me investment opportunities from time to time and to analyze investments referred to me which I reasonably request you to do.

3. As consideration for the services rendered by you to me hereunder, I agree to pay you 10% of the gross income received by me, as and when received, whether during the term hereof or afterwards, under any contracts entered into or negotiated by or for me during the term of this agreement, under any renewals or extensions of any such contracts, under any contracts substituted for or replacing directly or indirectly any such contract, or any renewal or extension thereof, or any contract made within a period of one year after the termination of this agreement. The foregoing compensation shall be payable to you irrespective of whether I have commenced or not commenced and/or completed or not completed the rendition of my services under the aforesaid contracts, renewals, extensions or substitutions thereof, or negotiated contracts. For the purposes of this agreement, compensation

-23-

EXHIBIT 3

15. This agreement cannot be assigned by you except that it may be assigned to any entity in which Al Ross has a proprietary interest.

If the foregoing accurately reflects our understanding, please sign in the space provided below indicating your acknowledgement hereto so that a binding agreement will exist between you and myself.

Very truly yours,

SPENCER HAYWOOD

Social Security No. 319-42-4191

AGREED TO AND ACCEPTED:

By _____
AL ROSS

Dated: October 20, 1970

_____
Witness

On this page, the beginning and end of the second and superseding pact between Spencer Haywood and Al Ross, and on the following pages, portions, including the first and last pages, of Spencer's contract with Sam Schulman and the Seattle Supersonics.

PLAYER CONTRACT

THIS AGREEMENT is made and entered into this 28th day of December, 1970, by and between FIRST NORTHWEST INDUSTRIES d/b/a SEATTLE SUPERSONICS (hereinafter called the "Club"), a member of the National Basketball Association (hereinafter called the "Association") and SPENCER HAYWOOD, whose address is shown below (hereinafter called the "Player").

WHEREAS, the Player contacted the Club without the solicitation of the Club and has told and represented to the Club:

That the Player (while legally a minor) on April 1, 1970, executed an American Basketball Association Uniform Player Contract with the Denver Rockets (hereinafter called the "illegal Denver contract");

That the Player executed said illegal Denver contract while a minor without independent legal counsel as a result of misrepresentations to him of, among other things, the amount of compensation he would be paid;

That except for the confidence and faith which the Player placed in said misrepresentations he would never have executed said illegal Denver contract;

That as a result of said misrepresentations Player has been advised that said illegal Denver contract is of no force or effect and is grossly unfair;

That, since said illegal Denver contract is unenforceable, the Player is a free agent and is also not under contract to any other Association member;

That the Player no longer is willing to play basketball for the Denver Rockets because of certain acts of personal abuse which he has suffered while playing basketball for said team;

That the Player now desires to play basketball only in the City of Seattle;

WHEREAS, the Club believes that the Player, who
is not under contract to any other Association member,
should be permitted to play basketball where and for whom
he desires.

NOW, THEREFORE, the parties hereto promise and
agree as follows:

1. The Club hereby employs the Player as a skilled
basketball player for the term commencing on the date of this
Agreement and continuing until September 30, 1977.

2. The Club agrees to pay the Player for rendering
services described herein the sum of $1,500,000.00 (less all
amounts required to be withheld from salary by Federal, State
and local authorities and player contributions to the Association's players pension fund, participation in which is
mandatory) in one hundred and eighty (180) monthly payments
beginning with the first of said payments on January 1, 1971,
and continuing with such payments on the first of each month
until said sum is paid in full.

3. The Club agrees to pay all proper and necessary
expenses of the Player, including the reasonable board and
lodging expenses of the Player while playing for the Club
"on the road" and during training camp if the Player is not
then living at home. The Player, while "on the road" (and at
training camp only if the Club does not pay for meals directly)
shall be paid $10.00 per day as meal expense allowance.

4. If the Player is chosen "Rookie of the Year", he
shall receive a bonus of $10,000.00. If the Player is chosen
as the league's Most Valuable Player, he shall receive a bonus
of $10,000.00.

5. During the following periods of time, during
the employment term of this Agreement: (a) after the date of

-3-

9. The Club agrees to indemnify the Player, and
to hold the Player harmless from, any and all costs, liabilities
and expenses (including but not limited to attorneys' fees)
resulting from his execution of this Agreement; provided,
however, that the Player must give to the Club prompt notice
of any claim, action or proceeding covered by this paragraph;
and provided further that the Player shall not incur any expense in prosecuting or defending any such claim, action or
proceeding until Player has afforded the Club a reasonable
opportunity to select the counsel to conduct such prosecution or
defense.

17. If any provision of provisions of this Agreement shall be void or voidable or illegal, the other provisions hereof shall be severed therefrom and shall be enduring and enforceable without reference to such void or voidable or illegal provision or provisions.

18. This Agreement contains the entire agreement between the parties and there are no oral or written inducements, promises, or agreements except as contained herein.

19. This contract is deemed to be a "no cut contract" for the term of the six-year playing agreement.

IN WITNESS WHEREOF, the Player has hereunto signed his name and the Club has caused this Contract to be executed by its duly authorized officer.

FIRST NORTHWEST INDUSTRIES
d/b/a SEATTLE SUPERSONICS

By Sam Schulman, Treasurer

SPENCER HAYWOOD

Player's Address:

1900 Avenue of the Stars
Los Angeles, California.

WITNESSES:

that it would benefit all if a new contract was drawn up utilizing this program. He said detailed statistical analysis revealed there was less than a one percent chance that the plan would produce less than the $15,000 per year desired and there was a great probability it would produce substantially greater returns. He said he believed it was a good contract Haywood signed with the counseling of Robinson.

Mr. Ringsby said Spencer sought a third contract after he had been "bothered" by a number of agents from the NBA teams who were trying to get him to jump his ABA contract and that he was very "unhappy" with them "because he wanted to play basketball and they were bothering his basketball and that he wanted to renegotiate his contract so he could release to the press a statement that he was being paid a considerable, great sum of money so that the agents would quit bothering him because they were interfering with his playing." He said the agents told him that he wasn't making as much money as Lew Alcindor and was as good a player.

Mr. Ringsby said Haywood said he wanted to sign with the Rockets to remain with them for 10 years, but that team attorneys advised management that contracts for more than seven years might not be legally binding, so they settled for a six-year pact. He said he told Haywood the Rockets had lost a lot of money in their first few years of operation and would like to recoup some of this before going overboard, so he would like to continue at $50,000 a year for the remaining two years of his original contracts, but then would pay him $75,000 a year for four additional years, and would increase contributions into the Dolgoff plan from $3,000 a year to $10,000 a year, and that Haywood said this was fine with him.

He said Spencer did ask for a "no-cut, no-trade" clause and they settled on a $50,000 outright payment to Haywood in the event of a trade, which in any event would not have negated his contract. Mr. Ringsby said Ben Gibson, named to represent Spencer, was a reliable banker and a person of the highest character, who had provided Haywood with the finest advice.

And when Haywood began to ask for more money, Ringsby remarked, "I couldn't believe it. . . . I said that we had signed a contract, that it had been renegotiated two or three times and that we were running out of patience ... we thought we had a legal and binding contract ... we thought he had a moral and legal obligation to perform under that contract." Ringsby said Spencer asked $75,000 a year right then and there. And Ringsby said he asked if he gave Spencer that wouldn't he want more in two or three weeks? And Spencer said he'd sign a pledge that he wouldn't. But Ringsby wasn't satisfied. And, sure enough, he said, shortly Spencer had increased his request to $100,000 a year.

Enter Ross. Ringsby testified: "He wanted Spencer's contract clarified and guaranteed and we asked him what that meant and he said, well, that meant paying him in cash over 15 years or some such thing. . . . The Dolgoff Plan, he said, wasn't worth anything. . . . It meant, actually, our contract was nothing, that we had to start all over again, negotiate a new contract with Al Ross, I guess." Ringsby reported that at an airport meeting, Ross requested $150,000 a year for his client.

Ringsby said he told Haywood, "I would certainly like to sit down to try to work this out with him. I also told him that I was sure we would be able to force him to live up to his agreement. . . . I explained to him that while I thought he was a fine young man and that I was his friend and felt like I could do more for him than someone else would, and that I was willing to assist him through life and help mould his character and mould his future the same as I would one of my own sons, and try to get him to come back to Denver, and I explained also to him that if he decided to proceed under legal remedies that I would have to proceed against him. . . ."

Concluded the elder Ringsby of Haywood, "I think he loves Denver and I think he was well treated there and I think he will come back some day. . . . He seemed happy . . . but Ross wanted something else. . . . He came up with some silly idea of wanting $312,000 a year or something, for a one- or three-year contract, and got off into all kinds of tangents." Ringsby decided in the end it was hopeless to reason with Ross, though he held hope for Haywood until the end and said he wanted to be like a father to him, and regretted that Spencer's head had been filled with nonsense by others that had made him feel insecure and dissatisfied.

Meanwhile, there was much manuevering behind the scenes. Denver and ABA lawyers were advising the Ringsbys and Dolph that there were too many loopholes in the contracts tendered a minor who had not had proper representation for the Rockets to have much chance of winning. Meanwhile, the conflict had placed the planned merger of the two leagues in jeopardy. Schulman had assured the ABA people that if the case was settled in his favor he would do everything in his power to speed up the merger, and the ABA people were applying considerable pressure on the Ringsbys to surrender. Haywood was outspoken that he had heard the Ringsbys use racial slurs against him; he said that he would never return to the Rockets no matter how the case concluded.

As the younger Ringsby, Don, took the stand, court costs were mounting, and he began to seem driven by desperation to salvage something from this mess. The pressure pounded at him. A handsome young man, husky, hearty, he soon seemed pale, distressed, drawn.

Soon it seemed his testimony was not doing good. Had he and his father taken advantage of a poor, dumb black boy from the deep south and northern ghettoes? Possibly. Very possibly not. But this was how it seemed on the surface to some. Opposing lawyers hammered away at every technicality in the last contract tendered the player which threatened not to pay him what it had been publicized it would pay him. Counsel slashed at every weakness in the Denver argument.

Question: "Did you ever enter any contractual relationship with Mr. Robinson?"

Answer: "Yes."

Question: "And what was the nature of that relationship?"

Answer: "I retained him to scout for the Denver Rockets and paid him $5,000 as a retainer and agreed to pay him . . . for a period of five years the fee of $2,000. . . . "

Even as he testified, settlement meetings began in late March. And on March 30, agreement was reached, the cases dropped, court action ended. The jury never got a chance to render a verdict, nor Judge Ferguson an opinion, on the contract; but Pfaelzer insists, "We were winning. We smelled victory. They saw it. Even the members of the jury polled privately admitted it. It was a victory for us and a defeat for them." Don Ringsby insists, "I'm not sure we would have lost. My father wanted to fight to the finish." He shrugs, "Anyway, we did not come out of it empty-handed."

Reportedly, Denver settled with Schulman for $300,000 plus court costs, but as part of the settlement they also got concessions from the ABA, including the ABA's first selection in the first common draft if the merger goes through. Curiously, although the court had ruled Seattle had the right to sign and play Haywood in the NBA, a federal appeals court had ruled that the league had the right to impose penalties on Schulman for violating its by-laws. Walter Kennedy announced a fine of $200,000. This seemed to insiders, however, a small sum for a superstar. The fine was mocked, and many doubted it ever would be paid. And it has not been. But Schulman did pay his moral debt to move the merger along. Swiftly, it became a reality—subject to Congressional approval which may never come.

7. Spencer's Side

"I wanted an education, but college ball didn't challenge me and I quickly got fed up with the way I was treated in college, so I was ready to leave Detroit and turn pro and start making an honest buck as soon as I found out there was a chance. Let's face it, you only have so many years to play, and the money I could make playing pro for a couple of years when I ordinarily still would've been in college is money I'd have lost if I stayed in college. And my best chance to make a big stake for myself in life has to be on my basketball ability, not my brilliance.

"I really didn't know if I was ready for the pros. I had awe for them. I played with Connie Hawkins on a playground once, and I couldn't believe it was me playing with him. I was scared and nervous and I didn't do good. But I played with him. And most of the top players I played with, I held my own. And the stories were going out how good I was. I was scared of them, but I was scaring them, too. And every step of the way, high school, junior college, the Olympics, college, I'd been the best.

"Milwaukee wanted me. And Cincinnati. All right. But they couldn't play me right away. I wanted the money, but I wanted to play, too. I wanted to improve. I didn't want to fool around playing in Europe or playing funny-man with the Globetrotters. Denver wanted me, and they said they could play me right away and pay me good, so that was it.

"I wanted to play in the NBA, not the ABA, because I wanted to play with the best and I figured the NBA was it, but I figured I could play in the ABA until I was eligible to play in the NBA, then jump to the NBA. I didn't tell Denver this. I asked for a two-year contract. They wanted more years. We compromised on three. There still would have been time for me to make my move. I would have been young. Later, it looked like there would be a merger so I wouldn't have to make a move to play with the NBA stars. And if Denver was going to pay me what anyone else was going to pay me, what was the difference? So I signed the six-year contract.

"One of the problems was the money simply wasn't what it should have been and the contracts simply weren't what they were supposed to be. The money sounded OK to me at first, but then I found out what others were making and that I was as good as anyone in the ABA and better than most in the NBA and maybe had a chance to be the best but wasn't making as much as others and had tied myself up to the point where I wouldn't even be making it later after I'd played for years. I was filling their building for them and making them the best team in the league, and I was having to ask and beg for everything. After the season, over the summer, I talked to guys like Archie Clark and Em Bryant and John Green and Fred Crawford. We compared notes, and I came out on the short end. Also, they asked me questions about my contracts I couldn't answer.

"I hadn't really read the contracts before. I acted on trust and you can't do that in business. But what did I know about business? I trusted Will Robinson, but what did he know about business? I trusted the Ringsbys, and I guarantee you they knew their business. I got out my contract and I began to study it and it scared me. If I was the best basketball player ever after six years, I'd still have been making $75,000 a year. Guys already were making $100,000 and $200,000 a year who couldn't play with me, and after six years some guys might be making $300,000 and $400,000 a year. And I wasn't sure I'd ever get more. If

132

they asked me to sweep floors for them for $50 a week for four years, I guess I'd have had to do it to get any of the later money, and then I couldn't get any until I was 40 and I couldn't get it all until I was 60, and there was nothing in there that really said what I'd get. And I didn't see any protection in there for me in case I was traded or the team or league folded.

"Robinson didn't know from nothing. It's just that simple. He got me to go to Detroit because they promised him he'd be coach there, and then he got me to leave when they broke their promise to him; and he got me to go to Denver because they made other promises to him, and I could see they were going to break any promises they made him even if he couldn't see it. Poor black man lives all his life on promises from white men that don't mean nothing. I feel sorry for Robinson. I know what he done for me. He made me a man. He gave me a lot. He also done me wrong. He got me to sell my future for promises. I should hate him, but I feel sorry for him.

"I have not spoken to him a long time, and I'm sure he feels I'm ungrateful. The fact is, I'm grateful for everything he done for me. And I love him. But he should have said that he couldn't give me the right advice, and he should have said we should get someone who could. That banker Ben Gibson who was appointed to represent me in the dealing for my third contract is the Ringsby's banker and the Rockets' banker, and he never read the contract to me or explained it to me or advised me in any way, except to sign, and he never argued with the Ringsbys over any point. And Robinson, who is a little older and presumably a little wiser than me, should have stepped in and said let's get this young man some help. I'm sorry. I don't square with a man who goes against his own kind. And the last time I spoke to him I told him that.

"The Ringsbys were looking out for their own interests. I never asked them for the third contract. Representatives from New York and Milwaukee of the NBA had contacted me or Robinson directly and guys from San Francisco and Boston had gotten word to us indirectly that they were prepared to give me a lot more money to sign with them when my college class graduated and my pro contract expired than I was getting with Denver. Milwaukee talked of a million-dollar package. This was before the Bucks signed Oscar Robertson. I thought it would be out of sight to play with big Lew. But the Ringsbys must have seen the scouts sniffin' around, and then the story of the offers broke in the paper—I didn't give it away—so they called me in and offered me more. They weren't looking to protect me, they were looking to protect themselves. By then they knew I was a valuable property. I figured I'd have to wait a couple of years to collect the big money from the Bucks, so I took what the Rockets offered. But, later, when I asked for more, they said nothing doing.

"I suppose I was wrong for re-negotiating and re-negotiating and asking them to re-negotiate some more, but I was just learning, my eyes were just being opened up, and I was just finding out what the real score was. Everyone tells you you're worth such and such, soon you begin to believe it. When you don't have it, you get depressed. When they tell you they'll give it to you, fine. Then when you're not getting it, wow, it turns you off. What the hell did they do for me? Pay me $50,000 when they were paying other rookies $200,000? Give me a car? They sold me an old car and took it out of my salary. Give me a bonus? They gave me an advance and took it out of my salary.

"After a while what became as important as anything else was the way they treated people. Not the most important reason, but one of the reasons I was ready to go to Denver was that the Rockets had a black coach, John McLendon, who I'd met when I played in JC ball in Colorado, and who I thought was a good coach and a nice man. As soon as I got there, the Rockets fired him. We'd gotten off to a slow start, but the season was still young and it upset me all to hell. They said it was our fault, the players'. Hell, we didn't fire the man. But the coach they brought in, Joe Belmont, was a nice man, so I let it go. We got hot under Belmont, went on a winning streak, and wound up winning our division going away. But then when I left and the team got off to a slow start the next season, even though the season was still young, they fired Joe Belmont right away. He was Coach of the Year one year

134

and out of work the next. They never even had the courtesy to tell him he was fired. He heard it on the radio, that's what I heard. And they wouldn't pay McLendon what they owed him. He had to hire an attorney and go to court. He had to promise his attorney a third. The Ringsbys told McLendon, settle out of court, cut the lawyer out and we'll give you two-thirds. That's how they operate.

"We did well under Belmont. I gave the team a big lift. The MVP proves that. And I worked hard. Any of the guys will tell you that. But some of the guys may have been jealous. And I can understand that. Everyone on that team was underpaid and I came along and before I'd proven anything they figured I was overpaid. I was getting fat and they were hungry. They resented me. What do you think, athletes aren't human and don't have human feelings?

"Larry Jones was their best player and the league's best scorer before I came along, but he came to them without a name. They had him hooked on a cheap contract for $23,000 a year, and there was no way they were going to let him off. You say, maybe, if a guy signs a contract he should be stuck with it and shouldn't expect to re-negotiate it, but when a guy has got nowhere to go and is desperate and gets an offer, any offer, he has to grab it. But when he does a job for them, the bosses should see this and say, hey, we appreciate what you've done, we want you to be happy, let's be fair. But not the Ringsbys. And Larry Jones let them take advantage of him. And he let it affect his play. I feel sorry for him. He let the system beat him. When he bent his back and demanded more, they said, 'Bye,' and sold him down the river. Julie Keye was making seventeen, eighteen grand. Julie Hammond was making eight. They just took it.

"Wayne Hightower helped them get their franchise off the ground. And he was trying to get a business off the ground for himself in Denver. When he asked them for a loan to help him out, they sent him packing. They got Larry Cannon and treated him so good he right away jumped them. There weren't very many players on that team had any respect for the Ringsbys. When we won, they were in there smiling and patting us on the back and

135

sharing the bows, and when we lost, they were in there whining to us and sticking knives in our backs and cutting us up. They were going up to the coach and saying if he had played this guy or hadn't played that guy things would have been different, but what the hell did they know about basketball. They made the guy play a guy like Byron Beck, then blamed the coach when they lost. They wanted to see some white guys in there, I guarantee you.

"There were good guys on that team. Ben Warley, I dug him. And Lonnie Wright. But everyone was underpaid. And they didn't get so much as a Christmas present out of the Ringsbys. And when they asked for more money, they were told, 'You got a contract, take it or leave it,' or 'We'll have to trade you.' The guys got more and more unhappy. By the time we got into the playoffs we weren't enough of a team to win. And the Ringsbys said we were outcoached.

"From the first time I met them I suspected their feelings about race. Old man Ringsby sounded off right away on how beautiful blacks had it in Denver, like we should get down on our knees and give thanks for being treated nice. But I figured maybe I was taking it wrong. Later, he called me 'boy.' I said, 'I'm no boy, I'm a man.' I didn't ask him to call me Mr. Haywood. I said, 'Call me Spencer.' I figured maybe I took it wrong. Being called 'boy' means a bad thing to most blacks, but I'm sure it's not always meant bad. One day the younger Ringsby, Don, said, 'Get your black ass out on that court.' But he was smiling. It really upset me, but I saw he was smiling and figured he was just funning and didn't mean anything by it.

"Then I saw white guys being kept while better black guys were cut. They keep the black stars, but not the fringe guys. Lonnie Lynn, Floyd Theard and Dwight Walker were guys who were cut who were better than Greg Wittman, Walt Piatkowski and others who were kept after them. And after I left they wouldn't cut Ralph Simpson because they'd paid him so much, but they wouldn't play him regular either, which was ridiculous, and this year when they got afraid of losing him, they began to play him. Now he is their best player.

"After the season ended, I told Robinson I was worried

about my contract, but he said not to worry. But I couldn't help it. I asked the Ringsbys to explain it to me, but they said they weren't going to go into it again. I'd signed it and they weren't going to change anything. People talked to them for me. Joe Belmont talked to them for me. I'm sure that put him in bad. They weren't listening.

"We hassled all summer. I'd blown most of the money I'd made. I spent a lot and was a soft touch for every hard-luck story I heard. I could see this was no good and I needed the sort of management help other guys were getting if I was going to leave this game with anything. I'd met guys who used Al Ross of All-Pro Management in L. A., like John Brisker and Rick Barry, and they thought he did a good job for them. A representative of his had contacted me offering to get me some deals, so I called him up. He got me a TV interview date and flew me into L. A. for the show. I asked him if he'd do some business for me, put me on a budget, take care of my taxes, things like that, and he agreed. So I signed a contract with All-Pro for 25 percent. I sent it to Robinson at Mr. Ross's suggestion and never saw it again until it showed up in court. He took it to the Ringsbys, and they took it to court.

"I also asked Ross to look over my contract and he agreed to do that, too. By that time, it was time to report to camp. I got through training and played some exhibitions, but my heart wasn't in it. It was a relief when I broke my hand. I flew to L. A. and he said, like, wow, you don't have much of a contract here. He'd gone through it and found out everything I was worried about, I had a right to be worried about. He asked me what I wanted to do and I said I wanted him to get it fixed for me if he could. I said I wanted him to handle all my business, legal affairs, negotiate all my contracts, protect my future and leave me free to play basketball. He said, fine, on that basis, let's sign a new contract for a straight 10 percent of everything, and forget about the old contract and I said, fine, and that's what we did. He said he would pay the accountants, tax experts and everyone else out of his 10 percent. That seemed fair, and I think it is fair.

"At first, we had not thought of leaving Denver. We just wanted to get this contract guaranteed or to get a new one that would pay us just exactly the one-point-nine-million the old one was supposed to pay me. But the Ringsbys didn't want to talk to Ross at all. And I didn't want to go back to Denver until it was all straightened out. So I moved in with Al and his wife and family and the Ringsbys suspended me. Then there was a story in the Denver newspapers that we were asking three-and-a-quarter-million. I don't know where that came from unless the Ringsbys gave it to them, although they deny it. So we had to call a press conference in L. A. just to let people know all we wanted was what we were supposed to be getting. That helped some, because we weren't trying to hold anyone up, we just wanted what was owed us.

"They refused. We met here and we met there and it came to nothing. They kept refusing. In fact, they got downright abusive. I was in an adjoining hotel room at one meeting and I heard old man Ringsby say right through the wall he wasn't going to let that black nigger push him around. And I knew Jack Dolph was in the room with him. Another time, I was in the same room with him, a few feet from him, talking to Ross while he was talking to Dolph, and I heard him say this just wasn't a good nigger and there wasn't any way they were going to be able to deal with me like they could with a white man. Well, I felt like kicking him, but what's the point, so I just walked right on out and kept walking. After that, there was no way I was going to go back. And I had no respect for Dolph anymore, either, for not calling him on his talk.

"I mean we are slaves and they have us in contracts of involuntary slavery, all jocks; but the blacks are put down even worse than the whites, and there is no way I am going to take that kind of crap from anyone. He knew I could hear him. He didn't care. Dolph didn't care.

"They wanted me to stay in their league. Carolina called up offering me a firm $350,000 a year for six years. They said they'd get rights to me, but there was no way they were going to get me. The Ringsbys weren't going to give me up. Indiana, New York and Utah also made pitches for me. We said we'd be interested if they could get rights to me, but there was no way. They turned down trade offers. I understand Dolph asked them what they wanted for me.

They said a million dollars. He raised it. They said they didn't want to sell. The other owners voted to try and buy the club from the Ringsbys. They raised two million. The Ringsbys wouldn't sell.

"It wasn't just that they wanted me as a ballplayer who could make them money, but that they wanted me to suffer. They didn't want to be embarrassed by a black man.

"NBA clubs were coming after me, too. Los Angeles, Seattle, San Francisco, Phoenix, Chicago, Cleveland, Cincinnati, Atlanta, Buffalo, Milwaukee, Boston, New York all had guys call me or Ross and expressed interest or made pitches. Ross said he felt we could get out of the Denver contract and get an NBA contract if I wanted to go that way, but we'd have to fight it out in court. So I said let's do it. He suggested I call Sam Schulman of Seattle and see him. So I did that, and the man impressed me. He wanted to talk to Ross and see my contracts and things like that until he figured it out, and then he was ready to go. We talked money and got to one-point-five. Others offered more, but Sam was the only one who offered to go all the way to court for me and pay all costs and take all the risks, so that settled it.

"So we went to court. They got lawyers and we got lawyers. They filed suits and we filed suits. The ABA wanted me and the NBA didn't want me. I got so sick of hasslin', I couldn't stand it any more. All I wanted was what I was supposed to be getting. If Denver had justified that contract when we asked them to, I'd have reported right to them. My heart wouldn't have been in it, but I'd have gone. Later, I said there was no way I would go back. But then when they were trying to stick it to Ross, when they got an injunction against him, and threatened to disbar him, I figured I'd dragged him into a mess that wasn't of his making and I told him I'd go back if it would take him off the hook, but he said, 'Forget it.' He said he was a big boy and made his own decisions and he was with me because he believed in me and my case and would be with me to the finish, win or lose. I spent Christmas day at Sam Schulman's house, and he told me he was with me, too, and not to give up. So I stuck it out.

"Even after the judge granted me the right to play with

Seattle, the court case and the hasslin' went on and on and on. I reported to the team, and the playing coach, Lenny Wilkens, and Bob Rule and Rod Thorn and some of the other players treated me well, but some of the players were cold and cautious and I felt some tension on the team. The club had been having its troubles, and I know some of those old pros didn't like the idea of me as a saviour who was going to turn things around for them. Anyway, I couldn't do it. I was flying back and forth and appearing in court and on court I was tired and I couldn't concentrate. I couldn't follow everything that was happening in court. I didn't understand it all. I felt like I was being pulled this way and that way. On and off, I've felt that for a long time. In Seattle, I was cheered, but in other towns I was booed. Other team owners and coaches were making the most ridiculous statements. And some of the players were baiting me. Some wouldn't speak to me. Oscar Robertson turned his back on me.

"Before it was over, I just wanted to get the hell away from it. The public was down on me. The press was down on me. The pressure was wearing me down. I didn't have anything left. I didn't know anything for sure anymore. I didn't know if I was a good man or a bad man. I knew almost everyone thought I was a bad man, so maybe they were right. I didn't think I could win. I didn't have any faith in justice. Then I won. I mean it was like getting my faith back. There was justice, after all. It was like being reborn. There was a place for me, after all. I still find it hard to believe. I stood up for something, and I'm still standing. I got smeared, but I'm all right. I could start to play the game again. I had me a good contract and a shot at a fine future. All of a sudden, it was a whole new deal.

"I didn't stand alone. Without Al Ross and Sam Schulman I'd never have made it. And they got smeared a lot for standing alongside me. Guys like Ross get smeared anyway. Agents. Hustlers. They're called all the cuss words. What are they? They're businessmen. They manage a man's affairs who can't manage for himself. And they do their best for him because whatever they're doing for him they're doing for themselves. Al Ross negotiates my contracts, manages my money, advises me on investments, builds me tax shelters, pays my taxes, gets me deals. Whatever I make, he makes 10 percent. Whatever I invest in, he invests in with me. He does a job for me. He gets paid for it. It's a fair fee. He don't steal from no one. He's a helluva businessman. And a helluva man. And he's a white man. And he's my friend.

"So is Sam Schulman. He's also my boss. He's made a helluva investment in me. He put his franchise on the line for me. He put his reputation on the line for me. He's a big man. He stood up to those other big cats and he fought 'em right down the line and he won. All right, I'm worth something to him. He's got a basketball team and I'm a helluva basketball player. But it's more than just that. He owns this and he owns that. He must be worth many millions. He's done big things with his life. What have I done? Who am I? But he treats me like a man. The first time he sees me play, I come into L. A. and I try so hard to do something for him, I can't do anything. Afterwards he puts his arm around me and he says all he asks is that I do my best. Right on, man. He's a straight soul. His contracts spell everything out. If you want a hundred advisors and lawyers and managers and accountants and what-have-you, welcome. He has nothing to be afraid of.

"I feel I have nothing to be afraid of, either. I been cheated and I been tricked. I been blasted and I been booed. But I find out if you hold yourself together and fight back you can win. You may not always win, but you can win. I won.

"I don't even care about the Ringsbys any more. They lost. Let 'em go their way and I'll go mine. There'll be other turns in the road, I'm sure. Other people will disappoint me. And I'll disappoint other people. You think what you think. You do your thing. You don't worry about what people think. You can't control that. If you're right, you fight. Sometimes you win."

8. Al Ross's Side

He sits, polishing himself like a jewel, in a setting of splendor, high atop the city. He would own it if he could. As it is, he'll take what he can get, piece by piece. He is Al Ross, who manages athletes, one of the men who has revolutionized sports. This is big business. Superstars are among the highest-paid entertainers in the world since revolutionaries like Ross began in the last decade to represent the faces on the bubble-gum cards.

He has been called "immoral," "unscrupulous," "a Hollywood hustler," "an ambulance chaser," "a quick-buck artist," "a parasite," "a vulture," "a barracuda," "a crook," "a cannibal," and worse. This bothers him. He was bothered when an adversary called him "a Beverly Hills bastard Jew lawyer." This was getting personal. He broke the man's back, in a polite business way, of course. He ducks the bad names as though they were bullets and carries on as though he were a medic on a mission of mercy at the front.

What really bothers him is when he is called an agent. "Don't call me an agent," he says, as though it were a dirty word. "I am an attorney and a business manager, and I head up a large organization with a large full-time staff of experts and access to the best brains in the country. We offer by far the most complete service in the field to our clients. We get them business, negotiate their contracts, bank their money, budget it for them, invest it for them, provide tax shelters for them, pay their taxes. . . ."

In a pinch, he will also deliver their babies, arrange their bar-mitzvahs—although few of his clients require this particular service—draw up their wills and bury their rivals. He will even bail them out of jail when necessary and go to court for them.

He says, "We do a helluva job for the guys. They are like my sons. Or brothers. Sure I make a buck off them. It is business. But they know where every buck goes. They know I care about them. That's the difference between me and some of the other guys in this business. *I care.* I worry. Some nights, I don't sleep."

His organization is called Al Ross & Associates, Inc., and its main arm is All Pro Management. He is proud that he was called by a black writer "the true attorney for black athletes." He is white and some of his clients are white, but most top athletes are black, so most of his clients are black. He says he has made it his mission in life to see that the color of his clients' skin does not affect the color of their money.

He says he feels for them as only a member of another minority could, although one suspects he has suffered more persecution from being a member of the minority of athletes' managers than from being Jewish. "All athletes got the short end of the stick until they began to get proper representation," he says, "but it's the black athlete who's really been screwed because he can't get as many fringe benefits and is more at the mercy of the team owners."

His fifty clients include Spencer Haywood and Carl Eller and have in the past included Deacon Jones, who departed after a disagreement, and Rick Barry, who wanted to be represented in New York after he was traded there. Ross and Duane Thomas, "the silent man" of the Dallas Cowboys, parted company when they had, of all things, "words," but Ross found Thomas a rare one who really was "unmanageable." He has remained loyal to Warren Wells of the Oakland Raiders, recently paroled from a prison term. "You don't turn on a friend because he gets in a jam," Ross says.

Ross says he scarcely slept for six months while he was getting Haywood out of Denver and the American Basketball Association into Seattle of the National Basketball Association, a landmark legal maneuver which has reshaped the sports scene. He has built on its base similar cases involving Charley Scott of Virginia and Jim McDaniels of Carolina of the ABA, two of the most highly prized prospects on the pro scene, who are now with Phoenix and Seattle, respectively. He is now negotiating for Jim Chones and John Brisker.

Those who have not held Ross in high esteem have learned it is unwise to underestimate him. He has products to sell that people want to buy. His athletes trust him and take his advice. So he wields power. He forced the trade of All-Pro football star Bob Brown from the Rams to the Oakland Raiders. He made the deal for Diron Talbert to jump the Rams for the Washington Redskins. He set the signing of Green Bay jumper Marv Fleming with Miami. He forced the trade of basketball's Elvin Hayes from Houston to Baltimore.

The contract he negotiated for Haywood may be the best in sports because it is so clean. Spencer gets $1,500,000 for six years' service. He is paid $100,000 a year over a fifteen-year period, cash. After his seventh season he is free to negotiate a new pact that may pay him as much or more into eternity. For Eller, Ross got Minnesota to tender a contract worth $250,000 over three seasons, the best ever given a lineman in pro football. He's even thinking of putting together a group to bid for the Rams.

He comes on strong. In his thirties now, his curly hair is greying, but he doesn't touch it up because he wants his guys to know how much he worries about them and how hard he works for them. We once wrote that he works twelve hours a day, six days a week. We showed it to him. He crossed out the figures and replaced them with sixteen hours a day, seven days a week.

Ross looks young and wears his hair modishly long to cultivate a youthful, mod image. He dresses extravagantly in $350 suits and leather sportswear, wears ties that will never die, and brags that he "must spend ten grand a year on clothes." He leases a black Eldorado which he drives at insane speeds and is unhappy it doesn't have a telephone in it. He wants to get a telephone in a briefcase that he can carry around, too: "The guys are always calling me. When I go to lunch at the Hillcrest Country Club, they're calling me—from Pittsburgh, Miami, everywhere."

He recently moved for the third time into newer and fancier offices high up in a building along the Avenue of the Stars in the swank Century City layout in L. A. His firm's fifteen offices sprawl over seven thousand square feet, with more than twice that amount available for further expansion. There is inlaid tile on the floor, paneling on the walls, and original oils on the wood. There is a built-in sauna he swears he has had time to use only once, a kitchen and dining room with bagels on display, and a conference room large enough to host an international peace conference. The rent runs five grand a month.

His new secretary is a statuesque redhead, who would seem to lack certain basic secretarial skills. "So she can't type and can't take dictation"—Ross grins—"she's a great bookkeeper and a great cook." He pleads with her to stop interrupting him when he is in conference. He is always in conference. The phone is always ringing. His wife wants to know if he will be home for dinner. He will be, but he will be late, and he has to fly out to Louisville later that night.

Ross lives with his wife, Sheila, and his two young daughters, Dawn Robyn and Paige Stacey, in a $100,000 Spanish-style five-bedroom corner mansion in Bel-Air, complete with swimming pool and a dog the size of a defensive lineman. He calls his wife "the youngest mother in the world," which is an exaggeration, but then he is given to exaggerations.

He sits between his briefcase and telephone on the couch with a happily harried look on his face, and he says, "Big things are breaking ... big ... Big ... BIG! You wouldn't believe it! The things that are going on! He shakes his head with wonder at the wonders he works.

In front of him is the MVP trophy Carl Eller was voted, which Carl gave to Al, and Al waves at it and says, "When a guy like Carl gives me a thing like this and says, 'Al, I

145

want you to have it,' what he's really giving me is love. The Minnesota team asked me for it for display and I said, 'Are you kidding?' Things like this make up for a lot of the stuff I have to put up with, guys calling me names and all. . . ."

When we referred to him as a "Hollywood hustler" once, it almost broke his heart. "Jeez, Lib, how could you do this to me?" he mourned. He had a point. He is a Hollywood types. He does hustle. But there is a lot more to him than that. It is under the surface where it isn't often seen, but it is why he wins so much. It is only the surface that others see. And he sees himself as others do not.

Al is convinced his enemies revere him. ABA commissioner Jack Dolph, whom Al beat in business, would probably cheerfully beat him with a large club for hours, but Ross tells of encountering Dolph at an All-Star game:

"Hi, bad guy," says Dolph.

"Whattayamean, bad guy? I'm a good guy," says Ross.

"I know you are. Only I can't admit it publicly," Dolph confesses.

This is the Ross version, not the Dolph version.

Ross reveals that after a month of negotiating Carroll Rosenbloom, the owner of the Baltimore Colts, into almost complete financial collapse in order to sign an end, Rosenbloom practically pleaded with him to do some investing for him.

This is the Ross version, not the Rosenbloom version.

Ross comes on strong, as though needing desperately to turn you on to him, so strong his own wife admits he turned her off at first. "He's pushy," she says. "And hard as a roll of nickels on the outside. But there's more to him than that. His ego is only slightly larger than his heart. He's a good man and a brilliant man. It's just that he runs so hard, as though he was afraid of getting caught, as though afraid something is coming after him. To know him is to love him. But not many get to know him. He doesn't stop long enough."

Can he stop? "I don't think I'd know how," he admits.

Doesn't he get tired? Yes. He admits, "I feel sometimes I'm stretched so thin I'm just going to snap."

Is he afraid? It is frightening the force that he exerts on franchises, which are, in a way, public trusts. He meets

146

mighty men head-on. And he controls the futures of the athletes who trust him. He insists, "I'm concerned about doing right for the guys, but I'm never worried about taking on the men I must take on."

Is he enjoying his money, his power, his position, his possessions? "I don't know," he says. "I haven't had time to stop to think about it."

He is a sort of Sammy Glick. What makes Ross run?

He was born on the Lower East Side of Manhattan. His father was a cab driver who held down a second job on the side to make ends meet for himself, his wife, and their five children. He was reared in a tenement and the kids played games on city streets, followed by fistfights, automatically. He says, "You had to hustle to stay ahead."

He had to make money to make out. He ran an elevator, drove a Coca-Cola truck, spent summers in Catskill Mountain resort hotels as a busboy, waiter, and basketball player. His high school skill on court landed him an athletic scholarship to Michigan State, but he fell shy of superstar status and later flunked pro tryouts.

He did graduate with a bachelor's degree in business administration in 1958, then took his master's in physical education and psychology, earning a teaching degree in 1960. After six months of army service, he settled in Los Angeles where he supported himself by teaching in special schools for delinquent boys under the sponsorship of the county board of education while he continued his own schooling, receiving a master of education degree from the University of Southern California in 1963 and a law degree from night school at L. A.'s Southwestern University in 1968.

At this point Al Ross, BA, MA, MED, JD, seemed committed to a career as a student, but he was dissatisfied with passive pursuits and ambitious. "It took me fifteen years in college to find out what I wanted to do," he sighs. For a while he operated some rest homes and then sought a killing in real estate, the stock market, and the international money market. Later he took a flier on some fast-food franchises.

A frustrated athlete, he was playing pickup basketball games in local gyms at night with some rock-'n'-roll performers who wanted some managerial help. He started with this. They turned him on to Carl Eller, who was as bad in business as he was brilliant in sports and badly needed bailing out by a manager. As he straightened out Eller's affairs, Carl turned others on to him, the word of mouth in dressing rooms was good, and an empire was born.

Ross formed All Pro Management in partnership with his brother Leonard's law firm in August, 1969, passed his bar exams and entered private practice in 1970, and re-organized his operation last year, buying out the interest of his brother, who, however, remains associated in the enterprises. In less than three years, it has become pre-eminent among the management firms that have flourished within the last ten years.

Ross's athletes swear by him. Carl Eller says, "I trust him completely. He straightened out my affairs when they were in a terrible tangle and has assured me a fine future. Athletes for years have needed men like him, and he's the number one man with athletes." Marv Fleming says, "He pushes, but not beyond reason. He lays it all out for you and encourages you to go to other experts to check him out. I love paying him his money because he repays me in a million ways."

Even Deacon Jones says, "We had a disagreement I don't want to discuss, over a business matter, but it was clean, a thing between two men. Forget it. We split. All right. But I have no complaints with him."

Ross says, "It's true that most athletes don't need managers, but I take from the guys only what I earn and they can afford, and I am getting more selective in accepting clients. It is a fact that by having more than a few of the fellows to pool their resources, we can enter into larger and sounder investments, which benefits us all.

"It is also a fact that, despite denials, managers have gotten better contracts for athletes than they ever got for themselves. We do not carry guns which we press to the heads of management. Our only ammunition is the worth of the player to the team. If the teams did not feel our clients were worth what they pay, they wouldn't pay it, it's that simple.

"Pro sports contracts so tie the player to his team as to

brutalize his bargaining power. These fellows have a limited time at the top to cash in on their special skill. Previously, management had all the best legal and business brains on its side in drawing up contracts and negotiating with inexperienced young men. Isn't it fair the athlete have this sort of help on his side in seeking his fair share of the profits?"

Ross says, "Most franchise-owners and team-managers are honorable men, sharp businessmen, but that's not bad. You don't hear many complaints about the contracts Jack Kent Cooke gives his Lakers, for example. On the other hand, there are some narrow-minded or closed-minded people in power in sports who are only interested in getting a guy as cheaply as they can and then discarding him when they no longer have use for him.

"It's not a sentimental business. Teams will trade or drop their greatest superstars without hesitation and without a tear when their time at the top is ending. So let's not pretend teams protect the players. It's not games these guys are playing. It's a tough business. And the players have turned to guys like me for protection.

"I'm a lawyer. I can't solicit stories on myself or clients, but if I do a job for a guy, he tells a friend. I sign a guy, I go into business with him. But it goes deeper than that. I wanted to be an athlete myself. I respect the ability of these fellows and the pressures they face. I respect them as men, not just players."

Ross says he collects from 10 percent of all a client's earnings to 25 percent of moneys from special deals arranged for them, but never in any event more than 25 percent in the end. It depends, he says, on whether a client wishes his complete service in the first case or only his help in arranging fringe benefits for them in the second case, such as endorsements, appearances, and books, such as this writer has done with his clients Haywood, Barry, and Jones.

Reasonably, it is asked why it benefits the athlete to have a contract based largely on invested funds withdrawn in favor of a cash contract which results in Ross's investing the funds. Ross says, "Because our investments do things the others do not—they provide tax shelters right now and fast returns for reinvestment." But are they any safer? "They're as safe as sound planning can make them," he insists. "There's a risk in any investment, but we haven't had a loser yet."

He explains, "We have gone mainly into the building of new shopping centers, apartment buildings and office buildings. Our initial investment in most of these has been a million dollars or more. On the average, they provide from 8 to 14 percent return annually, plus tax writeoffs of from 60 to 90 percent. Originally, we went a lot into 'leasebacks' wherein we'd buy the property, sell it, and lease it back. Now we are going more into straight ownership where we sell within five years or whenever the proper profit is offered us.

"Our organization has some of our own investments. Also, we are prepared to participate in our clients' investments. We buy the deal and lay it out for them and offer them whatever part of it we think they should have. They take only what they want. Where it is called for, we will arrange reasonable bank loans for them to help their participation. We keep anything that is left, if anything is left.

"Suppose a fellow was going to pay $26,000 in taxes. If he invests this money, he gets benefits that reduce his taxes to, say, $6,000. And he has that $21,000 working for him. He gets an annual return. When we sell for a profit, and our projects sell for profits, he gets his money back, plus his piece of the additional profit. Now he has newly taxable income which should be reinvested.

"We took over one player who was deep in debt. He was in hock to his club for salary advances, had cars being repossessed, couldn't meet his rent. He was making fair money, but had blown it with unwise spending and bad investments. We got him the sort of money he deserved with provisions for repaying the club, paid off his debts, and made him sound investments."

Pointing proudly to a figure on a ledger, Ross observed, "He owed money two years ago and now he's worth $64,175.60, and the amount is increasing annually.

Asked about avoidance of taxes, Ross shrugged and observed, "It's legal. Let them change the law. We operate

150

within the law. It has been said the men who make the most money pay the smallest percentage of taxes. What is most unfair about this is that these men get guidance not available to the average person. We give our guys the same sort of program the best businessmen have, which seems fair to us."

He invests for entertainers, such as Vikki Carr, as well as many doctors. Clearly, he is interested only in those in the upper income brackets. It was his ambition to make a million, and he hints he has made it, though his money is tied up in so many different directions it is hard to fix a figure. He says his moneyed status helps him deal with moneyed men on equal terms.

He admits that the responsibility he has assumed for the future of his clients concerns him. "It's got to," he sighs. "I put up a big front, but there has to be something behind it. I have to back it up. These guys' lives literally are in my hands, and if I blow it, I break them. That's one reason I run so hard. I'll have no punch-drunk prize-fighters who have blown a million bucks selling programs outside the arenas."

Other reasons he runs? He says, "I was hungry and I didn't ever want to be hungry again. I enjoy nice things and I want my family to have the good life I never had. Also, I'd be lying if I said I didn't enjoy prestige and power. Who doesn't want to be a big man? I admit it. I enjoy what I'm doing. I don't expect pats on the back, but I eat it up when a guy says, 'Gee, Al, thanks, you saved me.' It burns me up when a guy is ungrateful. But I thrive on those thanks. And I love the duels. The challenge is frightening, but I come through in competition."

So he runs—hard. He says, "I feel bad that I don't have more time to spend with my family, but they know what I do is for them, too. We socialize some, but I'm very restless. We have friends over. Some are business friends. We do business. My wife drags me to a movie, and I sit there and don't see it. I've always got big things brewing on my mind." He says, "I've caught myself sometimes lately wondering if it's worth it. I mean, maybe I could do with one less deal, spend one more day with the kids. Jeez, I don't want to die young. But I can't stop. I just can't."

The Spencer Haywood case carried him to his peak. He recounts it:

"When an athlete like Spencer Haywood comes into prominence, either one of the players in our organization or All Pro makes contact with him to explain our services and organization. A representative of ours spoke to him the first part of 1970 and gave him our card and certain literature. Thereafter Spencer called and said he was interested in joining our organization and I mailed him a contract. When Spencer first moved to Detroit, he was friendly with John Brisker of the ABA, who is one of our clients, and I guess John and some of the other players had said good things about us and what we were doing for them. In any event, this was strictly for endorsements, commercials, publications, and so on, and had nothing to do with Spencer's contract or our legal services.

"We didn't hear from Spencer until the end of September, or the beginning of October, at which time he indicated he would like to join our organization. I arranged a television appearance for Spencer. He stayed at the Hollywood Roosevelt Hotel, and we spoke for several hours. I took to him right away and he seemed to take to me. He's a straight kid with no pretenses. Spencer then told me he had a contract that was supposed to pay him $1.9 million from Denver over a period of years and he didn't think he was going to get it. He asked if I could look at the contract and let him know what I thought of the agreement. I said I could, and he subsequently retained me as his business manager.

"I reviewed all the documentation after Spencer left, and then I looked at it again and again. At first glance I thought it was one of the worst personal services contract I'd ever seen, and after a second and third study I thought it was even worse. I let several accountants review the contracts and got other legal advice from experts. We ran the projections and figures through a computer, and I prepared a 29-page analysis and summary of the agreement confirming every bad suspicion Spencer had about his contract. Considering the sort of money he was supposed to be getting, there wasn't much front money. He was tied up for six playing years at something less than a superstar's salary. Thereafter he had to serve the Ringsby Trucking Company for four more years at some unspecified job, for some unspecified sum of money, in order to receive the investment portion of the monies promised to him ($1,500,000). If Spencer got hurt, cut or traded or if the team or league folded, he had no guarantees, as promised, nor any protection against losing his money. He could not withdraw any of his money for twenty years after the initial ten-year investment was deposited. This meant he had to wait thirty years to begin to actually withdraw any of his money. Then he could withdraw for an additional ten or twenty years. He would be sixty or seventy years old before he received what was promised to him. There were absolutely no guarantees that Spencer would receive the $1.9 million that was represented. The Dolgoff plan that Spencer was put into by the Denver Rockets consisted of mutual fund investments that offered no guarantees whatsoever. All his money was tied up in this one plan, and if the economy went sour, too bad, Spencer.

"The contract was a farce and not as represented to Spencer or in the newspapers, magazines, and so on. He had been a minor when he signed it, and he could not have had any legal advice of consequence or he never would have been permitted to sign it. I asked Spencer what he wanted to do. He asked me if we could fight it, and I said I thought we could. I said I didn't think the contract would ever stand up in a court of law and the Rockets had to realize this. I indicated that we should attempt to restructure and renegotiate the terms of the contract with Denver so that he received the guarantee that was promised prior to executing the contract. Spencer then stated, 'Let's do it.' There was no talk of wanting more than $1.9 million, for six seasons. That was all we wanted, though there was talk that maybe we could receive more money up front so we could invest it. However, we mainly wanted the terms of the contract clarified and restructured so that Spencer was guaranteed the monies promised to him.

"When I first got together with Spencer, he told me that Will Robinson had been his guardian, advisor and friend and he wanted me to meet with him to review the contract and give his approval. I agreed and met with Will at the

Chicago airport where he reviewed our contract, and he subsequently gave his full approval. He asked me if I could help Spencer. He also asked, 'What's in it for me?' That surprised me. Later he said, 'I can get you other guys.' He seemed to want to be cut in for a percentage, but we weren't interested in this kind of relationship. We also weren't looking to cut Robinson out of Haywood's life. We never said anything against Robinson to Haywood. But if Spencer was retaining me to advise him, it had to be me he listened to in these matters.

"Spencer was going to stay in a motel when he came to Los Angeles, but I suggested that he stay at our house and he accepted my offer. I wanted to get to know him better and have more time to discuss all the details involved with his contractual situation. We came to know him so well that my wife cried when he left. He's the kind of person you really get to like when you really get to know him. Anyway, we figured it would be only two or three days before we would have everything ironed out with the Rockets, but almost instantly I could see it was going to be something else. I called the Rocket owners to notify them that Spencer was in Los Angeles and that I was representing him as his attorney and financial advisor. I indicated that I wanted to get his contract clarified and guaranteed. They said there was nothing to straighten out. They stated they were going to notify the ABA commissioner, Jack Dolph, about the situation, and I said I would do likewise. I also indicated I would meet with them and had no objection to meeting with Dolph as well.

"Dolph sent out Martin Heller, a New York attorney who represented the ABA, and we met at a neutral location in Las Vegas to explain our objections to the Denver contract. Heller relayed our objections to Dolph in New York. Later we met with the Ringsbys and with Dolph on several different occasions. We had one meeting at the O'Hare Airport Hotel in Chicago that lasted three days and must have covered sixty hours. The hours passed, but we couldn't get anywhere. They kept saying a contract is a contract, and we kept saying, not if it's not any good it isn't. Along the way, there was a story in the Denver newspaper that we were asking $3,250,000, which simply wasn't so. We were beginning to get a brutal press, so we called a press conference in Los Angeles to indicate that we just wanted to get the $1.9 million contract clarified and restructured so that the sum would be guaranteed to Spencer. That's all we wanted, and if the Ringsbys had agreed to it, Haywood would still be with the Rockets.

"Spencer had broken his hand in an exhibition game, so he couldn't play anyway, but the Rockets suspended him and accused me of trying to induce a breach of contract by taking him away from them. By then, others were trying to take Spencer away from Denver. The story was out that Haywood had jumped the Rockets, was hiding out in L. A. and was ripe for the plucking; and almost everyone in pro basketball was ready to reach for him. By then, also, Spencer was ready to go somewhere else. He didn't want to return to the Rockets. He felt they favored white players over black. He'd heard the Ringsbys speak of him as a no good black nigger, and call me some names, and he didn't want anything more to do with them.

"My phone was ringing every day with offers we weren't at first free to take unless we went to court to rescind the contract, which we decided to do. After we were in court trying to rescind the contract, the offers were still being made for Spencer's services. Even after we accepted an offer from Sam Schulman of the Seattle team, the offers kept coming in. Even an offer from Bill Ringsby. He stated he would pay 15 percent more than Seattle offered. I then asked Ringsby whether he would guarantee the contract and guarantee not to call Spencer and me names, and he didn't respond, which leads me to believe he got the message.

"Many team representatives called us over the long period of negotiations and court hearings. Marshall Boyar, who had represented Joe Caldwell in his negotiations with the ABA Carolina Cougars, I believe, called us on behalf of both the Carolina and Utah Stars teams in the ABA. The president of the American Basketball Association, Don Sherry, called us on behalf of the Kentucky Colonels team of the ABA and on behalf of the ABA itself. Others called us on behalf of the New York team of the ABA. All indicated they wanted to know if they could make a deal if they could get rights to Spencer. Carolina indirectly said they would make Spencer the best deal ever made a basketball player and offered him $350,000 a year for six years plus other incentive provisions. Kentucky offered us a $100,000 bonus up front and $200,000 cash per year for a five-year period. It was all a little hard to believe. It was hard to pin some of these clubs down to exact terms, but I believe some were sincere and really were prepared to bid high for Spencer's services.

"Meanwhile, we still were negotiating with Denver. We felt we could win in court, but you can never be sure. Spencer was anxious to start playing basketball again and tired of what he called all the hassling. We arrived at a figure of $150,000 a year for six years, plus $15,000 a year for the next fifteen years whether or not Spencer played for Denver thereafter. We also wanted a no-cut contract, with a no-trade provision unless Spencer consented, as had been promised to him, but which was not in his contract. We also negotiated for a guarantee of outright payments of $50,000 for the duration of the contract if the team folded and Spencer had to go elsewhere in the league and $75,000 if the league folded. We actually agreed in principle with the Denver attorneys regarding these provisions and we waited for the formal contract. When the contract was completed, it was for $125,000 a year with none of the side agreements and provisions included. I couldn't believe it. The Denver lawyers said the Ringsbys had changed their mind regarding some of the provisions and they could not control their client. So it appeared that we were right back where we started, nowhere.

"The Rockets insisted his standing contract was good. I insisted it was no good. I said, all right, if it's so good, will you give us a total of five hundred thousand dollars for it right now? And they said, no. How about a total of one hundred thousand dollars, I asked. They said no. So I said, so how can you say it's any good and anything is guaranteed? And they just smiled and shrugged. Dolph told me the ABA was cooking up a deal where one of its teams would buy Haywood from the Rockets for $1 million or more. He also stated that new owners were attempting to buy the Rockets from the Ringsbys for $2 million. One of

156

the members on the ABA Board of Trustees asked whether Spencer would return to Denver if the Board of Trustees operated the team, or if the franchise was put on probation. I stated all we wanted was the contract promised to Spencer for $1.9 million, guaranteed. Nothing ever came of these discussions.

"I didn't like the way Dolph dealt. I got the impression he was willing to make a lot of different deals. I didn't trust our negotiations. I told Dolph I did not want to see Spencer or any other player abused by the Ringsbys anymore, and whether he returned to Denver would be decided at a later time.

"Meanwhile, NBA teams were approaching us for Spencer's services. Sam Schulman of Seattle contacted us to inquire about our situation. Richard Bloch of Phoenix also inquired about Spencer's status. Both men live and operate businesses in Los Angeles. Allan Rothenberg, Jack Kent Cooke's lawyer, contacted us on behalf of L. A. Representatives of the Buffalo, San Francisco, Chicago, Milwaukee, Boston and New York teams all made inquiries directly or through third parties. Some of the guys wanted to wait until they were sure we were free of our Denver contract. Others wanted to wait until Spencer's college class had graduated. Some were ready to enter into agreements. The Lakers implied that, if we would wait, money would not pose a primary problem. We preferred to place Spencer in L. A. or New York because of the greater potential for side money in commercials, endorsements, films, and so on, but we didn't want to wait. Phoenix suggested they would pay Spencer $150,000 dollars a year, plus a percentage of the gate, and asked whether we would consider this offer.

"Sam Schulman was willing to talk turkey, to put it in writing, and to move right away. He was also willing to pay all court costs and agreed to indemnify Spencer and me against all lawsuit claims that might be imposed on us. He swore he would fight to the finish with us, with all his resources, and he is the sort of man you believe. Thereafter, we negotiated seriously with him for a contract with the Seattle franchise. We finally settled on a $1.5 million contract covering six years of basketball services to be paid in cash, payable $100,000 a year for fifteen years, plus

157

certain incentive provisions, and a no-cut guarantee. We even agreed on additional payment for the remainder of the year if Spencer played for whatever of the season was left, with the full pact to begin the following season, 1971-72. It is, I feel, as equitable and firm as any contract any professional athlete has, considering the additional expenses the Sonics were obligated to pay. Some may seem to be more so on the surface, but few are as free of entanglements and as guaranteed as is this contract. I also feel it is an excellent contract for the Sonics, and the fans of Seattle will benefit in the long run. Obtaining Spencer has made Seattle a true contender.

"There were times along the way when Spencer was ready to surrender and return to Denver. There was a time when he thought my future was endangered and offered to give up the fight as a favor to me, but I would not let him sacrifice himself when I knew we were right. And there were times when he was tired of fighting and missed playing and bent under the pressure and cringed at being regarded badly by the public. He had to see it to believe that I would stand alongside him all the way. Of course, we both had a lot to gain and to prove. But I guess he felt at first we'd melt from the heat. But in the end you can only be called a black bastard so many times before you get angry and begin to fight back harder than ever.

"More black athletes should stand up for their rights when they are right and not be pressured by the establishment or management. Spencer had one beautiful saying to think about, 'If you don't stand up for something, you'll fall for everything.'

"When Spencer got the right to play and began to play for Seattle, some of the clubs that had sought his services started to protest against his playing. The hypocrisy of it sickened Spencer, Schulman and me and caused us all to fight harder than ever.

"We all felt we were prevailing in court and we felt the feeling was prevalent among most persons present in the courtroom. When the case was settled out of court, Spencer and I really weren't happy at all, because we knew we would have won, and Ringsby would have gotten what he deserved—no player and no compensation—but everyone else seemed happy to settle all lawsuits. Seattle now had a superstar and Denver received compensation from both Seattle and the ABA. Since I was only concerned with Spencer's welfare, I really don't know all the details of the settlements. I believe Sam paid Denver and the Ringsbys something for Spencer's contract, which was worthless. And the Virginia Squires of the ABA were supposedly going to pay Ringsby another five hundred thousand dollars, although I understand Virginia did not have to pay the franchise fee required as part of an agreement with the league when it bailed out the Oakland franchise. Sam was fined by the NBA, but I do not know if he had to pay it. I know the ABA waived rights to all legal expenses and agreed to pay their own, which were considerable, perhaps $150,000. Around $500,000 was spent on legal costs for Haywood, Ross and Schulman. Victories don't come cheap and neither do defeats.

"We are investing some of Spencer's money for him. What is the difference between our investing his money and the Ringsbys or the Dolgoff Plans investing it for him? With us, he has a say in each investment, gets advice on it, can get other advice any time he wishes, has control over it and can withdraw it at any time. And we invest in programs such as income-producing real estate investments with maximum tax benefits. Spencer reaps the benefits from year to year, not twenty, thirty, or forty years from now. He is investing a substantial portion of his income and banking most of the rest. He is on an allowance and gets enough to enjoy life, but as long as he is with me, he is not going to squander his money. He is not going to wind up like some punch-drunk fighters who had it all at one time and wind up with nothing when they retire. He is an intelligent individual, maturing rapidly, and he has a high potential for his future beyond basketball, but we are not going to waste the high potential of his basketball years.

"It was a messy case. It soiled him and it soiled me. I'm used to it. He wasn't. He's getting used to it. It hasn't turned him as hard and tough as you might expect. Sam Schulman is tough. Some people we had to fight were tough, but compared to Sam Schulman they were cupcakes, and they crumbled. I'm tough. I'm not going to crumble and blow away no matter what some club-owners want. I'm going to do something for the guys, and in the process I'm going to do something for myself. Out of this case, a lot of good came. Out of some of the rulings, some doors seem to have opened through which some athletes can walk in freedom. What we did was for Spencer, but it worked out for a lot of other guys, too. We have to open more doors. We have to do more. We have to help more guys.

9. Sam Schulman's View

Sam Schulman was a Brooklyn boy, educated at New York University and the Harvard School of Business, who made it big in business. Former director of the Bergen Trust Company, vice president of Peninsula Savings & Loan, president of Mission Pak and George McKibbin & Sons, and partner in Executive Car Leasing, he was then chairman of the executive committee and vice-chairman of the board of National General Corporation, which operates Great American Insurance Company, Bantam Books, and Grosset & Dunlap, publisher of this book. He also is one-fourth owner of the San Diego Chargers of the National Football League and full owner of the Seattle Supersonics of the National Basketball Association.

When the NBA sought expansion prior to the 1967-68 season, Sam Schulman was set up as sponsor of a new franchise in Seattle. Despite the troubled economy there, research convinced him the area would support a major league basketball operation, and he has been rewarded with an average attendance of between 9,000 and 10,000 fans per game although the new club has not yet become a contender. Only New York, Los Angeles and Milwaukee draw better. An absentee owner who seldom sees a contest in Seattle's splendid Coliseum, he nevertheless has achieved popularity with the public by not interfering with his manager, Bob Houbregs, or the black player-coach he appointed, Lenny Wilkens, and by bidding boldly for Spencer Haywood and standing up to NBA commissioner Kennedy and the league owners.

Short, shrewd, turning 61 at the time he was rebelling against the establishment, angering the owners who had admitted him into their private club, Schulman shook up the status-quo. ABA attorney Fred Furth called him the key to the resolution of the Haywood case and the accomplishment of preliminary merger plans despite the opposition of the NBA: "The reason is simple. He's tough enough to see it through and NBA commissioner Kennedy is not." Shortly after the settlement of the disputes, the maverick Schulman sat in his office and reviewed the situation:

"Spencer Haywood's availability was called to my attention by a mutual friend of his manager and myself as the new season was beginning in the fall of 1970. I was immediately interested because I knew by his reputation he was the sort of superstar who is not often available and my operation in Seattle needed help. In the three years the Sonics had been members of the NBA we had finished 36 games under .500, 22 games under .500 and 10 games under .500 and, while I was pleased with our progress and continued improvement, I knew we would have to add someone special if we were to make the final jump into contention for championships. Considering the sort of team we had been able to give them, the fans in Seattle had supported us handsomely. If we wanted even greater support, we had to reward them," Schulman explained.

"I told this fellow we were interested and the next thing I knew a meeting was arranged with his attorney, Al Ross, in which Haywood's problems were discussed and papers we wanted to see were presented to us. I had my attorneys go over Spencer's contract with the Denver team and the NBA by-laws, report and make recommendations to me. Their report was that Spencer's contract with the Rockets was a poor one with many weaknesses and that NBA rules which might work against our getting Haywood into a

Sonics' uniform were poor ones with many weaknesses and that we could overcome both obstacles, but only if we were prepared to challenge authority and engage in a difficult fight which might last a while and cost a lot.

"We discussed the details. I decided in my own mind that the youngster had a right to rebel against his Rockets contract. And I decided also that we had a right to sign the youngster against existing NBA rules on several counts: One, when the four-year rule was put in, I was not a member of the league, I'd never had a chance to argue against it, and there was not another league operating in competition with us partly by disregarding such a rule. Two, Spencer no longer was a boy being tempted to leave college, but already a professional who could not return to college competition even if he wanted to. Three, the four-year rule seemed legally unfair to youngsters who had a right to earn a living with their special talents. And, four, members of the league already had violated their four-year-rule and draft regulations in signing and being permitted to keep Elvin Hayes and Wes Unseld prior to the completion of their collegiate eligibility, and signing and assigning to Phoenix Connie Hawkins, who never had been drafted.

"The fact that the league hushed up the signing of Hayes and Unseld so as not to disqualify them from NCAA post-season tournament activity did not in my mind eliminate their responsibility in the matter. And I had been a prime negotiator in settling with Hawkins and luring him from the ABA. Milwaukee won Lew Alcindor in a coin flip. Phoenix was awarded rights to Hawkins. We were the have-nots whose turn it was to land a player of this level and the fact that the other owners fought me on this seemed then and still seems now to me to be dreadfully unfair and hypocritical.

"I had to find out if Haywood would be available to us at a price I considered to be reasonable according to that paid other players of his level, and preliminary discussions with Ross convinced me of this. I then still had to decide if with his background Spencer was the sort of person we wanted to make a major investment in, staking much of our future on, and I asked for a meeting with him. Around Thanksgiving he called me and said he would, indeed, like to play for us, and after we met and talked, I decided, he was, indeed, the sort of lad I wanted playing for us. I felt he had been dealt with unfairly in the past, would respond to fair treatment in the present and could be trusted in the future. At this point, I determined to make every move possible to obtain his services, and gave Haywood my promise to stand by his side in a fight to the finish.

"I did first seek to obtain rights to Haywood through normal channels. I asked NBA commissioner Walter Kennedy for permission to sign him along the lines of the Hawkins case, but was denied. Later, I asked for and got a league vote, and again was denied. All this time I knew the other owners of the league were seeking to sign him for their teams, and I knew owners of the other league with whom we still were in competition were seeking to sign him for their teams, and I could not understand the denials of my partners. What was right for one seemed not to be right for another. I got angrier and angrier and more determined than ever to fight this to the finish.

"We signed Haywood and went to court to fight for what we felt were our rights. And I was sickened by the response of many of my fellow owners and by the commissioner of our league, who would even have denied us the right to prove our rights. What is wrong with going to court? Isn't this the American way? If we were in the wrong, we would lose. No, Mr. Kennedy and other owners did not want us in court because they knew they were wrong and would lose. And Mr. Kennedy fined me $1,500 for criticizing his administration. It seems free speech is not one of the rights of NBA owners.

"Well, we were right on every count, and we won every decision that was rendered in the end. We did settle out of court because the longer the case went on, the greater the pressure on this young man and on my team and the wider the division between two warring leagues at a time when peace seemed essential to the future of professional basketball and because it was a settlement in which we were granted the right to employ Spencer Haywood. It was a costly settlement, but then it was a costly case. It cost me

There was a lot of waiting and wondering as Spencer Haywood sought to separate himself from the Denver Rockets of the ABA. He signed with and sought permission to remain with the Seattle Sonics of the NBA. Here he looks out of his high hotel room window at misty downtown Seattle and the bay beyond.

(PHOTO BY DUDLEY, HARDIN & YANG)

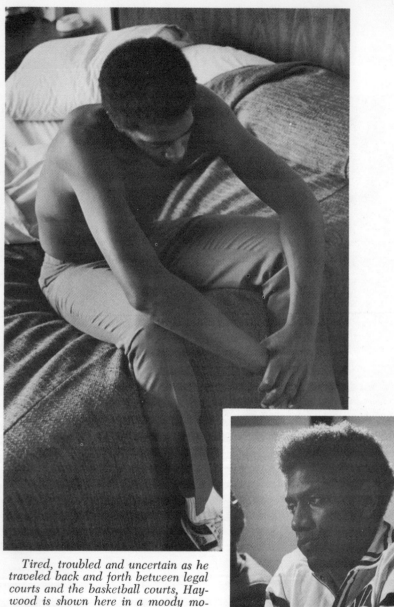

Tired, troubled and uncertain as he traveled back and forth between legal courts and the basketball courts, Haywood is shown here in a moody moment on a bed in a hotel. At another reflective time he stays on the bench in a game in which he was not permitted to play in Sonics' uniform.

(PHOTO BY DUDLEY, HARDIN & YANG)

Flanked by the bags of a man on the move, Seattle Sonics' owner Sam Schulman stands in front of Spencer Haywood outside a federal court building on a happy day. Their case had gone well.
(PHOTO BY BILL RAY, LIFE MAGAZINE © TIME, INC.)

An intense Spencer Haywood, wearing a souvenior shirt from Kutsher's in the Catskills in upstate New York, listens to the thoughts of Seattle coach Lenny Wilkens.
(PHOTO BY DUDLEY, HARDIN & YANG)

Casually garbed, Spencer Haywood and Seattle Sonics' players scrimmage with other players at the Seattle University gym. In the top picture, Spencer feeds off around the leaping defense of Bob Rule (later traded). In the middle picture, he gives a shot to a little girl who had been watching. In the bottom photo, he has his back to the wall, Bob Rule standing alongside him, as the weary warriors take a break.

(PHOTOS BY DUDLEY,
HARDIN & YANG)

Spencer sits on the stone wall outside his apartment house, which towers behind and above him, and stands outside his double apartment on a balcony overlooking downtown Seattle, the World's Fair Space Needle and the adjacent Seattle Center Coliseum, home of the Sonics. (PHOTOS BY DUDLEY, HARDIN & YANG)

Relaxing at home, in his Seattle apartment, Spencer raps with teammates Don Smith, Fred Brown and Garfield Heard in the top shot and below, dances in front of his hi-fi set and records with a sweet "sister."

(PHOTOS BY DUDLEY, HARDIN & YANG)

Janice Shephard

The new Sonics' superstar Spencer Haywood goes high and higher for a couple of one-hand jump shots against the Cincinnati Royals, displaying perfect straight up-and-down form, the ball held high on a slightly cocked arm and cushioned in his large hands. Below right, with a referee watching in the foreground, he gets well above 6'10" Sam Lacey (44), while to the left he gets not only above the reach of Tom Van Arsdale, but also the ten-foot-high basket. In both, he uses his free arm for protection. (SEATTLE SONICS PHOTOS)

Most Valuable Player in the ABA All-Star Game, as well as the Olympic Games' basketball tournament and the annual off-season Maurice Stokes Benefit classic contest in the Catskill Mountains involving all-stars of both the NBA and the ABA, Spencer Haywood happily holds his trophy aloft. The youngster was especially proud of his performance in the latter contest since he showed his best against the best while bridging the gap between the two leagues.

(PHOTO BY KLUETMERY, SPORTS ILLUSTRATED © TIME, INC.)

$10,000 a day in court. But it is wrong to think we would not have won in the end, because we would have. However, it would have been unwise of me to indulge in the personal luxury of going through to the ultimate triumph considering the sort of turmoil the case was inflicting on all concerned.

"It was one of the most frustrating periods of my life because I found myself losing respect for men I had respected. No sooner had they lost their own fight to acquire Haywood than they turned on the winner. Men like Elmer Rich of Chicago turned around completely. A man like Jack Kent Cooke of Los Angeles, for whom I certainly hold no personal friendship, still should not have turned on me and sought to have the league penalize me. The head of our league, Walter Kennedy, should have congratulated me, not sought to impose penalties on me.

"There were times I toyed with vengeful pursuits which might have been profitable. I never considered signing Spencer for any city other than Seattle, but I did seriously contemplate the establishment of a new professional basketball franchise in the Sports Arena in Los Angeles with such UCLA stars as Sidney Wicks and Curtis Rowe, whom I felt I could sign, as our stars. The Lakers do not operate in Los Angeles, you know. Their home Forum is in Inglewood. I did not pursue the project because I recognized my motives as spiteful and did not consider that a proper basis for beginning a business venture.

"I predicted four years ago that if the American Basketball Association remained in business, it would pose a threat to us by the early 1970's, and my forecast proved correct. In any such venture, owners inevitably suffer heavy losses at first. If they have the resources to persevere, their chances of succeeding in the end grow increasingly greater as time passes. My fellow owners ignored both the lesson the NFL learned in the success of the AFL and my warning, and they did not begin to act appropriately until the ABA had begun to hurt the NBA heavily in the acquisition of new talent and the cost of this talent.

"It is not well known that at one point in these

proceedings I offered to sign Spencer Haywood for the league, sacrifice my own rights to him and expose him to a league draft simply so our league could have this player instead of the other league having him. This, too, was refused, and in the end it was up to me to keep him in our league. Now I think a merger is in the best interests of both leagues and can be achieved without denial of legal rights to the individual players, and I have worked and am working to this end.

"I would be less than honest if I said I emerged from the fray without some hard feelings. I regret these. But I carry no grudges, and I will not show my scars in my future operations within the league. I still want our joint success as well as my individual success. Strangely, I have harder feelings for some of my fellow NBA partners than for some of my real opponents in this case. I think Jack Dolph, the commissioner of the ABA, and his fellow owners operated understandably and ethically in seeking to keep a valuable property within their province. I think the Ringsbys are hard-nosed businessmen, basically decent and honorable, who may have made a mistake in the legal structure of their contractual relationship with Spencer Haywood and may have been carried away by passion in pursuing the problem, but did not do many things differently than I would have done had I been in their place.

"I think Al Ross is an intelligent and imaginative person, who can represent athletes responsibly and to their mutual benefit without working what should be any hardship on management, and I think he was diligent and fair in carrying his responsibility to Spencer Haywood to a conclusion insofar as this case is concerned. I think Spencer Haywood is a simply splendid young man with great desire to use his talents to their fullest and to do good for his fellow men, whether he be black or white. I think circumstances conspired to cheat him of a swift start toward realizing his full potential as a person and that he has had to go through an intense and difficult period of confusion and adjustment, but he is no more greedy than you or I or any person, whether he be a star athlete or a clerk, in seeking to get the greatest possible rewards, at the least the going rewards, for his services, and in wishing to be treated with dignity and respect. I want to make it clear that I do not demand he become the greatest of players in return for our investment in him. I ask only that he try his best to be the best he can, as a player, and also as a person. I see that he is trying. That in itself is satisfaction enough for the suffering all of us in this have had to endure."

10. As Don Ringsby Sees It

When the ABA was begun prior to the 1967-68 season, a franchise was awarded Jim Trindle of V.T.N., a Los Angeles engineering firm. He sought to locate it in Kansas City, but when he could not obtain satisfactory arena dates there, he shifted into Denver. In short order, he hired and then fired Vince Boryla as his general manager. Boryla subsequently sued and collected on a three-year contract before the first season had been completed. Meanwhile, Trindle sought local Denver money to ease the financial strain of launching his operation. Jack Ashton of the Denver Chamber of Commerce contacted H. R. Berglund, who had put together the 1960 Denver Open golf tournament, who in turn put Trindle onto local trucking magnate J. W. (Bill) Ringsby. Trindle originally sought a one-third partner, but wound up with a two-thirds partner as Ringsby put up $170,000 to gain control of the infant franchise. Shortly, Ringsby paid another $85,000 to take over the entire operation.

J. W. (Bill) Ringsby was driving a coal truck in Denver before and after school when he decided to go into business for himself in the 1930's. His company was incorporated in 1940. Today, Ringsby-United, his transcontinental truckline which operates from the Midwest to the entire West Coast and Canada, grosses $100,000,000 annually. It is an enormously successful operation and he is an enormously successful man. The road to success in pro basketball has not been smooth for him, although he will tell you no road to success ever is smooth, in trucking or anything else, and obstacles must be overcome in any endeavor. Actually, he and his two sons, Don and Gary, who also are with him in the family trucking business, are equal one-third partners in the basketball operation. While the elder Ringsby is chairman of the board and an ABA trustee, Don was president and Gary secretary. Don also served as the team's general manager until Alex Hannum was hired as president and general manager and coach prior to the 1971-72 season, and it was Don who originally sought Spencer Haywood for the Rockets.

Don Ringsby

"I'd heard a great deal of favorable comment about Spencer Haywood as a budding basketball superstar. My father for one had seen him at the Olympic tryouts in Albuquerque in the summer of 1968 and been tremendously impressed. Anyone who saw him was tremendously impressed. The ABA needed superstars desperately not only to upgrade its own level of play, but also to force the NBA into a merger, which the ABA franchise-holders wanted. But the ABA had been losing the bidding war for graduating college stars such as Elvin Hayes and Lew Alcindor at that time and had not yet begun to lure established performers from the old league—with the exception of a Rick Barry. Since then, this has changed. The ABA has signed some of the best collegians, such as Dan Issel, Charley Scott and Artis Gilmore, and has lured such as Zelmo Beaty and Joe Caldwell. Then, however, there was a bit of desperation in it when Jim Gardner, the owner of the Carolina Cougars, who was serving as ABA president—we didn't have a commissioner at that time—called an emergency and secret draft meeting during the summer of 1969 with the idea that we could fix bidding rights to some players the ABA might obtain. It occurred to me then to draft a Haywood with the idea that with a year or two to work on him we'd have a better chance of taking him away from the NBA than had other ABA clubs in the last-minute bidding for Alcindor. We had just lost Lew, and there was some feeling then that this might be fatal to our league's survival.

"I remember I passed Denver's first turn around the table and postponed my pick to the following day. I went back to my hotel—this was in New York—and called John McLendon, who was our coach at that time. I asked him, 'If you could draft any college player in the country, who would you take?' He said, 'Spencer Haywood.' McLendon was a scout for the US Olympic team and was in Mexico for the 1968 Olympics, thus he knew Spencer personally. This confirmed what I'd heard about Haywood. Mind you, I'd never even seen him play, personally, at the time. And I really didn't have much experience in basketball or basketball business. We knew he was about to begin his second season at Detroit University, but we knew he'd prepped at Trinidad Junior College in Colorado, so we figured he had three seasons behind him. Usually, you play for two years in junior college before moving up to senior college. We were wrong here. You can move up after one year if you have a B average, and Spencer had gone that way. He was further from being eligible than we realized. In any event, I decided to go ahead and draft him. In our first two seasons we had finished second and third in the Western Division and it didn't look like we'd ever get a shot at drafting one of the two or three best graduating collegians in the normal order of things, so this early draft and a selection of Haywood seemed to be the only chance we had to get a player of his caliber. He'd played JC ball in Colorado and we hoped we could convince him that when he turned pro it should be in Denver.

"We had not even made preliminary contact with Haywood when we were contacted by Steve Arnold, a business agent for athletes who was working for the ABA in the procurement of players. Arnold knew we had draft rights to Haywood, and he said he'd been in contact with Haywood and Will Robinson his high school coach.

178

Haywood was unhappy at the University of Detroit and might be tempted to leave college to turn pro. My first reaction was fine, wonderful, this might be an unexpected bonanza, so I told him to come to Denver to talk about it. He did. He'd investigated and he said Haywood's unhappiness at Detroit was compounded by the hiring of a new coach who was supposed to be very tough who Spencer didn't want to play for. He also said Spencer was very afraid the ABA would merge with the NBA and eliminate the big-money contracts before he could turn pro.

"Although it had never been done before, he suggested there was no reason a college player shouldn't have the right to quit college and turn pro if he wanted. The ABA by-laws, like the NBA by-laws, prohibited signing a player until his college class graduated, but this seemed an unfair violation of his personal freedom, as the courts later ruled in the Haywood vs. NBA case. It was Arnold who came up with the 'hardship' gimmick whereby we could plead for a waiver of the rule on the basis of financial hardship. He knew Spencer came from a poor family in the deep south. Arnold just invented it. It was just a gimmick. And Jim Gardner, president of the ABA, OK'd it. It had no real meaning. If Spencer ever really used his money to help his family, I never knew anything about it. To be honest about it, the ABA was just looking for ways to land top talent even if it meant bending the rules here and there, but in this case this probably was an unfair rule which deserved to be bent. Ball players like Haywood should have a right to earn a living at what they do best whenever and wherever they can.

"Steve Arnold offered to make arrangements to bring Haywood to Denver for negotiations. He came back with Spencer and his high school coach and mentor and guardian, Will Robinson. They met with my father and me, and we tried to work out a deal for Spencer to sign with the Denver Rockets immediately. I want to say right here and now that not only did Spencer have a tough man, Will, helping him, but Spencer was pretty tough himself. He may have been underage and from a limited background and of limited education, but he was and is an intelligent young man and a very astute, able negotiator. We had a long, difficult negotiation, about 12 tough hours.

"Spencer finally agreed to sign a contract for three years on 8/16/69 worth $460,000, approximately. It called for $51,800 yearly salary with deferred payments of $15,000 per year for 20 years starting on his 40th birthday. It was a very good contract, in my opinion. It was twice what any other player on our team had gotten, and this was a player who hadn't proven himself as a pro, though we all knew he had the highest sort of potential, of course. You also must remember this was a few years ago and judge this and the later contracts we renegotiated with him by the standards of that time, not the standards now, which are much higher, though I seriously doubt some of the graduating collegians of the last year or two have contracts worth as much as reported. These things are sometimes inflated by the media. In discussing Haywood's contracts, we are talking facts. It was more than fair compensation for an untried sophomore in college.

"Anyway, Haywood signed and joined us, and I might also note here that such a fuss as was kicked up over the signing of an underclassman was fought strictly in the newspapers. The Denver Rockets never got a single telephone call or letter or direct comment of any sort of complaint from the University of Detroit, the NCAA or any other official body over our action. The NBA expressed outrage, but not to us. Of course, they weren't talking to us at the time. I wonder if the NBA didn't think all along it would get him eventually. Spencer later testified in court that he intended to stay with us only until he could go over to the NBA, which explains why he wanted only a two-year contract originally. We didn't know this at the time. We wanted a five-year contract because we wanted to build a franchise around a player of his stature, not because we thought we'd lose him. We were signing a contract with him. We assumed that would bind him to us for the length of the contract at least. We settled for a three-year contract with an option on his future services. This is a standard ABA basketball contract. It is similar to the pro football contract. A player can play out or sit out his option year,

180

then try to make a deal for himself with another team. The reserve clause in pro baseball is different in that it denies the player the right to simply go to another team and make a deal for himself. Baseball teams own their players for the length of their careers in their sport. Our system is far fairer to the player. We naturally assumed Spencer was ours for the length of his contract.

"We got off to a disappointing start that season and made a change in coaches when our record slumped to 9-19, replacing McLendon with Joe Belmont, and Spencer and the team almost immediately began to play better and to catch fire and we were very pleased with Haywood and the team. In the early fall we were informed of the Dolgoff plan, which Ralph Dolgoff had devised for the investment of contracted sums in a combination of mutual funds and life insurance in the form of a variable annuity. Carolina signed Billy Cunningham to an ABA contract utilizing this plan. Mr. Dolgoff made a presentation to us and we were intrigued, and he made a presentation to Will Robinson and Spencer and they were very impressed. We felt it was the best plan we'd heard of, both for us and the player, and we recommended to Haywood and his advisor, Robinson, that they might want to shift the deferred-payment portion of Spencer's contract into this plan. They agreed and this was done. This was Spencer's second contract with us.

"The basic monies were the same, only the way of handling the deferred payments was different. Previously Spencer's future compensation had been fixed with no growth pattern whatsoever. The money we put away for him was taxable to him as regular income now even though he couldn't take advantage of the money until he reached his 40th birthday. The Dolgoff plan was based on projections of an increase in value of mutual funds in the future calculated from the historic growth of such funds in the past, and it had certain tax-writeoff benefits both to the paying party, the club, and the player. And the projections were reasonable. It is very important to understand this. It was conservatively calculated for a 12 percent growth in its first year, whereas in actuality it had a 20 percent growth. There is a certain risk involved in any investment, but this seemed as sound as any, and the potential was high.

181

"When Spencer signed with us, he was given my father's year-old Cadillac El Dorado. He moved into a modest apartment on East Colfax which he shopped for for 2 weeks since he wouldn't pay more than $150 a month. He wanted a television set and he preferred to buy an old set probably worth $50 from me for $25 to paying for a new color set. In other words, he started out very conservative. However, he rapidly became less conservative as time passed. He soon expressed dissatisfaction with his car, his TV set, his apartment. He didn't have to buy a new color TV, as he won one as Most Valuable Player in the ABA all-star game. He wanted a new Fleetwood Cadillac and we arranged it for him. It cost approximately $9,000. He got $5,000 credit for the Caddy we'd given him, leaving $4,000. We paid this with the provision that he repay it from his contract over its three-year life. Thus we reduced his $51,800 per-year pact to $47,000 a year. This was calculated by showing the advance of $10,000, which he received upon signing his first pact, as a bonus for tax purposes.

"The first contract was $51,800 per year for 3 years, or $155,400. After subtracting the $10,000 bonus, it was worth $145,000. We then subtracted the difference between his first Cadillac and the new Fleetwood, or $4,000. This added up to $141,000. This sum was divided by the three year term and equaled $47,000 per year. However, since he only played one year for us, we only got $4,600 back. As far as we are concerned, he still owes us over $9,300 (for the car and the $10,000 advance), which is why there is a dispute now over who owns the car he still is driving as far as I know. He just drove it away to Seattle without our permission or the title to the car when he jumped. Loyalty and responsibility toward his obligations are two qualities Haywood doesn't possess.

"He moved into the Brooks Towers, which is the plushest high rise apartment in downtown Denver, and where his rent had to be twice what it was before, and I guess he began to live pretty high. As the season wore on, it was obvious he was having a tremendous rookie year and seemed on his way to leading our team to a divisional pennant and maybe the league title. He was a tremendous performer, make no doubt about that, and he was playing as well as or better than such far more experienced stars in our league as Rick Barry, who was coming back from an injury, and Mel Daniels. Possibly it went to Spencer's head.

"The team was playing tremendously well, yet there was friction, I knew, between Spencer and Larry Jones, who had been our high scorer and our star and our leader before young Spencer came along and who may have been envious of him. I saw scouts from NBA teams hanging around Spencer and I heard some NBA teams including Milwaukee were in contact with him, which made us nervous even though we had him under contract. He was still a minor at the time. This was war, after all. And they were telling him what a super player he was and how much more he could be getting and should be getting, and Spencer began to come in regularly and try to get some of this money out of us. No one else on the team was trying to renegotiate. We were having the good year, but everyone else was willing to wait until the usual off-season contract negotiations to seek raises. If there was any other player, Jones or anyone else, who was unhappy, we did not know it because we did not hear it from them. Only Spencer. First he wanted a raise to $75,000 a year. The next time it was to $100,000 a year. Will came in a couple of times on Spencer's behalf. Spencer put a tremendous amount of pressure on us.

"We didn't want anything to spoil the season. And we wanted good relations with a player who figured to be a major factor in any success we'd have for years to come. My father and I discussed the matter and we decided that while it might be a poor precedent to renegotiate a contract in mid-season, Spencer had by then established himself sufficiently, so perhaps it would be wise for us to give him the best contract we could afford and one which would be as good as or better than anything any NBA team could reasonably be expected to offer. Mind you, we weren't exactly rolling in money in basketball at the time. We'd lost $200,000 or so our first year of operation, around $150,000 our second year, and while we then were beginning to draw sellout crowds to our small auditorium, there was no way we were going to be in the black for this third season. Still, we were investing in the future.

"J. W. Ringsby was called on the phone by Spencer who

wanted to renegotiate right then and get his mind back on basketball. He claimed the agents wouldn't leave him alone and he wanted to be able to tell the world he was the highest paid ball player. We signed him to a six-year contract with a projected worth of $1,900,000 over the life of the agreement. He was to get the previous $47,000 a year his first two years and $75,000 a year his next four years. The rest of the money was deferred to the future, some of it, admittedly, the far future, but for six seasons of basketball he had awesome secur i i   ar the rest of his life. We would invest $10,000 a year in the Dolgoff plan for ten years, which figured to be a very sound investment for him. It was a good contract, the best i t e ABA and one of the best in all of sports at the time, I believe.

"We wanted Spencer to be happy, and he seemed happy when he signed, but what we did not know then and what we know now and what we should have been able to see, is Spencer never is going to be happy; he will never be satisfied with any contract, any amount of money, any amount of prestige, possibly any amount of anything in his life. He is by nature a demanding and dissatisfied person. He almost drove us crazy before he got the third contract out of us and, as good as it was, it wasn't long before he wasn't satisfied with it.

"You have to look at the facts. Here is a young man born in Mississippi who moved to Chicago, who was going to go to high school in Chicago and play basketball in Chicago who wound up playing basketball in high school in Detroit, who was going to go to Tennessee, who was sent to Trinidad Junior College by New Mexico University and wound up going to Detroit and stayed there only a year before he jumped to us, Denver in the ABA, and then jumped to Seattle of the NBA. Do you think he's going to be happy in Seattle? No way. It has nothing to do with Seattle. It has to do with Spencer. There is no way he is going to be happy anywhere. Or satisfied with anything. One day he wants $75,000 a year. Then $100,000. If he's getting $150,000, he'll soon want $200,000. If he ever hears anyone is getting more, he wants more. He has no respect for a deal, an agreement, a contract.

"It took time, but I finally began to see this.

184

"We won the pennant, but were upset in the playoffs by the Los Angeles Stars team, which now is the Utah Stars. Haywood was dissatisfied and contributed to internal conflict on the club. By the time the playoffs came around he was thinking more about money than winning. We lost the playoffs because of Haywood's attitude and I think because Joe Belmont was outcoached by Bill Sharman. I think even Joe Belmont would admit this. Joe inherited a lot of talent when he took over the team in an emergency, and it played with   for him, but he had no previous coaching experience and when matched against a veteran like Bill Sharman it showed. We made a temporary change the next season early then brought in Alex Hannum, for what I hope will be forever, after the season.

"Hiring and firing coaches isn't a pleasant chore, but this is a business and you have to make the moves that will help you. Until we could get a man of Hannum's experience and ability to take over the whole show for us, we were grabbing at straws. When Haywood jumped, Denver became just another team, of course, but Belmont was replaced because we felt we could better ourselves, not because our best player left.

"On October 19, 1970, Spencer came to me and said he wanted the title to his car and the cash back from some personal investments he'd made in mutual funds. I finally realized what sort of person he was, and I saw he was getting prepared to skip town. I went to my father and I said, 'Spencer's checking out,' just like that. It didn't take any genius to put two and two together.

"Spencer had spent the summer with some players from the NBA who filled his head with fancy notions about what this player was supposed to be getting and that player and they convinced him he was the greatest thing going and was underpaid. Then Al Ross got together with Spencer and the next thing I know Will Robinson had called me to tell me Spencer had tied up with Ross. Then Ross and Spencer began to come at us for more money, for another contract yet. My God, we'd given him three contracts in one year and now he wanted another one! Where was this going to end? When I told my father Spencer was surely leaving, he said, 'Good, good riddance.' By then, we were

185

all fed up with his discontent and his demands. But practical considerations overruled emotions. He was a very valuable property, he *was* our franchise, he *was* our future, and we had a right to him. So we couldn't just wash our hands of him. Reluctantly, we began to negotiate with Ross.

"Ross said the Dolgoff plan wasn't worth the paper it was printed on, which is ridiculous. The fact is the money Spencer wanted back from his personal investments was money he'd put into mutual funds along the same line as the Dolgoff plan because he was so impressed with the plan. Ross wanted Spencer paid in cash so Ross could handle Spencer's investments, thereby receiving the commissions himself. Ross said he wanted the $1.9 million estimated value of Haywood's contract paid over five years in cash. Good Lord, what is that, almost $400,000 a year! What athlete is worth that? It's ridiculous.

"A professional team can offer an athlete an attractive contract and provide for his future by making investments for him promising x returns over a period of years, but there is a limit to what can be paid out in cold cash. There is a limit to the returns a team can get from a franchise with only 6,800 seats in its arena, and if salaries keep going up, few if any in basketball will ever break even. Most are losing money now; I'm sure. And what's the point if you're in the red? The athlete should be paid every cent he is worth in the overall scheme, but if you're playing to capacity at top prices and a player's demands will throw you in the red, you have to back off or go to an institution. Our investment in Spencer exceeded $100,000 the first year, yet at that point he wanted a raise to $400,000. That's absurd!

"I have no idea whether Al Ross wanted out of the contract so he could peddle his hunk of flesh named Haywood on the open market or whether he was prepared to let him stay with us, but I suspect Ross wouldn't have minded if we met his demands. I believe he was ready to go wherever the money was, Denver or anywhere else. Agents like Al Ross take advantage of situations as they present themselves. Most of them do not have the interests of their clients at heart. They're opportunists who capitalize on the situation. They are not easy to do business with. We offered Haywood through Ross a five-year contract calling for $100,000 in cash; we felt it was a damn good offer and he didn't. You have to understand that we didn't think we had to offer him anything. We had a contract and our lawyers told us it was valid and we believed that. And we still believe it was valid. The fact is the court never got to make a ruling on the contract, so we'll never know. We settled out of court, for reasons which I'll explain.

"The negotiations were pretty bitter. We were pretty fed up with Spencer by then, for what I think are understandable reasons, and Ross came on strong. He came on pretty strong accusing us of selling out secret negotiations and lying when a Denver sportswriter put in the newspaper that we said they were asking for over $3,00,000—but that wasn't our doing. I don't know where the sportswriter got that figure—we never gave it to him—and I raised hell with him about it when I saw him, because it jeopardized the real negotiations. It simply wasn't so. Ross and Haywood, too, I understand, accused us of using racial slurs toward Haywood, which also isn't so. I never used any and never would; I have never heard my father use any and I do not believe he ever would. Race never entered into my dealings with Spencer or anyone else. I'm proud of the fact that I was the first general manager in pro basketball to hire a black coach, John McLendon. Bill Russell and Lennie Wilkins were hired as coaches before I hired John McLendon; however, they were basically players hired for convenience or financial expediency. Neither had any previous coaching experience as far as I know.

"Jack Dolph, the American Basketball League Commissioner by then, did his best to mediate the dispute and settle the issue. He wanted to save Spencer for the ABA, understandably, and he acted accordingly. After he felt we weren't going to come to terms with Spencer, he wanted to place him with another franchise in our league such as Carolina. Marshall Boyar also entered the picture as a sort of volunteer negotiator trying to set up deals for both sides. I'm not sure what he expected to gain from the situation, but I think he just wants to exercise power. Will Robinson tried to speak to Spencer. He was working in Spencer's best interest. We made Will no promises. But Spencer turned on him too.

"It has been said that the ABA tried to get us to sell out so other owners might come into Denver who would meet Spencer's demands, but this didn't come to pass, because we were never made a legitimate offer for our franchise. We did get offers for Haywood. Carolina offered us $1,000,000 in cash for him. In retrospect, I wonder if we shouldn't have taken it, but you can't play dollar bills on court, and you just don't buy or sell superstars in sports these days. We offered Spencer to Kentucky for Dan Issel and Lou Dampier, and generous Mike Storen made a counter offer of Cincy Powell and a fourth-round draft choice, which was, of course, utterly ridiculous. Bill Daniels of Utah offered us Zelmo Beaty for Spencer, and in retrospect I think that was a deal we should have made, because Zelmo has turned out to be the best center in this league, but he's no Spencer Haywood. In any event, we weren't able to make a deal we could accept, so we didn't make one. We still thought we'd keep him.

"So we went to court. And the situation got messier and messier with name-calling and character assassination by Ross and Haywood. We hired the best lawyers we could find. It was expensive and time consuming. We had a trucking business to run, besides our basketball business, and our public image was being destroyed. Through depositions and personal testimony, we began to see problems with our contract. By that I do not mean it was a bad contract, because it wasn't. What I mean is that there was stress being placed on the fact that this was a poor, ignorant black kid from the deep south and the northern ghettoes who had signed contracts with us before he was of legal age. We began to wonder if the court might not prove sympathetic to his case in spite of legality. We still thought we'd win, but we no longer felt sure. There was an area of doubt which influenced us. All of these things influenced us. And perhaps the greatest influence on us was worked by our fellow ABA partners, who felt the case was endangering their chances of a merger with the NBA.

"Along the way, Sam Schulman had signed Spencer for the Seattle Supersonics and he was a member of the NBA merger committee. He promised us that if we settled out of court he would do everything in his power to accomplish a merger. And he did, I am sure, because shortly after we did settle and drop the case, a merger agreement was reached, though it has not been finalized. Because the rules of the NBA forbid the signing of undergraduates and Spencer theoretically still was an undergraduate, and because Schulman signed Spencer without having gained rights to him in any draft, Sam is supposed to be persona non grata in the NBA today, but I believe he still had influence then, and used it to live up to his promises. And I imagine he still has great influence today. And I have no bad feelings about Sam at all. He is a businessman. If he felt a player of Spencer Haywood's calibre was available, it was his business to go after him. I've heard that he's paying him $150,000 a year for ten years for playing only 6 years. That's his business. If he feels Spencer is worth it, fine. I doubt it. And I won't be surprised if Sam comes to regret it.

"For the men in the ABA, the merger was the important thing and individual feelings and rights just weren't that important. My father didn't want to settle and still doesn't think we should have. He thinks we were right and would have won in court. But what would we have won, an unhappy player who will be dissatisfied forever? And we got something out of the settlement, you know. We got money from Sam Schulman, and we got money from our fellow ABA owners. We got $250,000 from Sam and $500,000 from our league, if and when there is a merger. And we also got the first ABA pick in the first common draft between the two leagues when that comes to pass. I suppose they'll flip a coin to see whether an ABA or NBA team goes first that year, so we'll wind up with either the first or second-best college player in the country, who could be another Spencer Haywood. After Spencer jumped ship last season we lost another $200,000 operating and we had to start building from the ground up all over again. He virtually destroyed our franchise. And he destroyed our peace of mind. And harmed our reputations.

"I don't hate Spencer Haywood. It doesn't serve any purpose to hate anyone. I'll admit I don't like him very much. I think we did right by him and he did wrong by us. I think we gave him three increasingly valid and good contracts and bent over backwards all along the way to please him and got stepped all over and smeared in the end. Spencer lost sight of the fact that we gave him the opportunity to play pro ball two years before anyone else would have done so. We took on the NCAA, our own league and public opinion nationally to give both of us the chance to succeed in pro basketball. I'm not sure why we're still in pro basketball, except that we have a considerable investment in it now, and I think we now have an organization that promises us a fair return for our money in basketball and I think anyone who goes into it thinking he will make money is kidding himself. We hoped to at least break even. Basically, we went into it because we thought it would be fun. Spencer took a lot of the fun out of it."

11. Other Points of View

Walter Kennedy

"We have a league, in effect a partnership of franchise owners who are in competition in most areas but agree to certain restrictions in the common interest. We are bound by our own rules. These may be changed, but only by agreement. We have certain orderly ways of procedure. Without which there would be chaos. It is my job to see that our rules are followed and to enforce the rules and to impose penalties on violators and to mediate disputes. There are rights of appeal. I am hired by the owners and I may be fired by the owners, but as long as I am in power it is my job to oversee the league-wide activities of the owners without partiality, and this I have done to the best of my ability.

"I have been in office since September first, 1963. In that time, the National Basketball Association has grown from nine to 17 teams and attendance has risen from less than two million persons per season to more than six million. Recently, I was granted broader powers which grant me the right to impose fines of up to $25,000 or to suspend any person who in my sole opinion has been guilty of conduct prejudicial or detrimental to the Association and $250,000 fine on any club for tampering with a player under contract to another club in the NBA. I believe I now have power comparable to and probably greater than any other sports commissioner, including Pete Rozelle of the National Football League.

"I assume the granting of such power indicates the majority of the owners in the NBA are satisfied with my performance of my duties, although some have suffered rulings which went against them. We have survived several crisis situations. Our common bond is our strength. Did the authorization of new, broader and stronger powers to me stem from the Haywood case? That you will have to decide for yourself.

"Certainly, it was a most distressing case and one which was not settled to my satisfaction, but the courts ruled against some of our rules. We have had to adjust these. We are a body that believes in legalities, and we will, of course, always abide by the law, no matter how we may disagree with its application on a given point.

"I regret mainly that one of our own members chose to go outside our own circle to impose his will on the majority. Certainly, he did not have the well-being of the majority in mind. It was not his decision to make alone. I respect Sam Schulman, no matter what he has said about me, but I regret his actions in the Haywood case. Here, I believe he was wrong. He charges that I did not grant him the same rights granted other owners. The fact is I made the same denial to him I made to others. There is hardly a week goes by that I do not get a request from one club or another to do something a little unusual, where it may not be clear how our rules apply, and I consider the case and render a decision, and unless it is appealed, that is that, and the owners usually abide by my decisions.

"Many cases are different from other cases and each must be weighed on its own merits. You mention the Hawkins, Hayes and Unseld cases. Well, Hawkins had long since passed the time when his original college class graduated, and he was eligible for the draft; he had not been drafted, and an award of rights to him by league agreement had to be made. This was not comparable to the

192

Haywood case. Hayes and Unseld were taken through the draft and, to the best of my knowledge at that time, were not signed while still eligible for college basketball. These cases were not comparable.

"Around October of 1970 I got calls from two or three clubs asking if Haywood was eligible. The answer was no. This had nothing to do with his Denver contract. His original college class had not graduated, so he had not been eligible to be drafted and was not now eligible to be signed to play in the NBA.

"This rule was put in to protect the youngsters who are getting college educations on scholarship from being tempted by lucrative offers to turn professional prematurely. Most would be quite young and perhaps immature. Also, we have no minor league system; the colleges develop talent for us. We have enjoyed a good working relationship with the colleges which we do not wish to destroy. This may work against an occasional boy not suited to college or in financial need, but we think it is best for the majority, in the interests of the good of all.

"At our fall meeting it was proposed that a change in our four-year rule be considered, but consideration of rules changes requires 13 votes and only eight or nine of our 17 members indicated they wanted it brought up, so it was not. Later, in December, I got telephone calls from Sam Schulman of the Seattle team and Jack Kent Cooke of the Los Angeles team each telling me, in effect, that Haywood should be eligible because of certain special factors in his case. I said this could be brought up at our all-star meeting in San Diego in January. Subsequently, Mr. Cooke sent me a letter outlining various reasons why he felt Haywood was eligible. I replied that after considerations of these reasons I still did not consider him eligible, but that the matter could be put on the agenda of the January meeting.

"Then, on a late December night, I got a telephone call from attorney Eugene Wyman advising me that Seattle was signing Haywood. I explained to him that I considered Haywood ineligible to be signed and played. He insisted they considered it within their legal rights, so I suggested he put his reasoning in writing for me to consider and present to the league as a whole. Two or three days later I did get such a letter. It stated that since Haywood already was a professional he was no longer restricted by the four-year-rule, which he felt would not stand up in court, anyway, that Seattle felt he had an invalid contract in Denver, which it proposed to prove in court, and that Seattle felt it had a right to sign and play him, regardless of any draft, much as players have been lured from NBA clubs by ABA clubs without having been exposed to any ABA drafts.

"Shortly, I got a telephone call from Haywood's legal advisors that they were going to court to seek an injunction against our preventing him from playing in our league. I immediately notified our law firm, and we took counter-action. Soon we were involved in action and counter-action, in court hearings and court sessions, which imposed an enormous strain on all concerned. Frankly, I do not believe our particular problems are completely understood in the courts. I do not believe this is the best place to settle our differences. I would say this even if the rulings went in our favor. I believe that we deal with a special set of circumstances in our operation that require us to regulate ourselves for survival.

"I believe the majority rule is a democratic way of decision-making. I believe the draft has been the salvation of professional sports, the only way to distribute talent equitably over a period of time, the only way to approach parity logically over a number of years, the only way to avoid a single wealthy and greedy owner from buying up the best players and dominating the circuit. If there have been cycles of domination in the past, they simply have come from one team having come up luckier than another or perhaps made smarter trades or moves than another, but not from mere misuse of money.

"I believe the four-year rule was a good one. The court rulings have compelled us to alter this. We now have a hardship rule in which boys may apply for eligibility, be approved or disapproved, then exposed to a special draft. I would have preferred that we considered and drafted change in a more orderly manner, under less pressure.

"We must live with the times. These are changing times.

Perhaps changes must be made. The Players' Association wishes certain modifications in the standard contract. We must consider these. But we must consider them as a group. We must somehow balance individual freedoms against potential group chaos. We cannot have players simply jumping from team to team. This would defeat the sensible system of the draft and the structure of trading techniques in which a team may seek to strengthen itself where it is weak at the expense of weakening itself where it is strong.

"I have been castigated in some quarters for not simply barring Haywood from playing in the NBA. Well, we took a vote at the request of Mr. Schulman and voted heavily against his being permitted to use Haywood at that time. Mr. Cooke and other members of our group who may have wanted to sign Haywood and may have disagreed with our rulings, nevertheless abided by them, and when one of our members simply disregarded them, they voted almost unanimously against him. Mr. Cooke and others asked that penalties be imposed on Mr. Schulman, and I agreed and I did. As to whether these have been collected, this is our private business. The courts granted us this right. When they also granted Mr. Schulman the right to play Haywood, I had to abide by that decision, we had to abide by it. We were powerless to do otherwise.

"I'm glad it's over. It was a deplorable thing. I do not believe the action was in our league's best interests, nor do I believe the rulings that emerged from it were in the best interests of professional sports as a whole. I can only hope we all profited from the experience. I can only hope Mr. Schulman will abide by our rules in the future and I have now broad powers to see that all our owners do so. I want him to be a happy and successful member of our group, but I want him to arrive at this by the same common means as the others.

"I want Spencer Haywood to be happy and have a successful career. Certainly his abilities are an asset to our league. And I regret the problems he has had. But we were only concerned with his eligibility to be signed and to play with Seattle at that specific time and did not feel he was then eligible. Well, it is done now. And perhaps if a merger between the NBA and ABA becomes a reality we can have a return to orderly procedures and a sane operation. Our members have approved merger, pending Congressional approval, and if that is the way to better professional basketball, and if the Haywood case hurried this along, well, then, that was the one good thing which emerged."

Jack Kent Cooke

"I was interested in signing Spencer Haywood. I am interested in acquiring any player who will help the Los Angeles Lakers. But I will do so only within the rules of our Association. When I heard of the possible availability of Spencer Haywood, I asked Allan Rothenberg, who has done much legal work for us, to investigate it for us. And at first his reports indicated that it might be reasonable to consider signing Haywood. However, on presenting the case to Walter Kennedy, our commissioner, and to the league as a whole, we were told that it was against the by-laws of our league, so that was that. We did not, thus, ever get down to making any concrete bid for Haywood's services.

"I did not actually take our man off the case. I wanted to be informed of all developments up to the last possible moment. If at any time the situation had altered and it had been possible for us to sign Haywood, we then would have given serious consideration to entering into negotiations for him. I am not sure how high we would have gone. This would have depended on how high an estimation our officials placed on his worth. But if we were free to go after him and wanted him enough, the Los Angeles Lakers would not have been outbid. This was not the case. We were not free to go after him. There were 17 NBA teams and I presume all had some interest in him, but there was only one willing to break our rules to sign him.

"The vote went against Sam Schulman by 15 to two I believe. Now that is a strong vote. To say that I asked strong penalties be imposed on him is to underestimate the strength of the wishes of the vast majority of our entire Association. We all felt some action should be taken against one who had acted in direct violations of our by-

196

laws and against the wishes of our majority. But once that is done, I am not a man to bear grudges. Sam Schulman remains a fellow franchise-holder in this league, and I am perfectly prepared to treat him with courtesy and respect as a business partner in the future. The courts have cleared Spencer Haywood to play for Seattle, and I hope he has a long and fine career in our league and proves a worthy challenge for our players.

"I do not feel it was an incident which cast any credit on many of the persons concerned, but it is now a closed incident and we must look to the future."

Allan Rothenberg

"I believe one of our players, Jerry West, had spoken to us about Haywood's possible availability. When Mr. Cooke asked me to look into it, I went to see Haywood's attorney, Al Ross, and we discussed the situation and he showed me some of the legal papers covering it. I advised Mr. Cooke that it was possible the way might be cleared legally for Haywood to be signed to play in the NBA, but that existing NBA rules appeared to preclude it. I know he then approached the NBA to inquire how the rules applied in this case, to present the particulars of this particular case to see if the rules perhaps did not apply, and so forth, but the NBA judgement was its rules did prohibit the signing of Haywood.

"There was never any question of our breaking NBA rules. Mr. Cooke never asked me if there were loopholes in the rules or if we could go to court to get them overthrown. His position always has been he wishes to operate within the rules. He is a very competitive person. He pays his players and coaches very well and seeks the best he can get. His desire to capture the NBA championship which has so narrowly eluded him in the past is clear. But he never empowered me to enter serious negotiations with Haywood or make any firm offer. And no one can ever point to a single instance in which he has disregarded the rules of the group to better himself personally.

"We wanted Haywood. We just didn't want him that bad."

Jerry West

"If, besides what we already have, the Lakers had Spencer Haywood in one corner, we not only would win the championship, we might never lose a game."

Jack Dolph

"I would say I went through the three hardest months of my professional life in the Haywood case. It was the most difficult sort of negotiations. Nobody was really in the right in the situation. And to be honest, I think everyone involved behaved badly, and that includes the teams in our own league. I think everyone involved acted in less than good faith. There was a lot of undercover maneuvering that was most deplorable. Some of it can be excused on the basis that this was war and everything goes in war, but not a lot of it, not all of it.

"I believe the Denver Rockets, Bill and Don Ringsby, and Spencer Haywood could have and should have resolved their differences. As ABA commissioner this was my first aim, and I am deeply disappointed that it did not work out. Spencer was underage when he signed his first three contracts with the Rockets. He was of age when he resolved to get a better contract. If his last contract with the Rockets was not all it should have been, the Rockets should have been willing to straighten out one that would then be binding because of his age, and he should have then been willing to accept it.

"Bad feelings interfered. I believe Spencer received a lot of bad advice along the way. By the time this matter peaked, he was a badly confused young man. He simply was not equipped to handle the pressures placed on him. Ever since he was a teen-ager beginning in high school he has been given a constantly increasing sense of his own value, which grew all out of proportion to reality, and all of us in sports share a responsibility for this. We keep doing this to other young men. The war between the two leagues and the outlandish dollar bidding for services keeps doing it.

"I believe Al Ross operated opportunistically, as all

198

agents do, and I am not sure he had the young man's best interests at heart. He wanted to make the most money for his client, possibly so he could make the most money for himself, but money itself will not heal all the wounds this young man suffered. I believe young players should have expert legal and managerial advice, but since it is difficult for them, being inexperienced, to be selective, I can only hope they will be fortunate in their choice of counsel.

"I believe Bill and Don Ringsby were too rigid in their approach to this problem. I think they are fine gentlemen and good businessmen, and I believe they feel they were pushed too far by Haywood and then by Ross, too, understandably, and were carried away by their emotions.

"Unfortunately, I must admit there is some truth to Haywood's charges in regards to the use of racial terms in this incident. In simple honesty, I concede I was standing there when I heard Bill Ringsby use the term 'black nigger.' But I do not believe he meant anything by it. He is a man of the old school, given to basic emotions, a gruff western man who speaks in terms not acceptable to much of society, and what he might say in passing or in anger is no worse than any of us might say or many of us have said in moments of frustration. The Ringsbys hired the first black coach in our league. They have paid heavily to employ black players. I believe them to be less prejudiced than many.

"Still, I can understand Spencer's resentment in overhearing such things. I wonder if Spencer does not sometimes say some things about white men in moments of anger which he might not mean or might regret. It is unfortunate that such basic passions erupt under such pressures, but this was a most arduous ordeal for most of us, with a great deal at stake. We have turned much of our lives over to the sport, and the resolution of this crisis was of critical importance to us.

"I was the man in the middle. I sought first to have Haywood honor what I considered a very real obligation to the Rockets and the Ringsbys, then, seeing this slip away, I sought to save him for our league. He was a precious commodity to us. There were good offers made to the Rockets and the Ringsbys for Haywood's contract by franchise-holders in our league who were prepared to pacify Haywood with a new contract, but these were refused. There were some offers to buy out the Ringsbys and hopefully solve the problem by placing new ownership in Denver, but unfortunately these did not turn out to be hard offers.

"I can understand the interest of NBA teams in signing Spencer out of the ABA. The ABA has signed good players out of the NBA. This has been war, make no mistake of it. I can understand the motives of Sam Schulman in signing Spencer for his Seattle franchise in the NBA. Here was a player who could help him, who seemed available to him. I cannot understand the motives of the NBA in resisting Mr. Schulman's act. Perhaps there was in this a pretense of propriety that in reality did not exist.

"I do believe Spencer should have recognized a moral obligation to the ABA. He and Ross could see where we were seeking to straighten this mess out, and had they not taken it to court, there is every possibility we could have done so. We gave Haywood his chance to play pro basketball. We opened up opportunity to many basketball players, including blacks. We could have used his sympathy and support in helping to spread the sport. But, I suppose, it always is every man for himself.

"The court rulings generally favored Haywood, Schulman and the Seattle franchise. Still, the most critical matter before the court, at least on the surface, the matter of the legality of Spencer's contract with the Rockets, never came to a ruling, so we never will know how that would have come out. It is not impossible, you know, that Haywood would have been ordered to play out or wait out his Denver contract. The fact that the court permitted him to play with the Sonics in the meantime does not rule this out. In the interests of speeding up the merger and ending a most messy situation, an out-of-court settlement was reached; and as far as I'm concerned it ended there.

"The people who launched the ABA believed that there was a need for a broader scope to professional basketball in this country. They believed there were more good players around than there were opportunities for them to play and more good cities around to support major league basketball

200

than there were teams for them. And the continuing expansion of the NBA itself supports the ABA position. It has not been easy for the ABA. It never is in ventures of this sort. Much money has been lost. Franchises have had to be transferred. But the league has been gaining in strength steadily since its formation in 1967, and now it is strong enough to survive and prosper whether or not the merger with the ABA is finalized, though we in the ABA believe a merger with the NBA is the only sensible solution to our common problems.

"I left CBS-TV to become commissioner in 1970 and soon was thrust into this Haywood case. I am left with some scars from it, but I am paid to do battle on behalf of the league and accept such wounds as may come my way. I believe myself and my counterpart in the NBA, Walter Kennedy, and all other sports commissioners and men in our position are bound to be caught in the middle of controversies and inevitably will have to make unpopular decisions at times and from time to time will be made to look bad in the public light, but this is the nature of our job.

"I am sorry we lost the Haywood case—and in a sense we lost, though there were some victories in the settlement—but it was not a loss which crushed us. We're sorry Spencer no longer is in the ABA, but the ABA goes on. It consists of its people, but it is bigger than any individuals. And the rise or fall of merger plans are not greatly affected by the court cases of the Spencer Haywoods, the Rick Barrys and the Billy Cunninghams. Each is important in its own way. But in reaching decisions on a possible merger, we are concerned with the broad, long-range view, not incidents of the moment.

"We had reservations about the four-year rule and already had created a hardship clause in which needy players could apply for certification and exposure to a special draft. This was used not only in the Spencer Haywood case, but the Ralph Simpson case and others. This seemed a way to protect the rights of the colleges, to protect players from undue temptation and yet protect the rights of the individual to use his special talents to pursue a paying profession. In the summer of 1971, we had 15 applicants, approved 12 and drafted four. I assume the other eight are now ineligible for college ball. Clearly, there are dangers. The rule is imperfect. But we have not found a better one.

"And I might note that Judge Ferguson's ruling might be overturned if appealed to a higher court. I don't know that it will be or even should be. I am just saying it is not necessarily the final word.

"Basically, we believe in the right to enact regulations to govern ourselves. But we also believe in the right of the court to rule on the legality of these, and we will abide by all such court rulings. In all honesty, I must say we have adjusted our league rules to fit our needs, as do all leagues, especially in this wartime situation, in hard competition with another league, and we will do so again and again to gain all the reasonable advantages we can if no merger goes through. We hope to become a partner of the NBA. We are not now that, however, and must act accordingly. We must, for example, bid against them for the best players. And in doing so we must pay a price beyond reason and give young men a false set of values.

"The real danger in this Haywood case, it seems to me, is that it may give owners, managers and players the idea they can ignore contractual obligations and do whatever they want to do. Once a bond is signed, it should be honored. Beyond this lies chaos and, possibly, disaster for sports."

Pete Pfaelzer

"The settlement stopped us from getting a decision on Spencer's contractual obligation, but I believe the ruling would have been that he had no obligation to a bad contract imposed on him when he was incapable of judging it on its merits. A bad contract is a bad contract and should not have to be honored. A good contract is a good contract and should be honored. Rules a league sets for itself are fine so long as they are moral and legal. A bad rule is a bad rule and a good rule is a good rule. Professional athletes should be entitled to the same freedoms as other citizens and the same protections. If sports cannot survive without bad contracts and immoral or illegal rules, then why should they survive?"

Judge Warren Ferguson

"If this case establishes something—regardless of the legal conclusions—I hope I can impress on the legal profession that professional athletes cannot be treated as merchandise. There appears to be universal callous disregard for professional athletes."

John McLendon

"It's a very difficult business being a professional athlete. Many make very good money, but they are being judged every game, and the pressures on them to keep producing are much heavier than in most lines of work. And a great many do not make exceptional money; they are fringe athletes who have no security and live a life of always trying to hang on with one team or catch on with another. Players are traded and sold and dropped all the time, and they have to leave their friends and homes and uproot their families. They are treated well usually only as long as they are needed. In the end, they rarely are shown loyalty. Yet when they seek to get more freedom or more security or more money for themselves, they are called greedy or disloyal by the press and the public. It is similarly difficult to be a coach. The profession has been degraded by the way we are hired and fired so casually. And if you are a black man and you have special problems making your way in society anyway and then you are an athlete or a coach, too, it is doubly difficult.

"I feel I have been fortunate as a black coach to get an opportunity to coach in major league professional basketball. I wish it had gone further, of course. I coached the old Cleveland club in the old ABL and then this Denver club in the new ABA. I had mixed emotions about the signing of Spencer Haywood. I wanted a player of his calibre to help my team, and I felt I could help him, but I feel a youngster should delay his desire to make money until he has taken advantage of the opportunity to earn an education. He can only play basketball for a limited time, I know he has to go for the big money while he can, but an education will last him all his life. In any event, I was handed Spencer Haywood.

"It didn't work out, but I don't feel it was his fault or my fault. He was unusually young to be playing against proven pros, and it took him a while to adjust, although he had such remarkable ability he made a remarkably fast adjustment. I didn't have a center, so I had to play him at center. Later, when Joe Belmont replaced me, they credited him with shifting Spencer to forward, but he just changed the name of Spencer's position, Spencer still played center. And he had to face some bigger men, but he had the jumping ability to handle it and he didn't have a mastery of the moves a forward needs to play perfectly out of the corners. He was learning fast.

"My hands were tied a lot. The Ringsbys were novices in the sport, but they felt they knew it all. They signed a lot of players to no-cut contracts, mostly white players, and I couldn't cut them, or trade them, either, for that matter, and I had to make the most of what I had. And at first that wasn't much. But then we had to play 21 of our first 28 games away from home—and with a 20-year-old center breaking in. We lost four in overtimes. We lost a double-overtime on the last shot in New Orleans, but it was our best game and we were heading home for 15 of our next 19 at home. I felt sure we were ready to make a move. Only my release had already been written up.

"I woke up one morning and was called into the office and young Ringsby, Don, started saying there were certain things I did he couldn't understand. He was challenging my coaching moves, see. I looked on his desk and I saw my release there. I figured what's the point of discussing it? So I quickly cleared out my desk and left. They'd offered me the job of director of player personnel, but it was only a token thing. Within 24 hours I decided against it. I later landed a fine position with Converse, which keeps me close to basketball, but I miss coaching.

"I feel I got Haywood off to a sound start, and I believe if I had been permitted to stay with him, I could have avoided some of the troubles that followed. I wasn't surprised at the moves he made later. I kept seeing him and I tried to counsel him, to pacify him really, to keep him happy so he'd play to the best of his ability. He could be right about their feelings about black players. I'm not sure. I know one of the more militant black groups was sending representatives around the Rockets to create some commotion. I suggested to Spencer he cut them from his life, but he feels strongly about freedom for black people, for all people. And I know the Ringsbys were difficult to work for; after you were with them a while, it was hard to have confidence in them.

"But I like Spencer very much. I think only people who don't know him don't like him. I think to know him is to like him. He's really a very fine, sincere person. There's a lot of warmth to him, a lot of personality, and no put on. He's ambitious, but not greedy. He's bright and thoughtful. He's really a beautiful young man. I think he's reached only perhaps 65 to 70 percent of his basketball potential. I think he's going to be one of the great players. And I think he's reached only perhaps half of his potential as a person. He can be a great person who can do a lot of good for people. He wants to. If the pressures of his profession don't wear him down."

Joe Belmont

"I wasn't aiming at the opportunity to coach a pro team. I hadn't put myself in line and in most situations I wouldn't even have gotten the chance, so I guess I can't complain too much that it didn't come to anything, but it did seem like something. To have something given to you, to make something of it, and then to have it taken away, well, it hurts.

"I played for Duke in college ball and for the old Denver Truckers in AAUU ball and I had only one season of coaching behind me, with the Duke freshmen 13 years earlier, when I joined the Rockets in a front-office capacity. I had been an ABA referree. When the team got off to a bad start and they wanted to make a change, I was the only individual in the organization with any experience, limited though it was. When I was offered it, I felt I could do this.

Coaching is probably overrated. If you have the horses, anyone can produce. If you don't, forget it.

"I felt sorry for John McLendon because I thought he was a good man, but the Ringsbys have minds of their own and once they had made up their minds to make a change, why not me? Coaches get fired. That's the only way coaches get hired. The Ringsbys laid out a pretty picture for me. I was only an emergency replacement, but if I made good, the job was mine. Well, I made good. We won 18 straight at one point, we won 42 games and lost only 14, we turned things around and we won the pennant. I had the horses. I had Haywood. But we lost the playoffs. And I lost my job shortly after the next season began.

"I think I found the right way to use Spencer and he's such a tremendous player he lifted everyone up once he got going. He's a black man and I think he regretted the Ringsbys' firing the black coach, but he gave me everything he had and there was never any black-white thing between us. If there was anything, it was a black-black thing, between two black players, Haywood and Larry Jones. Or something between the Ringsbys and the players. A lot of players grew unhappy with the bosses. I mean, they were good when we were winning and not so good when we were losing. It was all right for a long time, but then maybe resentments that were smouldering beneath the surface began to come up and fester and hurt our team play. I'm not sure how much it hurt us in the playoffs. Sometimes the other team just wins and you just lose. We beat a good team with Rick Barry, but then lost to Bill Sharman's good team.

"I was disappointed, of course, but it never occurred to me the owners weren't satisfied. I knew some of the players were dissatisfied with the money they were making. I knew Spencer was unhappy and thinking about leaving, but I didn't really think he'd leave. I mean, he had a contract and all and I spoke to him and tried to keep him happy because with him I thought we could win it all the next season. But then I didn't want to interfere in what he felt were his personal rights. I really liked him, understand, and I think he liked me, and we had a good relationship, which wasn't built on preaching.

206

"We got to camp and Spencer got hurt. Then he disappeared and we opened the season without him and things began to go bad with him. When you have a player like Haywood, you build everything around him, maybe 80 percent, and without him this 80 percent just doesn't work, so you have to make adjustments, but you don't want to make too many because you figure he'll be back. But then he isn't coming back. I tried to talk him out of leaving because I feared it might be bad for him, make him an outcast, and because, hell, I knew it would be bad for us, but it's his life, and I have no authority over him and can't play God. So he goes and our chances go with him.

"If he stays, I keep my job. I don't blame him. I don't hate him for it or anything like that. He has his own life to live, and he has to do what he thinks is right for him. He was always straight with me and a nice boy under a lot of pressure, being pulled this way and that. I should have thought that the Ringsbys would see how hard it would be to win without him and give me time to straighten things out, but they didn't. The season had just started, ten games or so, and we were losing close games we'd have won with Haywood, and just when I figure I'm getting it figured out I get it in the neck.

"I don't want to leave with bad feelings, but you ask so I'll tell you how the operation went and you can decide for yourself. We were on a trip and we get to Miami and a friend calls me from Denver and tells me there's a rumor going around I'm about to be fired. I put it aside, though I couldn't ignore it, and I figured I'd see how it was when we got back to Denver. We got the win in Miami, our third in 13 games, and went home.

"We got in too late for me to go to the office and I had to drive my son to a football banquet so the family loaded in the car and off we went. And then on the car radio they announced I'd been fired. That's how I heard. And that's a hard way to hear. My wife started to cry and my son got upset. Couldn't they have told me to my face?

"We had to get through the rest of the evening and the night somehow. I said I'd go in first thing in the morning to find out what this was all about, as if I didn't know what it was. So I got through the night. But when I went to the office in the morning, they wouldn't even see me. Not at first. I got there at eight and I was told they were in a meeting. I waited outside for two hours, until ten, when they finally permitted me to see them. Then they told me the change was as a result of a unanimous vote of the board of directors and was in the best interests of the team.

"I said, 'I'm not going to defend myself. You've done this, so that's it.' They didn't say a word about regretting it or thanking me or anything. Well, we settled up, and that was it. They own the team, and they have a right to hire and fire as they wish. Perhaps they were right and I wasn't doing the job. I'm sure I'm not the best judge of that. I'd never been fired before. I'd be lying if I said I wasn't embarrassed and my pride wasn't hurt. You get your ass kicked and it hurts. It hurts you and your wife and your kids.

"They hired Stan Albeck to replace me, and then they fired him and hired Alex Hannum. I'm now refereeing in the NBA. And Spencer is playing for Seattle in the NBA. We had a short, sweet time of it with the Rockets and the Ringsbys. Well, that's the business."

Chet Nelson, Sports Editor,
Rocky Mountain News

"The short time Spencer played here was the brightest in our basketball history. Everything seemed serene. He was happy. The team was happy. The owners were happy. And, of course, the press and public was happy. We were winning. But then it turned out many were unhappy under the surface. I can't pass judgment on the merits of their unhappiness because I do not know all the details of their differences, but I can say it was a most unfortunate experience for Denver sports.

"I think Bill Ringsby was a good businessman but a bad basketball man. He was a neophyte in sports. The same goes for his son, Don. I respect the old man's accomplishments in life, but I think he may have been bullheaded in this controversy. I think it became a vendetta with them both, in which they placed their personal satisfaction ahead of the franchise and the city. But, on the other hand, I think Spencer may have been ungrateful to the team, the owners and the town that gave him an opportunity. Maybe he could have given a little, too. I like him personally. I like the Ringsbys.

"I think everyone wound up a loser."

Lynn Howell, Sports Writer,
Rocky Mountain News

"I printed the story that the Spencer Haywood camp was asking $3.25 million because that was what Don Ringsby told me they asked of him. Then Don Ringsby said he didn't say it and told me he never told it to me. Well, what can you do? Everyone does the best he can. I do and they do. I think they got carried away with this whole thing. I think Bill and Don Ringsby and Spencer Haywood are all good people who behaved badly in this situation and Denver basketball and all sports, really, suffered as a result.

"I doubt that the contract Haywood had with the Ringsbys would have cheated him in any way. Perhaps he could have had a better contract; but I think it is very important that when you or I or Spencer Haywood signs a contract, we should have to live up to it, and I think it is unfortunate he got out of it. I like him and I always believed him a very shrewd young man. Just because he does not have as much formal education as I do does not make him less intelligent and less responsible for his own acts.

"Bill Ringsby had very little formal education, too, but he, too, is a very intelligent person. And he's not a bad person. He's a very basic guy. But he's the kind of guy you can tell you think he screwed up this situation and he may not agree with you but he won't put you down for it. And I have told him this because I think it. I think he could have and should have said this player is so important to this franchise and this city I'm going to have to give in to him.

"Well, we're struggling now. The Ringsbys hired Hannum to run their basketball operation, and they moved their trucking offices into other offices far removed from the basketball offices. The Rockets no longer have Haywood, and they no longer are big winners. Crowds aren't what they were in Denver. It's a long road back. We miss Spencer. I hope he's happy in Seattle."

12. Seattle

Possibly no player has entered the NBA under greater pressure than Spencer Haywood had to endure when he broke in at the tail-end of the 1970-71 season. Probably more was expected of Wilt Chamberlain and Lew Alcindor when they began in the big leagues, but they only faced the physical challenge of performing up to expectations. Surrounded by controversy, Haywood was confronted by mental and emotional problems, too. He had to fly back and forth between court appearances and games, he never knew if he was going to play on a given night, he was always unsure how long he would be permitted to play in the league. He was wary of his teammates and they were wary of him. He was unsure of the reception he'd be accorded by the other players and by the fans and writers around the league. He was criticized in the public prints and on the airwaves regularly and booed and heckled from the stands. He was living out of a suitcase and in hotels.

He seldom demonstrated his true talents. There was the odd night when it worked for him, such as in Baltimore in mid-March when he hit 13 of 20 shots from the field, scored 35 points, and collected 16 rebounds, but his averages of 20 points and 12 rebounds per game for 33 games were below his potential. He was unable to lift his troubled team from its lethargy. Seattle finished six games below the .500 level and failed to make the playoffs.

He says, "It was a real hard time. I wanted so much to do well and for my new team to do well, but we had a lot against us. I was concerned about my case, naturally, and I never was sure how it would go. The courtroom stuff like to drove me out of my mind. Talk, talk, talk. It just dragged on and on and on. A lot of it was like Perry Mason. I couldn't believe lawyers really acted that way. You'd have thought the crime was murder. When it was my times to talk, I just told my story as best I could. Between times, I just sat there. And listened. I gained a lot of vocabulary. And learned a little law. But not much. To be honest, a lot of it just confused me. And I always had a plane to catch. And I was always late for it.

"The general manager, Bob Houbregs, and the coach, Lenny Wilkens, and a lot of the guys, Rod Thorn, Bob Rule and the rest, were real nice, but a lot of the guys were sort of standoffish, too. They had their own troubles, of course. They hadn't been going good. The playoffs were getting away from them. And they weren't sure I was good enough to turn things around for them. And at that time I wasn't. I mean, they knew I was getting a whole lot of money, a lot more than any of them, and they weren't sure I was that good, they were a little put off by it. They weren't sure I wouldn't turn right around and jump them, too, or maybe be taken away from them by the courts, and they were just gonna wait and see. You can't just walk in at mid-season with my kind of reputation and the press always hanging around you and the spotlight always on you and expect the guys to just accept you as one of them. I hadn't made any sacrifices for them. And I wasn't able to do anything great for them.

"I didn't have much time for sleep. When I had time, I couldn't sleep. I'd lay awake, tossing and turning. I took a lot of sleeping pills. And I'd still wake up at four in the morning in the dark room thinking about things. I couldn't get my mind onto other things, the things I like to do. I had no appetite to eat and I lost weight. I couldn't hear the music. I had no social life. I let the ladies go and didn't date. I didn't call home much. I didn't want no more

211

advice. I'd cut the ties with Will Robinson. I had Sam Schulman and I had Al Ross and I had my lawyers and that was it, but these were not people I went to bed with, if you know what I mean. I was very lonely.

"The phone kept ringing. And people kept coming around. Asking questions. Always asking questions. And there was no place I could hide. Like I said, I thought of running away. But I stuck it out. I played my games. Some of the other guys seemed to know what I was going through. They were competing against me on the court, but they went out of their way to make me feel welcome. When a man does this for a guy like me, well he's really a man, and they'll never really know how much it meant. Like Wilt Chamberlain moved up alongside me on court and said, 'Man, don't worry.' And Jerry West said, 'Don't let it get you down. You've got it. It'll come out. Don't press.' And Connie Hawkins said, 'Welcome to the club, my man.' Billy Cunningham said nice things. And Gus Johnson. And Earl Monroe. And some other nice people. And Lew Alcindor—Kareem Abdul-Jabbar, now—he rapped with me about other things like we was old buddies.

"But then Bob Lanier said, 'Hey, man, who said you were a player? You can't dribble and you can't shoot. All you can do is jump teams.' And Willie McCarter said, 'Look out, man, you don't belong in this league.' And Rick Roberson said, 'Bring the ball to his side. He can't play this game.' And when I went to talk to Oscar Robertson, he wouldn't even talk to me. I walked up to him and he turned his back on me and walked away from me. Now, here was a hero of mine. A guy I dreamed of playing against. A guy who had fought for his own rights. The head of the Players' Association. I was so surprised. I still don't know why he did it like he did," Haywood sighs, wistful with disappointment.

Robertson says simply, "I don't remember the incident." He will not say any more about it.

Haywood says, "Some of the fans were very abusive. They'd yell, 'Who do you think you are?' or 'We don't want you in this league' or 'Go back to Denver' or 'Go back to Mississippi' or 'Go back to Africa.' Some of the coaches baited me from the bench. Some of the managers and owners threatened to pull their teams off the court if I played, and most of them protested the games I did play. And the writers rapped me. And people wrote me letters saying, 'Nigger ape, don't you know your place? We don't need you in this country.' There were some nice writers, too, and some nice fans, too, who showed understanding, but the sad thing is these never wipe out the bad things. It's the bad things that stick and fill you with hatred. I had to overcome this. Overcoming it may have made me a better man.

"Lenny Wilkens helped a lot. He had every reason to resent me. He was not only the team's first star player, but the coach. He was used to getting most of the publicity. He had proven himself. And there were times and still are times when he seems a little cool. But then, hell, he's a coach and I'm a player and you can't be buddy-buddy. But he'd feel the vibrations and he sympathized. At first, I'd sit alone on planes. Then he'd sit with me and talk to me. He'd counsel me to try to take things in stride, to just do my best on the court and try to get through the stuff off the court and I'd come out on the other end before long. He saw when the guys weren't giving me the ball, and he smoothed things out with them. By the end of the season, it was beginning to get better.

"Then I win the case and we start this season fresh and it's a whole new deal. I settled down in Seattle and worked out with a lot of the guys who live here at the Seattle University gym over the summer. I went to camp with them and I opened the season with them. We're together now, we're a team. Lenny is a good coach and Rod Thorn, who retired to become his bench assistant, helps. The guys have a good spirit. I don't know how far we can go. We have weakenesses. We don't have a giant center. Bob Rule never recovered right from an Achilles tendon tear and lost a lot of the mobility he depended on and got unhappy and got traded. But we have strengths, too. We have some good players."

This was in the middle of the 1971-72 season, when he was speaking without knowing how it would come out.

"How good can I be? The best, I hope. But there are good players all around. When I first faced the pros in the

ABA, they weren't as tough as I thought they'd be, most of them, and I could do my things against them without too much trouble, though there were some good ones. Mel Daniels is a very solid center, perhaps not as strong physically as he might be, but talented. Rick Barry is a super scorer and a very mean competitor. He's almost impossible to defense. He's as good a forward as you'd want to see. Roger Brown has good speed and good moves, and he can go at either forward or guard and give you big games. Before he hurt his knee, Jimmy Jones was about the best guard, almost unknown around the country, but a fine inside shooter with a tough, solid game.

"The NBA players have been every bit as good as I expected, though they haven't scared me any. Lew Alcindor is a super center. He has the great height and reach and probably the greatest quickness and agility and coordination of any man his size. He's gaining beef and strength, and he has a great soft touch shooting and a lot of shots. He's unselfish and makes everyone who plays with him much better than they really are. So does Oscar Robertson, who is smooth and effortless and very smart and unselfish. Having those two together makes Milwaukee a great team.

"Nate Thurmond is an exceptional defensive player and team player and rebounder, perhaps the most underrated player, and probably no worse than second or third among centers. Willis Reed and Wilt Chamberlain are both great. Reed has tremendous strength and a good all-around game and a willingness to use himself for his team, but his bad legs have held him back. If it wasn't for those bad legs, New York would have a team that could challenge Milwaukee because they have a lot of balance with Jerry Lucas and Dave DeBusschere and Bill Bradley, strong guys up front, and Walt Frazier and Dick Barnett and Earl Monroe, quick cats in the backcourt.

"L. A. probably has the best chance to beat Milwaukee with Wilt and Jerry West and Gail Goodrich and a lot of good guys to go with them. They beat us several times during the record winning streak, which was just an unbelievable accomplishment. Bill Sharman really has them running, and if they don't run out of steam or run into injuries, they'll be tough in the playoffs, but the

214

playoffs are a whole new season, and the record isn't worth a single victory there. Wilt is supposed to be old. I guess he used to scare guys the way he used to score, which he doesn't try to do any more, but he still scares you with his size and strength and the way he dominates the boards and blocks shots and gets rid of the ball in a hurry. He's put down a lot, but he impresses hell out of me, I want to tell you. As for West, well, he may be the greatest. He also is supposed to be old, but he is so quick it is unbelievable and he does everything, absolutely everything. He contributes to a team in a hundred ways every game. And the tougher the going gets, the better he gets.

"Being voted to a starting spot at forward for the West for the All-Star game well before mid-season in my first full season in the NBA made me feel I'd shown something good. Writing in *The Sporting News*, Phil Elderkin listed me as one of the ten most valuable players in the NBA. This was before mid-season. I want to be one of these guys the other guys marvel at. I'm good, but I think I can be great. I'm just learning. I watch other guys and try to pick up things from them. In the ABA, I took a lot of close looks at Rick Barry. Here, in the NBA, I study Connie Hawkins. These are guys who can do things the way I want to do them. But I also have my own things I can do I'm working on. I work against smaller men like Lee Winfield, who is the quickest. I watch forwards because I'm playing forward, out here I've played mostly center until recently. The difference is the forward plays out of a corner instead of in the middle like the center, and the forward is usually facing the basket while the center has his back to the basket a lot. I think I'm a better forward than a center, but I'm just learning. I'm only 6-9 and it would be tough for me to play center against guys like Wilt and Lew, who go 7-2 and 7-4, but because we don't have a center of that size I still have the responsibility for rebounding with them. I'm up in weight from 215 to 230, I'm getting physically stronger, and it hasn't cost me any speed. I can jump, so I can go with them, but they have an advantage on me.

"I can handle the ball. I can put it on the floor and go with it. I have good moves. But I'm not as good as I'm going to get. You have to be able to face a good man one on one and go with him, on both offense and defense. I can shoot from a lot of places. My problem is getting my hands on the ball. I'm not as good without the ball, getting to places where I can get the ball, as I should be. I'm double-teamed a lot, and I'm not thrown the ball as much as I want to be. I have a feeling lots of nights I can score as often as I can get the ball. Sometimes I don't look for the pass as much as I should. I'm not always sure yet when I should shoot or pass. The good players tell me this takes time. You need experience.

"I have a reputation for being a poor defensive player. All scorers do. I'm probably a better defensive player than most people realize. I'm working on it. It's mostly hard work and concentration and desire. I have the desire. I can see where if you scored 40 and your man scores 35, well you're only plus five, so what's the point? You don't stop the super scorers, but you have to make it as hard for them as you can. You have to outscore 'em as much as possible. And any basket you take from 'em may be the difference between winning and losing. I block a lot of shots and I'm blocking more all the time, maybe more than any forward in the league. I have the jumping ability and timing to do it. I can go up with any man on rebounds, but I have to learn to get better position on the taller men. I want to clear those boards and whip that ball out fast.

"It's tough under the boards. Hey, wow, it's rough in there, but that's the game. If I don't feel beat up physically when I get back to the dressing room, I feel like I haven't worked hard and earned anything. Guys like Gus Johnson and Bill Bridges and Dave DeBusschere really put it to you—they grab you and push you and hack you and body you—and you've got to give it back in turn. I enjoy it. I'm a physical player myself. I learned a lot from watching Tom Meschery right away after I joined Seattle. He was something else. He didn't have great ability, but he knew all the tricks. You'd go up to shoot and, wham, you'd be sitting in the stands.

"The thing is, it's really a physical game. The guys who designed it as a no-contact game didn't realize what they were doing. We're too big and that court is too small, especially that area under the basket. There's no way you can play this game right without jockeying for position. And these guys ain't jockeys. When Bill Bridges bumps you, you feel it. But that's not bad. That's the real game.

"Sure you can get hurt. But that's like crossing the street. Anything can happen to you any time. You just go in there and take your chances. But you got to play hard. That's the game. And, wow, it's an education watching and playing against some old pros. I'm learning a lot. How to grab a guy's belt or keep him off balance by bumping his legs when he goes up. I've gotten kneed and hipped. I've gotten into some fights. Mainly, I don't like it when the refs don't call the obvious. I get hell beat out of me sometimes and I like those free throws.

He had started talking about his game over sandwiches in a downtown Seattle coffee shop. Now we were driving crosstown and his enthusiasm was holding at a high level. He said, "I can't dominate the game the way a seven-foot center can. No forward can and no guard can, no matter how good they are. But I want to dominate games as much as I can and I'm having trouble doing it so far because my game all-around isn't yet what it should be. I want to be the Most Valuable Player in this league just like I was in the other league. And I will be. I'm not kidding. That's my goal. And I can reach it. I have to do everything I can do as well as I can do it and dominate games as much as I can and sacrifice myself for my team.

"It's the team that counts, it really is. Let's be honest, up to now I've been concerned with proving Spencer Haywood is a great player. Every player wants that when he's starting out. But I've always given to my teams, not taken away from them. My teams have always been winners and this one will be, too. It's not just the individual talents that count. You could have a team of all-stars that couldn't win a championship. It takes a team of guys playing together and sacrificing for one another to win the championship. Bill Russell taught me that. And I'm spreading his sermon around. I'm preaching love. And togetherness. And sacrifice. Diving for the loose ball. Passing up a shot to pass to a teammate who has a better shot. Even if you're black and he's white. Feeling free to tell him if he's doing wrong . . ."

"Even if you're black and he's white?"

"We're not to that point yet. But we'll get there."

"Is there really that much black-white feeling on court?"

"More than most players will admit. But we have to get over it. On a team, there can't be blacks and whites, only teammates. If you have love for your teammate, you can groove together, it's beautiful. We have to love one another on court. I'm not kidding. Off the court, maybe you can go screw yourself if you want, but on the court, you're my teammate, my brother and I love you, I'll do anything to bring you success, because your success is my success.

"You have to psych yourself up. It's a long schedule. Endless travel. Lots of weak opponents. It's hard to get up for every game. I used to have a tendency to relax. I'm resisting that now. You have to talk yourself into it. You have to be ready. The rewards are the greatest."

Through the first part of the 1971-72 season he was averaging around 25 points and 15 rebounds a game and blocking four or five shots a game, but he wasn't yet dominating games, though he had some big games against big teams. He was losing his temper some and raging at refs and facing up to foes menacingly.

After a game in Los Angeles, Jerry West said, "He's just on the verge of dominating games. It's hard for him because his team doesn't have a top center and he has to take on the big centers, but he can jump out of sight and he's got moves that don't stop and he's very strong and tough and talented." And the Laker coach Bill Sharman asked, "What is he, now, 21, 22 years old? Right now he should be just a rookie in this league but he's ahead of rookies because he's been playing pro. But he's made a big jump now and he has to get adjusted and figure out how to use best the things he does best. But he has as much going for him as any man who ever came into this game, and he could become the greatest in the game."

Now, at a practice session in Seattle, assistant coach Rod Thorn watched Haywood work out with wonder. Rod remembered, "When he first came to us, he created confusion because we didn't know if he would stay with us; we didn't know if we should make the adjustments to fit him in. As a guard, I welcomed him, but the forwards

218

were leery of him, he was going to take someone's job away. Most veterans want to see a guy prove himself before they accept him, anyway. And he didn't do it. He didn't show his stuff. He played just so-so. It was extremely difficult for him, of course. But he handled it very well. And he went out of his way to get along. He's a very open person. By the end of the year we could see that he was a super person. And now we're beginning to see he's a super player. I'm a queer for talent and this guy turns me on. He doesn't get the ball enough yet, but he's gaining size and strength and he just oozes power. One of these days he's going to begin pushing guys around and they're going to be begging for mercy."

Coach Lenny Wilkens, a skilled veteran and a more conservative sort, said, "He's very good and he has a chance to be great. He does a lot of things naturally, but he has a lot of skills to learn that have to be learned. He wants to learn. He'll listen. He's very coachable. He's not one of these guys who thinks he knows it all already. Too many guys want it easy. We got some on this team. He's not that way. But he still has a way to go.

"I was asked what I thought about maybe getting him originally. I'd watched him in the Olympic games and I'd seen he had tremendous talent. I said if we can get him, we can use him. I'd gotten to know Mr. Schulman first as a player representative, then as his coach, and I figured if anyone can get anything he wants, it's this man, but I didn't want our team standing around waiting for Superman to arrive. I kept saying to everyone, if he does arrive, don't expect miracles. And we didn't get any.

"He came and the situation unsettled all of us and put a lot of pressure on all of us. Of course, it was rougher on him than on anyone. I tried to help him, but I had to put the team first. I wasn't jealous of him or anything like that. I really wasn't. I never made his kind of money, but then I never made the kind of money a lot of players made in this league. And I can't play much longer anyway. I'm already coaching, and as a coach my success hangs on getting guys like him and fitting them into a team. So we just had to get through the hard time until we could get to a better time. There's no way of knowing if we'd have made the playoffs without him and the problems he brought. We didn't make it with him. But he brings with him hope for the future.

"He's got the kind of natural ability few guys have. But he does things naturally. He has a weak knowledge of the game yet. He doesn't play smart yet. He has a tendency to try to do it all alone. Maybe he tries too hard to live up to his reputation. He has a tendency to dribble too much and shoot too fast and give up the ball too often. He upset me at first and I began to doubt how good he was. But now I've gotten to see how good he is and how much better he can be. So have the other guys. There's a tendency to treat a first-year man like dirt. Veterans resent rookies. Especially high-priced, high-publicity guys. But when you see a guy has real ability and is willing to work and try to help the team, well, then you go all the way for him."

Bob Houbregs, the general manager, said, "When I was asked about Spencer Haywood and agreed we should go after him, I feared the sort of turmoil he might cause, and when he came, I regretted the turmoil he did cause, but I have never regretted his coming, because he's a fine person and the sort of player you don't get every year. I had confidence in Sam Schulman, but I didn't have confidence in Spencer Haywood. I had to be shown. And we actually played worse for a while after he came. But now we're much better for having him. I'm not sure yet if he's the sort of player who can turn a franchise around like an Alcindor can. Maybe only a center can do that. But a Haywood can do a lot for you. If we hadn't lost Rule, we might be ready now to challenge the best.

"The thing is, he had a lot of things against him. His case drove us up the walls. Everyone was attacking us. You'd think we'd stolen mother from home. Actually, I thought we were in the right. But Jack Kent Cooke was saying this and Franklin Mieuli was saying that and people were popping off and the press was pouring all over us. Now, finally, things have calmed down. The question may be how well Spencer has settled down. He has super talent. And he has an exceptionally engaging personality. But he's been pulled this way and that and pushed around a lot and been confused a lot and he hasn't really taken roots. The secret to his success in the long run lies in how well he fits in with the team and the town. He has to be happy here, and I think he will be."

Before the 1971-72 season opened, Spencer Haywood moved into a new double apartment on the eighteenth floor of a high-rise building in downtown Seattle. It is a very exclusive place. There is a doorman guarding the entrance. You must buzz to get a return buzzer for admission to the elevator, and while you wait in the lobby you can communicate with the tenants through an intercom system and can be observed by them through a closed-circuit television system which feeds a picture from cameras below onto channels on the tenants' sets above.

Wanting more room than one apartment afforded him, Haywood asked the owners to knock out a wall to provide him a double place, which they did. It is a sprawling apartment, done up basically in blacks and whites, but decorated by Spencer himself in what seems to be good taste. There is a large "liberation flag" on one wall. This is a symbol of "freedom for all minorities and all people," according to Spencer, and it is a flag he follows. Its basic colors are black and green and Spencer wears a beaded "liberation ring" in those colors on one finger. He has a diamond-studded ring on another finger. And he has handsome modern-art paintings on other walls. Many of these are by Vern DeSilva, his old teammate at Trinidad and Detroit. One has H. Rap Brown speaking as a city burns behind him. Another has Martin Luther King standing in front of two crying children. A third has one black man in chains while a brother is breaking his chains. There are a few trophies here and there, but no formal trophy case.

One end is given up to a hi-fi setup and an enormous collection of more than 1,000 jazz records. These are almost all pure jazz. There is very little rock-and-roll, contemporary pop, soul blues or classical music represented. Haywood is a pure jazz buff. "I need jazz music to get through the days," he says. He digs Miles Davis and John Coltrane and Freddie Hubbard and other giants of this music, and he always is playing this music loudly, at home, in his car, wherever and whenever he can. And he knows the music. He got many of his records free from past and present part-time pursuits as a weekend disc jockey taping shows for radio stations, such as KISW-FM, Seattle, but what he did not get free he was prepared to purchase. His immodest ambition is to "own every jazz record there is. If I hear one I don't have, I want it. I can't hear them all, but I want to have them all. I never know what I might want to hear or what a visiting friend might want to hear." He also wants to make his own jazz by learning to play guitar or other instruments. And he hangs out in jazz clubs, such as Shelly's Manne Hole in L. A., wherever he can find them.

If he likes anything better than basketball and jazz, it is the ladies. He calls them "sisters" and regards them with respect, as friends as well as lovers. When the wall was knocked down to form his apartment, it left back-to-back kitchen units, one of which now serves as a wet bar and the other of which usually is occupied by a couple of sisters fixing some supper for Spencer. "I'm a human garbage disposal for the slop they stir up," he grins. There usually are a lot of guys around his pad, but also a lot of gals, and he would just as soon have the company of the gals as the guys. There have been and still are one or two who are special, but Spencer is not especially ready to get married yet. He is willing to wait and he hopes they are.

"I like a lot of ladies. I don't lie about this to any of them so I don't feel I have to be accountable to any of them." He grins. "But I like them as people. I like the sisters for different reasons than I like the brothers. You can rap with both, but you rap in different ways. I really rap with the sisters, too. It doesn't have to be just one at a time. I am not always looking to jump into bed with one. I am trying to find out their ideas. I want 'em with me instead of scuffin' in the streets. I am turned on by their beauty, warmth, sensitivity. I enjoy being with them. I enjoy their companionship and their view of life, which is different from a brother's."

One day we wanted to take a picture of Spencer dancing with a sister in his apartment. We had missed an opportunity to do so at a party the night before and now at midday we asked him to have one come up. And he was agreeable. But after telephoning this one and that one and another one here and there and getting no response because no one was home at this time, we began to tease him. His reputation was on the line. "No sweat," he grinned. "I'll just go out in the street and find one."

"No way," we said. "You're not that good."

"You better believe I am," he was saying, and he was already throwing on an old Army jacket and an old floppy cap and heading out the door, looking a little like a bum and not too much like a cat who was going to attract a canary. From a balcony we watched him trot down the street, around the corner and out of sight. We assumed he was going after a girl he knew, perhaps one who worked in the area.

Within ten minutes he was back with a chick, and not just a chick, but a real beauty, mini-skirted and magnificent. And to our surprise, we found she really didn't know Spencer at all. She had never met him before. She had heard of him. He had spotted her entering a department store, hurried up to her, introduced himself to her, asked if she would mind posing for a picture for his book, got her agreement and had hurried her back. And she was a nice, bright girl, too, no tramp. "I was surprised, but it seemed like a fun thing to do," she smiled.

As they danced for the photographer, she looked up at Spencer and said, "Oh, my, you really are tall."

The picture appears in this book.

And when the picture-taking was done, he escorted her back to the department store, thanked her and bid her farewell. And when he returned, we suggested that our request had at least produced a new telephone number of promise for him. But he said he had not bothered to get her number. But she was beautiful and bright and nice, we protested. But he was already chest high in beautiful and bright and nice sisters, he said, and did not need any more. "I think I have my special lady picked out, but she will have to be patient a while," he smiled.

Possibly it is Janice Shephard. Possibly not. But he concedes she has been special for a long time and she concedes she has been patient for a long time. He says, "A lot of ladies are after me for what they can get out of me now. It is no special talent for someone like me to land ladies. Sports stars can be swimming in sisters if they wish.

But Janice was with me when all I could give her was crap. And she stood by me in the bad times. And we have broken up many times and always gotten back together again. And now we're far apart because she's living in Detroit and I'm living in Seattle, and yet we always feel close and, whether or not she's the girl I eventually marry, she's a person I always will feel close to."

She says, "He likes ladies because they don't envy him the way men do and they like him. I sure do. We met in June of 1968 and have gone together on and off ever since. We never had real fights, but as time goes on a girl gets edgy wanting to know where she stands. Well, a girl always knows where she stands with Spencer. He is not ready to get married. He may have a special girl, but he is going to be dating other girls, too. He tells it to you straight. He doesn't try to snow you. He gets mad when you ask him where he's been or where he's going. He puts it straight to you. He wants his freedom and he grants you yours. He doesn't get upset if he calls up and you can't go out with him when he wants to go out with you. He wants you when you want him, too. But he's always there when you need him. And he always calls you, on your birthday, on Christmas, and on days when you least expect it. He makes you feel like you are always a part of his life.

"He's a very brilliant person. He's very understanding. He doesn't tell you his troubles and not listen to yours. He's very warm and gentle. The girls at work ask me why I'm not afraid of him, but there isn't any meanness in him. He's a big man and he loses his temper sometimes, but I feel as safe with him as I would with a saint. He is very easy to get along with. That is because he has a way of getting you to like what he likes. Like jazz. He has a beautiful personality. He just charms you. But it's natural, not phony. There's nothing phony about him. I call him 'The Rich Man.' And he wanted his money. But it didn't change him.

"When he was going through hell, I used to cry for him and he said I was too weak. He feels you have to be strong to survive. But he doesn't impose his strength on you. You have an argument with him at night and leave him mad and the next morning you're still mad and you see him and

224

he's not mad and you realize he doesn't remember the argument at all. He's had his hard times, but he doesn't carry grudges. He just lives. He's really a beautiful person. I miss him terribly. I cry sometimes I miss him so much.

"He's not the kind of person you can ever forget. I know I'll never forget him. I'll wait for him as long as I can. I am working and going to school. I'm a dancer. I don't know if he'll ever marry me. Maybe I'll eventually meet someone else I'll want to marry. He's made me no promises. For all I know, he's made promises to someone else. But if he asked me to marry him today, I'd marry him tomorrow. And if he never asks me to marry him, I hope I'll always be his friend.

"I hope he marries some day. He'd make a marvelous husband. And father. I think he loves kids more than anything. He says he wants to have ten. His joke is he'll make the first four and the other six are up to the lady. Well, if the lady is smart, she'll work it out any way he wants it."

He says, "I want kids so bad I've even thought of trying to adopt some without getting married. I guess I want the kids more than I want the wife. I know I want the freedom more. I don't ever want to cheat on a wife or neglect my kids, and guys in sports are tempted to because they're away so much and chased so much. I enjoy the chase. I just don't want to be tied down. I want to go where I want when I want without punching a clock or checking in. I like a lot of people around me. I like a lot of ladies. I like a lot of parties."

The music was moving in the room, Charles Lloyd wailing for all he was worth.

There are bedrooms at opposite ends of his apartment now and one serves as the master bedroom, the other as a guest bedroom. The closets of both are full to the brim with Haywood's extravagant wardrobe of some 25 suits, 15 sports coats, 15 sweaters, 15 hats, 25 pairs of shoes and boots and 30 sports shirts. He often runs around during the day in dungarees, Army jacket and floppy cap, but when he is ready to dress up, he does it in style, and he styles many of his clothes himself. Most of his stuff is mod, but he is only modestly far out. There is "gangster" stuff and leather out-coats and Oriental and African things and a lot of things with a lot of color. He is concerned with the correct combinations. Because of his size, he must have many of his clothes tailored especially for him, and it is expensive. He is managing now on $500 every two weeks sent him by Ross, who has him on an allowance. His income is budgeted, and Ross pays all his bills.

He is driving his $11,000 custom red Cadillac, but wants to trade it in on a Rolls-Royce as "an economy," believe it or not, because he is convinced a Rolls-Royce is a sound investment, which he will not want to or have to trade in every year or two. He insists he is concerned with economizing these days because he blew so much money in his early days as a pro. He says, "I enjoy the good life. I like jazz, so I want all the jazz records. I like clothes, so I want a lot and the best. I have to drive a car, so I want to drive the best. I have a job where I'm free half the year so I like to be able to pick up and travel wherever I want whenever I want. I like to take pictures, so I want to have the best cameras. I'm still like a little kid in a lot of ways.

"But I want to grow up. I enjoy throwing parties. I like having people around. But I don't need a lot of hangers-on who aren't sincere. I need friends, not camp-followers. I know who my friends are, and I'm beginning to be able to recognize the camp-followers. I like helping people. It's nice to be able to play big man. I got money other people don't have. It's nice to be able to help people with loans. And you don't expect to get all of it back. But it hurts when you find out you get very little of it back. I'll never ask. So I got to stop giving.

"I'll give to my family. But even there I'll draw a line. Not around mama. She can have anything she wants. But she doesn't want anything. But I took one member of my family into my home and set him up in business and the next thing I knew he had driven my car to Detroit and taken my television set with him. I learned you can give, give, give, and they'll just sit back and take, take, take. You got to draw lines.

"It's been hard for my family. A lot of them never found no way out. I look at them and I look at me and I realize how lucky I am. Virg got married, had kids and began to drink too much. She's had it tough. She lives in Detroit,

226

just trying to survive. Lena lives in Chicago, married, making out all right. Joe has had a couple of marriages, a couple of kids. He fought in Vietnam, came home to a pretty good job in an auto plant in Detroit. I got Roy a couple of pro basketball tryouts, but his bum knees beat him. He's married with two kids and teaching and studying back in Michigan. I blew eighteen, twenty grand on a bumper shop I opened for Andy in Portland. He's stubborn. He's married and has responsibilities, but has got to go his own way. He blew a basketball career and a business career. Vern is a good girl, but she's strung out in Detroit and can't figure out what she wants to do with her life. I got Floyd into Trinidad Junior College, but he broke his elbow there, then into Tacoma Junior College, playing basketball. He's 6-4 and 210 and he's good and he's got a chance. The last kid, Ivory, lives at home with mama. She's a senior in high school, she has a daughter and I support the three of them.

"I'd like to do more for mama. She's never even seen me play. She's afraid to fly. Oh, she's traveled. She's been to Detroit and Chicago, but over the summers, seeing her sons and daughters and grandchildren. I tried to get her to move in with me in Denver or Seattle. I offered to buy her a home in Denver or Seattle or Detroit or Chicago. But she doesn't want to leave Mississippi. I offered to buy her a home in Mississippi, but she doesn't want me to spend my money. I'm fixing up her place for her, but she keeps putting me off. She still lives in the same old place I was raised in back there in that white state I hate. But she don't hate it. She don't feel prejudice. She has her friends there. She has work there. She finds things to do. She can hardly walk. We had her legs fixed up as best we could. We had her mouth fixed up. She's an old lady. She's tired. She won't ever want for anything any more, but she doesn't want anything from me and won't ever ask for anything from me. She doesn't understand about my kind of money. She worries about me going broke. She worries about when I can't play basketball any more. She worries about my future. All I worry about is talking her into taking a trip to the West Indies with me next summer so I can give her some pleasure for once in her poor life."

She says, "My children are my pleasure. They haven't all had it good, but they all meant good. Spencer's had it the best and he's been the best. He worries about me. He really cares. You know how mothers complain about their children never calling them? Well, I complain, too, but about my other children, not Spencer. He's I don't know how many thousand miles away and he calls me every week, at least once a week, without fail. The only time he didn't call was when he had his troubles and didn't want to trouble me. And I worried about him. It makes me so sad when people say bad things about Spencer. But I know he's not a bad boy. I think people done bad things to him. I don't think he's done bad to anyone. He never did bad to me, not ever. Or his brothers or sisters, and sometimes they've did bad to him.

"When he was in court, it almost give me a heart attack. I had no other way to live but through him. I am just dependant on him. I am old now and my health is not good. But I just want to take from him what I have to take, not any more, and I never have to ask, because he always gives, and he always wants to give more than I'll take. I think he's going to fix up this place some now. I hope so. It's coming apart around me now. But it's my place and I don't want to leave it and I don't have that much time left anyhow, to go traipsing off making a new home somewhere. I do worry about his future. I don't know how much money he's really making. Isn't that why he went to court, because he wasn't getting what he was supposed to be getting? What will he do if he doesn't have any money left when he can't play basketball anymore? What will happen to his fast and fancy life?"

Spencer sighs: "I've studied radio and television and I'm still taking courses in college, at the University of Seattle, whenever I can. I really hope to get enough credits to graduate eventually. I've worked as a disc jockey and I like it. I've always thought I could become an actor and I've taken some acting lessons, though I'm not right now. I know it sounds silly, but I had kind of a thought of becoming a black cowboy in movies or TV. I haven't had an opportunity to do any commercials, but I'd love the chance. Not just for the side money, but for the experience.

228

I've done some sportscasting, and if I can improve my speech enough, maybe I can go that way. Maybe I could go into a good business. Maybe if I make enough money and it's handled right, I'll never have to work again as long as I live."

Al Ross says, "A large part of his annual income is being put into sound investments which guarantee his future security. If he is able to play productively at a high salary level for a reasonable period of time, he really may never have to work again as long as he lives. . ."

"I do want to do something worthwhile with my life," Spencer says.

His apartment has two balconies, one overlooking U. S. Highway 5, a tangled interchange of freeway traffic, and, beyond, the Elliot Bay portion of Puget Sound; the other overlooking downtown Seattle and, beyond, the Space Needle, symbolizing the site of the World's Fair, and the Coliseum, where his team plays.

He stands at twilight in a cool breeze, resting on a railing looking over his new hometown, and says, "Denver and Seattle are a lot alike. They seem like old cities and their downtowns are dingy, but they are surrounded by beautiful country. However, this is not black man's country. There are not many black people in these towns, and it is hard to feel at home here.

"Times have changed. I'm young and I never lived through the bad times when a black man couldn't go into a restaurant or rest room or movie house, when he had to sit in the back of the bus. I guess I'd of just killed someone if I had. But I lived in Mississippi where I was regarded as a nigger until I became a national hero. When they gave me a day in my honor and a parade, I didn't go. I'm proud of that. When they do things here for me they wouldn't do for less well-known black men, I'm proud enough to resent it.

"I can go anywhere I want in Seattle, just as I could in Denver. There are black neighborhoods and clubs and places black people go I go to here just as there were there. And there are white neighborhoods and white places I go to here just as I did there, but there isn't an easy feeling about it yet. It is still sort of as if you were the stranger, the intruder. They cheer you on the court and ask for your autograph outside the arena and shake your hands in the street, but you don't feel they are your friends.

"Driving my car, I used to get stopped by the cops in Denver; and I get stopped by the cops here in Seattle. I guess because a black man in a big flashy car is suspect. Or perhaps I'm recognized and I have a reputation. But I don't break any laws. I've been stopped 17 times since I settled in Seattle. I'm counting. The cops suspect the car is stolen or you're pushing drugs. They search the car for narcotics or robbery loot. If you've got a sister with you, they think you're pimping for her. She may be a nice lady and they regard her as a whore.

"What happens? One time a cop car, lights flashing, pulls up alongside me and motions me over. He gets out and says, "Show me your license, son.' I say, 'I'm not your son.' He says, 'Show me your damn license or I'll have to take you in.' I show him my license and ask him why he stopped me. He said, 'Suspicion.' I said, 'Suspicion of what?' He said, 'I didn't know what you were doing.' I said, 'I was driving my car.' He said, 'Don't get wise with me, boy.' I said, 'I'm not a boy, I'm a man. I'm 6-8 and I play basketball for a living. I earn an honest living. I'm not a thief or a pusher or a pimp.' He said, 'Well, next time, watch yourself.' And he dropped my license on the ground and I had to pick it up. And he left.

"Another time I was driving some other players and we realized we were being followed. Then the cop car sped up and pulled us over and five cops jumped out with pistols drawn. I asked what the hell was going on. They said they got a report a car like mine was running narcotics. They frisked us and frisked the car. They didn't find nothing, so they couldn't do nothing. And they let us go. But each time you go away from these things with a little more hate in you. I'm not the only black player or the only black who faces this. Bob Rule, Walt Hazzard, a lot of the brothers have bitched about it.

"The average white person simply isn't harrassed like this, and so he doesn't sympathize with our feelings about it. But it's things like this that bind black men together. Whenever I see a sister pulled over, for instance, I'll stop to check it out to make sure she is treated decent. I'll risk involvement. I don't know her, but she is a sister. I want to be a witness to my people's troubles.

"Prejudice still exists. It is just more subtle now. When I first settled in Seattle, I moved into Lakeshore West, an apartment building that was right on the water, which I really dig. When I went to see about the place, I was put off. They told me it wouldn't be right for me. I went after it anyway. They gave it to me. Then my neighbors began knocking on my door complaining my music was too loud. I'd walk through the lobby with my friends and the white faces would look at the black faces funny. I'd have one girl up one day, another the next evening. The man would smile broadly and wink broadly and make some wisecrack about a different chick every night. I don't see him with his wife and say, 'Wow, the same one every night.' I respect him and expect him to respect me. I didn't get respect, so I moved out. Maybe I should have stayed, but you get tired of hasslin'. So I'm here now and the people seem friendlier."

We were sitting in his living room now, Herbie Hancock hammering away on the hi-fi. Spencer said, "Maybe I'm too sensitive. Maybe all black people are. Maybe we read things into things which aren't there, which maybe were there once but aren't there any more, but you feel the vibrations. Maybe my court case wasn't a black-white thing, but right away it degenerated into a fight against some black nigger trying to push a white man around, some black nigger who didn't know his place, some black nigger and his sharp lawyer. My sympathies, you see, don't just extend to blacks, but to Mexican-Americans and the American Indians and all minority groups who are prejudiced against and lack full freedom. That's what the liberation flag is all about. And then Jim O'Brien of the New York *Post*, which is supposed to be a liberal newspaper, writes in *The Sporting News* sarcastic stuff about my having a liberation flag symbol on my basketball shoes. What the hell's the difference?"

He sighed, his face solemn. He looked down at his large, empty hands. He said, "It may not be intentional, but it's a sort of conspiracy which drives us together. So most of my friends are black. We understand each other. And I don't date white girls. Not because I dislike white girls. Not because I'm prejudiced. Not because I give a damn what someone would think about it. But because my black sisters have gotten nothing out of life all this time; now that some of their black brothers are getting something, they deserve a share of it."

Although Ross was trying to get him to change his mind, feeling that it would hurt his future, Spencer, counseled by Kareem Abdul-Jabbar, was seriously considering adopting a Muslim name, as had Abdul-Jabbar, Muhammad Ali and some other athletes.

We asked him, "Do you belong to any organized black groups?"

"You mean like the panthers or something?" he answered. "No. But I'm a follower of the liberation movement and of Muslim teachings."

"Do you believe in violence?"

"No. But I understand it."

"You understand it?"

"The black people made some advances through nonviolence, such as sit-ins. They made more advances through violence, through riots. I do not believe in violence. I do not believe in rioting. I don't buy any excuse for burning and looting. But I see—and the white man is blind if he doesn't see—that it was through a show of muscle by the black man, through the white man being scared, that a lot of concessions were granted the black man. It was a bad means to a good end. They weren't going to give us anything. They'd had all the time and chances they needed. We had to take. We had to take the rights and freedoms we were as entitled to as the white man."

"But if you feel violence and rioting and crime is wrong, how can you defend those who do these things?"

"I don't defend them. I just don't put them down. I was born in the deep south and raised in northern ghettoes. I understand what the black man had and didn't have and how he came to hate and strike out. If I hadn't had basketball, I'd have gone the same way."

"But if you knew a black man was guilty of something really wrong, couldn't you condemn him?"

"No."

"Isn't right right and wrong wrong?"

"No. It's not that clear. It's not a matter of black and white. Or maybe it is," he smiled.

"What about a white person apparently guilty of the same crimes?"

He laughed. "I'd think him guilty, I guess. Unless he was a poor man. Or an Indian. Or a Mexican. You have to understand the reasons. I'm trying to understand the reasons. I'm trying to rap with white people. Like Dick Snyder of our team. We rap together a lot now. At first I didn't trust him. Now I've gotten to understand him some and he interests me a lot. And Pete Cross. But you can't just walk up to a white man and say, 'Be my friend.' Maybe after you get to know him, you won't want him to be a friend. And a prominent athlete is naturally suspicious of people who would be his friend easily. Black athletes accept the friendship of black fans because, without thinking about it, I guess, we figure they're entitled to a piece of the pie, a little rubbing off of the glory.

"I want to get to understand whites the way I feel I understand blacks. My doors are open. My mind is open. I want to see people as brothers and sisters, not black and white men and women. I've known some bad blacks I wouldn't trust out of my sight. And some whites I've trusted with my life. If it wasn't for fighters like Sam Schulman and Al Ross, I hate to think what my life would be today. You run into the odd fuzz who stops you for speeding and you think, 'What now, pig?' and he says, 'Hey, be cool. Don't do that or you'll hurt someone. Go on your way now.' And you see you can't judge everyone alike. You have to take each man as he comes."

He stretched out on a sofa, all arms and legs. "But I'm a black man," he said, "and my first responsibility is to help black men. Most whites don't need help. Most blacks do. And I'm a black in a position to help. I have to use my position to help. I'm not nineteen any more. I have to grow up. The money I was going to spend on a new suit today I can use better to help someone. The money I was going to spend on a new car tomorrow can go to a better cause.

"Me and John Brisker and some other fellows are starting a fund for sickle cell anemia, a disease which strikes mostly blacks, which kills about 25 blacks a week and has crippled youngsters across the country. Because it is a black-man's disease, there hasn't been much money donated to the cause. Because so many major league pro athletes are black, we feel we can get these moneyed guys to rally to the cause. With this, I've found something I can dedicate myself to, something worthwhile.

"I'm hung up with kids. I go to the ghettoes and rap with 'em and play basketball on the playgrounds with 'em. I take 'em to good eating places and give 'em a decent meal. I take 'em up to my pad to rap some more and I give 'em a few bucks and send 'em home to their mamas. I want to get 'em off the streets.

"In the summer my teammate Don Smith and I hope to run free clinics in the parks all week long—three nights of basketball and two nights of books. I want them to know about Malcolm X. He means more to a black kid of today than Abraham Lincoln. I want them to hear about the dangers of smoking and drugs and stealing from a man who's been there. And since athletics are a way out for a lot of kids, I want other athletes to help me teach them so they can have a chance. And since music is a way out for many of them, I'd like to ring some musicians into the act. I want to start an Academy of Music."

He is driven by dreams. "I can't be just a jock," he says.

"I want to make Seattle work for me, and this might be a way of giving something to the city, to kids, and to my people. And I don't want it to be closed. I want it to be open to poor white kids, too. And Chicanos. And Indians. And anyone who needs it. I want to help my brothers out of hell. I been there. But it's hard.

"You see," he said, "I don't have much to give. I have a bad background and a limited education. I have a name and a little popularity in my community and a lot of money and a little influence and I want to try to do some good with it.

"I'm trying to improve my background and complete my education. I buy books and read them instead of standing on street corners waving at ladies. I buy books by Baldwin, Mailer, anyone who is supposed to have something to say. Sometimes I have to read a sentence three times to understand it, and sometimes then I still don't have it straight. It's hard for me, but I'm trying hard.

234

"I use the wrong words sometimes. When you have an idea of what you want to say and you can't communicate, it's frustrating, it's humiliating, it hurts, like it makes you less than a man.

"I'm sorry I quit school. If I had chosen another school and been happier there, I wouldn't have quit. The money is important, but the education is the way to more money, the way to everything good in life," he concluded.

A sad song of Nina Simone surrounded us.

Referred to in a story in *Sports Illustrated* as "The Big One Who Stayed," one of the few undergraduate collegiate superstars who did not jump at the chance to become a hardship recruit into professional ranks, Jim Chones of Marquette said, "I can't go anywhere without people bringing up this professional business. But I weighed the negative and positive aspects and I've done the right thing.

"People from the ghetto say I blew it, but they don't know how much my father wanted me to get an education. Or how much Spencer Haywood and Ralph Simpson actually lost by leaving school. On the other hand, businessmen downtown say, 'Oh, you've made a fine choice.' But they never had to watch their mother sweep up roaches and piles of rats in the summer, or had to eat biscuits for two weeks because their father was on strike. I'll admit I'm still confused.

"College opened up a new world, the world of whites to me. Then my father died and I thought about leaving school. Marquette couldn't solve all my problems. We needed stability. My sisters weren't too worldly. I didn't want them going wild or my brother going into a shell or my mother falling apart. I didn't see how we'd make it if I stayed here. But we have.

"I do want to make it big in basketball in time. I'm trying to take the best things from everyone and put them together—Kareem's hook, Hayes's turnaround, Russell's blocking shots, Chamberlain's team defense. Especially, I want to play the all-around game, smooth it, get a rhythm and a beat to it, like Spencer Haywood. He's patient and mean at the same time. He plays the total game. It's a smooth passage from beginning to end."

But before the end of the 1971-72 basketball season,

after he had led Marquette to twenty consecutive victories, and with a month left to play, Chones changed his mind. He jumped. Pursued by NBA teams and pressured by the ABA to sign before a merger broke his bargaining power, Chones deserted his teammates and college ball to join the New York Nets, opening the floodgates for others to follow.

The ABA had a rule prohibiting players from playing college and pro ball in the same season, so Chones would not yet be eligible to play for the Nets, and signing a professional contract would make him ineligible for college play. Chones made his move anyway. He said, "It was the kind of offer I couldn't afford to pass up. It does everything for my family that I wanted it to."

His college coach, Al McGuire, said, "I have said all along and I say again now, I couldn't tell him not to take that kind of money. It was up to him. I hope he continues with his education. I just say to myself, he broke his leg. The team will have to go on without him." His new coach, Lou Carnesecca, said, "He came to us. We've lost good ones before. We couldn't be burned again."

Chones's new boss, Roy Boe, said, "We don't approve of signing undergraduates, but others are doing it, and you have to keep up with the competition. It's a good contract. It's not in the back, it's out front. It's not in investments, it's in cash. It's well over a million dollars." Reportedly, it was $1,500,000, which seemed to be the new standard, set by Spencer Haywood.

That is approximately what Jim McDaniels signed for with Seattle, jumping from the ABA to the NBA as Haywood had done, going to Ross and coming out with a $1,800,000 contract for six years' service with payments spread over eighteen years, a pact almost identical to Haywood's. The Haywood case did this. It blazed the trail and established the guidelines.

McDaniels had been drafted by Utah of the ABA, and by Seattle of the NBA, but Carolina obtained rights to him through an ABA intraleague agreement based on its ability to sign him. Thus, on completion of his college career at Western Kentucky in 1971, McDaniels announced he had signed with the Carolina club, which had courted him successfully. The situation was similar to that of Howard

Porter's, the Villanova star who had signed before season's end and denied it. Porter was caught out, and the NCAA forced Villanova to forfeit its victories and runnerup position in the NCAA tourney.

McDaniels's contract with Carolina was announced as $1,375,000 for six seasons. McDaniels said later it was supposed to be for $1,500,000 spread over fifteen years with payments in cash, but it turned out that payments were spread over twenty-five years. Thus, he said, where he had expected to be drawing $100,000 a season, he was actually drawing $60,000. He said he complained to the club but received no satisfaction from them.

In January, 1972, Ross attended the ABA All-Star Game to see several of his clients in action. McDaniels, who made a sensational showing in the game, was not a client, but he approached Ross and told him of his dissatisfaction with the Carolina contract. He wondered if Ross would look at it and consider working out the player's troubles as he had for Haywood. Ross said he would consider it, telling McDaniels to carry on for the time being.

Ross took the contract back to Los Angeles, studied it, and decided there was merit to McDaniels's complaints. He says, "I was very hesitant about taking on another Haywood case. Possibly, it could be profitable. Clearly, here was an attractive client. But I didn't solicit him, and I could see how others would suppose so, which could cause me legal troubles I didn't deserve and didn't need. Also, I didn't want to be branded as a heavy, as a contract-breaker whose main role in life was to cause trouble for team owners. We do so many other things for our clients, but this is the publicized thing. And I have to live with these owners. It could be ruinous to my reputation.

"On the other hand, the kid had come to me and he did have a case. What was I supposed to do, turn my back on him? I decided if I was in this business, I was going to have to accept the responsibility for the rough stuff, too. The kid was worrying himself sick over his troubles. He'd lost weight and was in bad shape."

Ross approached the Carolina club and tried to straighten out the tangle. The club took the position that it had a valid contract with the player, that he had not been misled in any direction, and that he was receiving everything he was supposed to be getting. They said he had already received $50,000 bonus and the first of a series of new Cadillac Eldorados he was to get every other year for six years, and his mother had begun to receive her payments, which were to amount to $7,200 a year for six years.

Norman Blass of New York, who represented McDaniels in his original negotiations with Carolina, said, "I don't see any loopholes in his contract and I can't see how it can be voided. But in this day and age, who knows?"

Seattle owner Sam Schulman said, "We'd love to have the young man, and if his contract with Carolina is illegal and invalid, then I can assure you the Sonics will assert their draft rights to him, but I will not be a party to breaking his present contract if it is valid."

Discussions were at an impasse when McDaniels jumped the team in February. Where did he wind up? With his wife he moved into the Ross house, as Haywood had done. When the story broke and everyone was seeking him, he was hidden in Bel-Air.

Ross says, "I didn't tell him to leave, but he just wasn't willing to wait any longer for his problem to be resolved. When he turned up at my front door, I wasn't going to slam it in his face." McDaniels says, "I was sick of sweating it out. I felt they'd had their chance to do right by me and hadn't done it. So I made my move. I trust Ross to do what is right for me."

Carolina then announced it was willing to talk about the contract. But by then Seattle had its lawyers looking at the pact, and they determined it had weaknesses. Zollie Volcok, a Sonics board member, said, "Our attorneys are confident several provisions make the Carolina contract invalid."

When Carolina brought a million dollar damage suit against Ross through attorney Frederick Furth and got a court order restraining Ross from "interfering" with McDaniels for the time being, Ross turned the youngster over to a Seattle attorney, Charles Burdell, and McDaniels moved out of the Ross home. Sam Schulman and Sonics attorney Mel Monheimer negotiated with McDaniels, and Burdell signed him to the $1,800,000 contract for six

238

seasons, with the payments to be in cash over an eighteen year period. They reported that NBA commissioner Walter Kennedy promptly approved the contract.

Without a center, even with the splendid Haywood, the Sonics had been struggling with the Golden State Warriors for the second playoff berth in its division, behind the L. A. Lakers. And a realignment for the 1972-73 season would add the powerful Phoenix Suns to an already strong division. The Seattle franchise was in fine financial condition, averaging more than nine thousand fans a game, but Schulman figured he needed another player like the seven-foot pivot to play competitively in this power-packed group. The Sonics were prepared to play him at once. Introduced to the Seattle crowd at a game in mid-February, he received a standing ovation.

Munchak Corporation, owner of the Carolina Cougars, and its boss Todd Munchak, promptly obtained a court order in Greensboro, North Carolina, temporarily restraining McDaniels from playing for the Sonics. A few hours later, the Sonics' attorneys obtained a court order in Seattle restraining the restraint. And so the battle was joined, bound, apparently, for a court fight. And the war between the NBA and the ABA had erupted anew, a duel of millions of dollars for top talent that could conceivably hasten the merger which would bring peace or, just as conceivably, end all hopes of a merger and peace in our time. Fortunes and franchises were at stake.

McDaniels was followed by Charlie Scott, the rangy guard from North Carolina. Scott, who had made the ABA All-Star team his first two seasons in the infant circuit, jumped the Virginia Squires before the completion of his second season. He went to Ross, asked for representation, and signed with him. Ross comments, "Charlie had the most iron-clad case of all. He said they simply had not paid him what had been promised him, and when he followed regulations by writing them letters requesting fulfillment of the contract, they stalled him, saying they needed time to come up with more cash."

Having taken on McDaniels, Ross saw no reason why he should not take on Scott, too, but he did so in secret to postpone a public outcry as long as possible. It was some

239

time before word leaked out that Scott, too, was an All-Pro addition. Ross sought Sam Schulman's help in arranging NBA negotiations for Scott's services. Sitting in his part-time retreat, a plush apartment at the Palm Springs Tennis Club, Schulman detailed his part in the ensuing transaction:

"I felt Scott had a right to make his move, and I felt the NBA should try to secure such an outstanding performer, but I did not feel my Seattle team should take him on in addition to Haywood and McDaniels.

"I called NBA commissioner Kennedy and I said, 'Walter, circumstances are not now what they were when you and I first locked horns over the Haywood case. A lot of owners in the NBA now see as I did that we have to go after these players if they are free to come to us. Al Ross has Charlie Scott. The Virginia team appears not to have lived up to its contract with him. I believe he would be cleared in any court case to sign a new contract, and I believe the NBA should sign him. I can help arrange it. Ross wants only a fair price for his client.'

"Well, Kennedy agreed, but he said Scott was one who had been drafted by the NBA and on that basis he felt the team which had drafted him, Boston, should be considered to have rights to him. I said, 'That is fine with me. If Boston wants to sign him and can reach an agreement with him, fine. If not, they can trade rights to him to a team which can reach agreement with him. I make only one stipulation. He can go to any team except Los Angeles. I make no secret of my dislike for the owner there, Jack Kent Cooke. I'll help negotiate for him with any team in the league, even teams in my division, teams which could hurt me with Scott, but I will not help sign him for Jack Kent Cooke in Los Angeles.' Well, Kennedy said that was up to me.

"We called Red Auerbach in Boston and Red did not want to take on Scott, but he was willing to make a deal with someone for him. I suggested Phoenix, which had signed Connie Hawkins, and whose president, Dick Bloch, was a business associate of mine. I knew Bloch and Phoenix would be interested in Scott, so that's the way we went. They made a deal with Red and signed Scott. Naturally,

240

the Virginia Squires screamed bloody murder and filed suit, but I believe they have a losing hand."

Ross says, "I'm not sure what Phoenix gave Boston for the rights to Scott, but I think it involved both draft choices and cash. Scott is not a center or even a big forward, but he is a big guard and tremendously talented. The Suns agreed to pay him $1,650,000 for six seasons to be spread in cash payments over thirteen years, and they also agreed to pay him $270,000 for his option year, a seventh season. He broke in with them brilliantly, playing the last six games and averaging more than 18 points a game. I believe he will be among the scoring leaders and top players in the league in the 1972-73 season. McDaniels played only in spots through the last twelve games and didn't score much, but he is going to be outstanding."

In the last stages of the season Artis Gilmore, Julius Erving, Dan Issel, and John Brisker, four of the ABA's outstanding survivors, were among others reportedly considering leaps to the NBA. Erving openly admitted he was considering it, and he was drafted by Milwaukee. Jack Kent Cooke's Los Angeles team had indicated it wanted him, but decided not to go after him because of the legal difficulties which might obstruct their path before they could secure him. Meanwhile, Chicago drafted Simpson, who, however, broke with Ross and signed with the lawyer of his manager and coach in Denver, Alex Hannum, and the Mark McCormack management agency.

Bob McAdoo, star junior of the University of North Carolina's NCAA tournament team, which finished third in the final round, signed with Virginia of the ABA, with Ross of All-Pro, and then was drafted by Buffalo of the NBA, which said it would seek to sign him. He was one of those who came under the "hardship" classification, an unnecessary device still employed by the leagues. It was rumored he had "turned pro" prior to the completion of the NCAA tourney, as Howard Porter had done in 1971. Ross said that he, at least, had not signed the youngster until after the season.

The NBA suffered a setback, however, when a federal Appeals Court in Richmond, Virginia, ruled that Billy Cunningham had to honor a contract with Carolina of the

ABA. Cunningham had signed with Carolina before the 1971-72 season but then had negotiated a contract with Philadelphia for $275,000 a season. The court held that the contract with Carolina was binding on Cunningham and that he would have to play for Carolina until the contract expired in October 1975.

On the other hand, the NBA managed to gain an advantage in the Rick Barry case. Barry, a forward with the New York Nets during the 1971-72 season, was signed to a contract that expired at the end of the season, and a San Francisco court in mid-1972 ruled he could not remain with the Nets for 1972-73 and would have to return to the NBA to honor a contract that he had signed with the San Francisco Warriors prior to the 1970-71 season.

Barry had been making $50,000 a season, and bonuses, by playing with San Francisco of the NBA until the 1967-68 season. Then he jumped to Oakland of the new ABA for $75,000 a season and bonuses for three years. When a court ruled that he had to wait until his San Francisco contract expired before he could join Oakland, Rick simply sat out the season. He joined Oakland for the 1968-69 season. Then the Oakland ABA franchise was sold and shifted east prior to the 1969-70 season. Not wanting to leave northern California, Barry signed a new contract with San Francisco of the NBA for $544,000 for three seasons. Then the court ruled that Barry had a contract with an ABA franchise, not just an Oakland team, and he had to accompany it wherever the franchise went.

Discontented, Barry rejoined the team, but he then forced a trade to the New York Nets. There he felt he could be happy. So he signed with the Nets for $110,000 in additional moneys for the remaining two seasons of his existing contract, and for $540,000 for three additional seasons—providing the way was cleared for him to play with the Nets. However, Franklin Mieuli of the Warriors had meanwhile shifted his team from San Francisco to Oakland and renamed it the Golden State Warriors. Mieuli resisted settling with Roy Boe, owner of the New York Nets, and persisted in a court case seeking to compel Barry to live up to his "new" Warriors pact after his original ABA pact expired.

242

Ross explained, "Until the ruling in the Cunningham case, Rick was the first one ordered by the courts back to his original contract. He is the one player who seems to have lost every ruling and been compelled to go everywhere he did not want to go. I have not been involved in his litigation. Possibly, his clubs honored his contracts completely, and he did not have a case against them as have Haywood, McDaniels, and Scott. Possibly, he simply had bad luck as far as he was concerned in how the courts ruled. You cannot always predict how the courts will rule. Each is different."

It was pointed out that it sometimes seems that when a player jumps a club in one state and goes to a club in another, his original club can get a ruling in its state that he must return, but his new club can always get a ruling in its state that he does not have to do so. It was also pointed out that it seems strange, that, no matter how bad a contract may be, or how poorly it may be fulfilled, a player is permitted to ignore it before it is put to a court test and is then able to play for a new contract with a new team.

Ross said, "In each case, the original club presented its side of the case in court in its state and the player presented his side of the case in court in the state of his new club. In order to obtain a ruling that McDaniels, for example, was free to play for Seattle, we had to present to a court in Washington sufficient evidence that his Carolina contract was invalid to make it clear we had a reasonable chance to win our case. McDaniels did not have to go with his Seattle team to North Carolina, or we might have encountered trouble there."

It was pointed out to Ross that if others of the stature of Artis Gilmore, who succeeded Haywood as Rookie of the Year and Most Valuable Player in the ABA during 1971-72, followed Haywood, McDaniels, and Scott out of the ABA, it could cripple and conceivably kill the league, which then would eliminate half the jobs available in pro basketball, and that would put a halt to the rising salaries, thus working to the disadvantage of his clients and himself.

"I'm aware of that," Ross said, "and I don't like the thought of it, but I represent individuals; and if their basic rights are being denied them, and if contracts being given them are not sound or are not fulfilled, then I have to act accordingly. If the ABA's contracts were ironclad, we would not have been able to make the moves we have made. A league is only as good as its contracts, and that's the story right there.

"I'd like both the ABA and the NBA to survive, but I'd like them to survive with the right kind of contracts, fair to the rights of the individual and fulfilled. I've been frustrated in my negotiations with the ABA. I'd like to feel I could negotiate with both the ABA and the NBA for my clients with confidence. It's not my place to pass judgment on the merits of a merger, but I would not like to see one which had built into it any legislation which enslaved the performer."

Some of these same questions were put to Schulman. And the shrewd, crusty campaigner was more outspoken on one point, saying, "I feel we've had right on our side in each contract case, but I'm not sure this was critical, because I'm not sure any personal services contract is binding. I can sign you to a contract to do a piece of work for me, but if after a period of time you are unhappy with me or the work and decide you don't want to do it, I don't believe I can compel you to do it, nor do I believe I could stop you from earning a living with your particular skills if you wished to go to work to do the same sort of job for a competitor."

Schulman added, "Until there is a merger, we must remain in a competitive situation, and each franchise owner must do everything legal and above board to strengthen his side and succeed. And if there is a merger, I do not believe it will work unless it comes with contracts permitting the players to bargain for themselves with similar freedoms enjoyed by other individuals in our society. I have expressed this as emphatically as I know how to the other owners because I believe they will be taken to court and beaten badly otherwise. These are changing times, and we have to go with the times.

"If we can't survive in free and open competition, then I am not sure we should survive. Whatever it costs to operate a team profitably on the new level, well, that's what it costs, and anyone who can't meet that price will be unable to compete and will have to drop out."

And so it stood in the off-season, as summer came on in 1972. With the help of an Al Ross and a Sam Schulman, Spencer Haywood had blazed a trail through the wilderness and come out on the other side to find himself and everyone else in pro basketball and possibly in all of professional sports still in a jungle and hacking away in an effort to find the route to survival.

In his first full season in the NBA, his third season as a pro and what would ordinarily have been only his rookie year, Spencer Haywood was sensational. He finished fourth in the league in scoring, with an average of better than 26 points a game, surpassing Jerry West, and Gail Goodrich, Bob Love, Elvin Hayes, Lou Hudson, and Billy Cunningham, and he just missed the top ten in rebounding, with an average of nearly 13 a game.

He was selected to the official NBA All-Star first team, along with Kareem Abdul-Jabbar, John Havlicek, Walt Frazier, and West, and while he did not win the MVP trophy he coveted, he was fifth in the player balloting, trailing only Abdul-Jabbar, West, Chamberlain, and Havlicek, and leading Love, Frazier, Dave Cowens, Nate Thurmond, Bob Lanier, Connie Hawkins, and other heralded superstars.

In announcing the honors in *The Sporting News*, Phil Elderkin wrote, "Haywood is one of those marvelously coordinated big men who can do almost everything a little man can do. He's fluid on the drive, strong inside and a natural rebounder. Among today's top players, he easily answers 'yes' to the questions: Can he run? Can he score? Can he rebound? Can he defend? If you were starting a new team and had first shot at the game's best forwards, chances are you'd go for Haywood first. He's only 22."

Sam Schulman said, "I must admit, now, when I first saw him play after signing him and he played poorly, I thought, 'My God, why did I go to all this trouble and expense? For what?' But I should have seen that he was just being kicked around from court to court and tense and nervous. He came on this season, and by season's end he was just unbelievable, as good a basketball player as I've ever seen. He was outrebounding bigger men, blocking shots like the greatest of the giant centers, outshooting small men from outside, playing defense and dominating games." Len Wilkens said, "He was coming fast, no doubt about it. He is unselfish, was learning his trade and getting the most out of his tremendous natural ability. He was dominating games the way only a Jabbar or Chamberlain can. And then he got hurt."

Haywood slipped on a wet spot on the Seattle Center Coliseum court and tore up his knee. Encased in a cast to his hip, he missed the last twelve games of the season. Schulman sued the city on the grounds that requested repairs had not been made in the arena roof to keep the city's inevitable rains outside, but it did not regain for his side the services of Spencer for the remainder of the season. The situation depressed the youngster deeply. "It was a bad break—for me, for the team, for Lenny," he said. With him, the Sonics had been battling the Warriors for second place in the division and the last spot in the playoffs. Without Haywood, and regulars Dick Snider and Don Smith, also injured, they fell out of contention and finished four games back, despite a respectable record of 47-35, which was better than half the teams in the league, including some that made the playoffs in other divisions.

When rumors spread that Wilkens was on his way out as coach, Haywood made a public statement: "Wilkens is an outstanding coach, has done an outstanding job, and should be retained as coach." However, Schulman confidentially confirmed the rumors: "It's just too difficult for a top player to be a top coach, too. A man can't handle both jobs at the same time without one suffering. Wilkens remains too fine a player to retire, so he has decided to remain with us as a player, while surrendering the coaching job." The next day Wilkens made such an announcement.

A few days later he smiled and shrugged and said, "I felt I did the job, but long before we missed out on the playoffs I realized I'd have to decide whether I wanted to continue as a player, and I decided I did. I feel that without injuries we'd have made the playoffs. But I've been around long enough to know you have to produce results. I feel attendance and comment in Seattle and comment around the league reflect favorably on my coaching, and I can only hope that some day I'll get to coach in the NBA again. I learned a lot from the experience.

"I feel indebted to Haywood for standing up and saying what he did. We're not close, personal pals, you know. He's just the sort of person who speaks his mind. And you soon learn that he stands up for what he believes in. He's not afraid to be counted. And you know you can count on a man like him because he will always be there."

And so the season ended, in turmoil and frustration. The new season will bring a new coach, Tom Nissalke, formerly of Dallas of the ABA. "And what else?" Haywood wonders wistfully.

The merger remained only a dream. The troubled ABA folded two franchises, the ones in Florida and Pittsburgh. Dolph resigned as commissioner.

Here is the way it was for Haywood one night last season:

Driving to a game, one eye out for cops, Spencer Haywood squeezed a device to strengthen his hands. Not that his hands needed strengthening. But he is going to do whatever he can to help himself. Parking at the arena, he paused to rub his right heel, which throbs with bursitis. He was taking four pills a day and shots to ease the pain and permit his play.

The arena was as yet almost empty. He stood and looked over the nearly deserted stands. He said, "I got to be good tonight. I got to be good every night. Everyone is always watching me."

His brother, Roy, says, "I am jealous of him. I am happy for him, but I am jealous of him. He has what I wanted, what a lot of us want. I had my chance to get it, but I didn't get it. I had pro tryouts, but my knee gave out. My knee held up at my tryout in Denver and I thought I made it, but they cut me. It was that close. It hurts to come close. Oh, well, I'll make out somehow. And I'll be rooting for Spencer. He is a beautiful person. He never forgets his people. He never uses his fame and fortune to rise above people. I came to his town and he moved me into his apartment. He put me in his bed and he slept on the

247

couch. I wasn't the one who took his car and television. But people done that to him. They done a lot to him. They've made it hard on him. He's paid his dues. He's got good times coming to him."

Will Robinson says, "I was his father and he was my son, and I dragged him out of the ghetto and made a man of him, but he let other people pull us apart, he let hard times turn him hard. We went through a lot together. He came out of it with a lot, and I didn't come out of it with anything. But I'll be his friend forever. When he decides he • needs me again, when he wants to come back to me again, I'll be waiting."

Spencer sits in a deserted dressing room and says, "Will was like my father and he did treat me like a son. He did do a great deal for me, but he wanted too much from me for it and he failed me in the end. No one pulled us apart. I turned on him. I'm sorry about that, but it had to be. My troubles cost me a lot of friendships. But the real ones remain. What Will and I had was real. I'll get back to him someday. I can't hate that hard. Not as hard as I can love."

He played his game and the fans loved the way he played it, cheering him. And afterwards, there were kids waiting for his autograph and he treated them tenderly. "I think I like kids because I don't mistrust their motives," he said. "Some of 'em been turned bad, but none of 'em began bad and a lot of 'em can be saved from ending bad."

A lovely lady waited for him, too. He said, "I don't really smoke or drink. I have a cigar or a beer now and then. A sip of wine, maybe. I don't gamble. The thousand bucks I blow at poker could save some kid. My worst vice is the ladies, if you call that a vice," he said, flashing that Bill Cosby grin and smothering one of her hands with one of his.

"You played good tonight," she said.

"I got to play good," he said. "I'm making 'em pay me good."

"I was really cheering for you," she said. "Everyone was."

"*Tonight*," he said. "*Tonight*, they were cheering."

In the quiet night it almost seemed as though you could still hear the cheers. Their echoes vibrated in the stillness.

"It's good to hear the cheers," Spencer Haywood said. "But you can't live off 'em."